Social Media Marketing

by Shiv Singh and Stephanie Diamond

for
dummies®
A Wiley Brand

Social Media Marketing For Dummies® 4th Edition

Published by: **John Wiley & Sons, Inc.**, 111 River Street, Hoboken, NJ 07030-5774, www.wiley.com

Copyright © 2020 by John Wiley & Sons, Inc., Hoboken, New Jersey

Published simultaneously in Canada

For general information on our other products and services, please contact our Customer Care Department within the U.S. at 877-762-2974, outside the U.S. at 317-572-3993, or fax 317-572-4002. For technical support, please visit https://hub.wiley.com/community/support/dummies.

Wiley publishes in a variety of print and electronic formats and by print-on-demand. Some material included with standard print versions of this book may not be included in e-books or in print-on-demand. If this book refers to media such as a CD or DVD that is not included in the version you purchased, you may download this material at http://booksupport.wiley.com. For more information about Wiley products, visit www.wiley.com.

Library of Congress Control Number: 2019957434

ISBN: 978-1-119-61700-6

ISBN: 978-1-119-61701-3 (ePDF); ISBN: 978-1-119-61702-0 (ePub)

Manufactured in the United States of America

V10016909_011520

Table of Contents

Introduction

Social media has transformed the Internet and society as a whole. It has impacted global revolutions, elections, and the way we communicate on a daily basis. Social media also presents unique marketing opportunities that force marketers to revisit the core guiding principles of marketing while providing new ways to reach social influencers, thereby encouraging people to influence each other and do the marketing for the brand. Social media marketing (SMM) forces companies to rethink how they market online, whom they market to, and how to structure their own organizations to support these new marketing opportunities. For anyone involved with social media marketing — and Internet marketing, more broadly — this is indeed an exciting time.

Social Media Marketing For Dummies, 4th Edition, is written to help you make sense of the madness. Because it's such a hot topic, the press and the experts alike are quick to frighten marketers like you and introduce new terminology that confuses rather than enlightens. This book cuts through all that noise and simply explains what social media marketing is and how you can harness it to achieve your objectives as a marketer. It also aims to help you prioritize what's important and what isn't.

About This Book

The social media marketing space changes rapidly, so by the very definition of social media marketing, this book can't be completely comprehensive. It does, however, aim to distill the core concepts, trends, tips, and recommendations down to bite-sized, easy-to-digest nuggets. As social media marketing touches all parts of marketing and all parts of the Internet, too (from traditional websites to social platforms to the mobile web), based on your own experiences, you'll find some sections more valuable than others.

As you read this book, keep in mind that the way people influence each other online and impact purchasing and brand affinity decisions is similar to the way they've done for thousands of years in the real world. The technology is finally catching up, and social media marketing is fundamentally about allowing and encouraging that behavior to happen in a brand-positive manner online, too.

This book helps you understand why social media matters to marketers and how you can harness it to directly impact your own marketing efforts in meaningful ways. Targeted at both marketers in large organizations and those of you who work in small businesses or run small businesses, it includes advice for every business scenario.

Foolish Assumptions

In writing this book, we imagined someone pulling a copy off a bookshelf in a Barnes and Noble and scanning it to see whether it's a valuable guide. And we wondered what that person would need to know to find this book interesting. Here are some of the assumptions we came up with about you:

» You have a computer and/or mobile device with Internet access.

» You're using social media sites such as Facebook or Twitter.

» You're working in marketing or want to join the marketing field.

» You have customers or prospective customers who use the web frequently.

» You sell a product or service that you can market online.

» You're curious about social media and how it changes marketing.

Icons Used in This Book

In the margins of the book, you'll find these icons helping you out:

TIP

Whenever we provide a hint that makes an aspect of social influence marketing easier, we mark it with a Tip icon.

REMEMBER

The Remember icon marks paragraphs that contain a friendly reminder.

WARNING

Heed the paragraphs marked with the Warning icon to avoid potential disaster.

Whenever we get technically inclined, we mark the paragraph with a Technical Stuff icon. If you're not technically inclined, you can skip these nuggets of info.

TECHNICAL STUFF

Where to Go from Here

This book is designed so that you can quickly jump to a specific chapter or section that most interests you. You don't have to start with the first chapter — although if you're new to social media marketing, we recommend that you do so. Understanding the foundation of social media marketing (which we explain in the early chapters) helps you better apply the techniques that you learn in the later ones to the specifics of your business.

You can also find the cheat sheet, complete with additional nuggets of information, for this book by going to www.dummies.com and searching for "Social Media Marketing For Dummies cheat sheet."

1

Getting Started with Social Media Marketing

IN THIS PART . . .

Find out how to begin practicing SMM.

Learn how to find your SMM competitors.

Discover what goes into developing a Social Media Marketing mindset.

IN THIS CHAPTER

» Understanding social media's role in social influence

» Discovering the different roles played by social media participants

» Knowing what types of influencers you're marketing to

» Coordinating your efforts with other types of marketing

» Moving beyond corporate marketing

Chapter **1**

Understanding Social Media Marketing

When marketing online, you design websites, run display banner advertising, publish videos to YouTube, and push your website listings higher up in the search engine rankings to promote and sell products. It's easy to forget how people actually buy. It's easy to assume that the potential customers are lonely people crouched over their computers late at night, choosing what products to add to a shopping cart — isolated from the real world and their family and friends.

But in reality, that's not how people buy online today. It might have been the case in the early days of the web, when the people spending time online were the early adopters and the mavericks, the ones willing to take the risk of putting their credit card numbers into a computer hoping for accurate charges and secure transactions.

In those days, few people bought online, and the ones who did were on the fringes of mainstream society.

Those days are over now. With over 300 million people using the web on a regular basis in the United States alone and approximately 3.2 billion users globally, using the Internet has become a mainstream social activity. Consumers approach purchasing online differently, too, and as a result, you need to approach your marketing online differently as well. Your approach must incorporate influence and the different roles that people play in the realm of social media, especially because social media itself has changed over the last decade with the rise of smartphones.

This chapter discusses the fundamentals of social media marketing: what it is, how it works, who the players are, and what it means in the context of your other marketing efforts.

Defining Social Media Marketing

A discussion of any subject needs to begin with a definition, and so here's the one for social media marketing: *Social media marketing (SMM)* is a technique that employs *social media* (content created by everyday people using highly accessible and scalable technologies such as social networks, blogs, micro-blogs, message boards, podcasts, social bookmarks, communities, wikis, and vlogs).

Social media (which has probably been one of the most hyped buzzwords of the last decade) refers to content created and consumed by regular people for each other. It includes the comments a person adds at the end of an article on a website, the family photographs she uploads to a photo-sharing service, the conversations she has with friends in a social network, and the blog posts she publishes or comments on. That's all social media, and it's making everyone in the world a content publisher and arbitrator of content. It's democratizing the web. Facebook, shown in Figure 1-1, is the most popular social network. It allows you to connect with friends and share information in a matter of minutes. Facebook has 2.41 billion monthly active users around the world.

FIGURE 1-1:
Facebook is just one example, albeit the largest, of the many media platforms.

Learning about the Roles People Play

To look at the framework of social media marketing, we need to look at the different roles played by those engaged in social media. They are as follows:

>> **Marketers:** They publish and share content online to achieve an organization's marketing and business needs. Today's marketer looks nothing like the marketers of the twentieth century. Customers now own the brand conversation. The opportunity to interrupt and annoy those customers has dwindled. Customers now meet businesses on their own terms. In the following section, we discuss the new role that marketers have to play.

>> **Influencers:** Several types of influencers contribute to the decisions customers make. They may be everyday people who influence the consumer as he makes a purchasing decision. Depending on the decision, the social influencers may be a wife (or husband), friends, peers at work, or even someone the consumer has never even met in real life. Simply put, the people who influence a brand affinity and purchasing decision are the social influencers. They may exert this influence directly by rating products and commenting or by publishing opinions and participating in conversations across the web. Anyone can be a social influencer, influencing someone else's brand affinity

and purchasing decisions, and you, the reader, are probably one, too, without realizing it. We discuss the specific types of influencers in the section "Understanding the role of the influencer."

>> **Platforms:** We used to believe that the social media platforms on which marketers, influencers, and consumers published content were neutral technologies without playing a role in whose content got promoted and shared the most. However, in recent years, the actions of the major social media platforms have shown that their leadership has an active role to play in what gets promoted, shared, and inversely censured on a social media marketing platform. If you're a small company, their influence may not be noticeable but for larger companies who market and sell many products online, understanding how the platforms and their leaders think about content is important.

It isn't enough to market to the consumer anymore; as a marketer, you have to market to your potential customers' social influencers as well so that they, in turn, influence either overtly or just by what they publish and share online. And that's what social media marketing is about.

Changing roles of the social media marketer

Anyone who has worked in online marketing for a while has watched amazing changes take place. Starting in 1994, one of this book's authors, Stephanie, worked at AOL, watched that company and other online services help start a social media revolution that continues to change the world. At that time, the other author, Shiv, created his first website using HTML 1.0 and added the ability to comment at the end of each page.

Since then, a lot has changed, and today many marketers are looking for a specific set of rules to follow to be successful. We can assure you that there aren't any, but there *are* some guidelines. Following are some of the actions that social media marketers must take if they want their company to compete successfully in the new social marketplace:

>> **Become the top persuader.**

When you lead an SMM team, you need to understand that persuasion is your most important tool. You persuade your team that you can help its members achieve success, and you persuade your customer to buy your product. Throughout this book, we discuss the role that influence plays in social media and in the art of persuasion. Before you influence, you need to figure out the persuasive message that will sell. When you do that, you can unleash the groups that influence your customers.

>> **Use a variety of distribution channels.**

The key mistake that some new social media marketers make is to focus solely on social media platforms to carry their message. This does half the job. Although it gets people's attention, it doesn't always get them to the sale. For example, imagine that you have just tweeted about a solution for stain removal. Unless you provide a link to your product and a place for discussion and reviews, you have a missed opportunity. Draw a map of all your channels (blog, website, Facebook page, newsletter, and so on), and use it whenever you plan a new campaign. You need a link to all your venues.

>> **Reinvent your strategy to emphasize value.**

Value is a secret weapon in this economy. When you boil away all the other ingredients of a product sale, you uncover value. This is a tricky concept because value is in the eye of the beholder. Understanding what imparts that value should underlie your entire marketing strategy. Think about your current SMM campaign. Are you focusing on features and benefits or on how the product makes your customer feel? For example, some companies focus on making people feel smart and sexy when they buy a certain model car. By the same token, others may focus on models that emphasize safety and responsibility. If you understand the value, you can establish a bond with your buyer.

>> **Market to inspire.**

The globalization of our world via the Internet has given us a window into the lives of others. It's hard to ignore the poverty and disease that plague much of the world's population. Many companies are seizing the opportunity to use their businesses to help make an impact. SMM encourages awareness of the connection we share with others. Think about how your business can participate.

In fact, in the last few years alone, purpose driven marketing, which is about defining why you do what you do, has become one of the most important ways to engage customers. Dove's #speakbeautiful movement Twitter campaign, which encouraged women to speak positively about themselves, is a perfect example of this type of marketing as it flowed naturally from Dove's broader purpose of improving the self-esteem and confidence of women. It wasn't just about selling a product but demonstrating that the brand has a more meaningful role to play in people's lives.

>> **Create and curate content.**

Offering engaging content is a big part of any SMM campaign. You need an editorial calendar that lays out your topics, creation tools, and deadlines. You also need to focus on curating content already published on the web. Becoming a trusted source of information is key to getting your customers to visit often. It's important to remember that your customers are leading highly engaged and entertaining lives in the social media world. Your content can't just be about your product. It needs to be valuable to them and their lives.

>> **Know when to resist the next shiny object.**

As you well know, new web tools pop up daily. The best way to avoid being distracted is to write down your objectives. The last thing you want to say to yourself is, "Everyone is using such and such, so we should use it." Place your objectives in a prominent place and refer to them often. If they change, revise the document. But whatever you do, don't try to do something on every social platform — you'll quickly discover that you don't have the tools, training, and — most critically — the resources to support all the tools.

>> **Be prepared to be wrong.**

This is a tough one. In your role as marketer, you want to lead your company to successive victories. SMM is not a sure thing. You need to be prepared to experiment and change course using the feedback that you get from customers. You may start with a small idea and develop it into a full-blown campaign. It's unlikely that you can start out with a very expensive big effort and not have to correct along the way. When management and staff start out with the notion that they are testing and experimenting, changes in direction won't seem as shocking. This cuts down on wear and tear of the psyche for everyone. It also limits the risks to your core marketing efforts while you learn this space.

Understanding the role of the influencer

To understand how social influence works, you need to look at how people are influenced in the real world, face to face. Social influence isn't something new. Long before the web, people asked each other for advice as they made purchasing decisions. What one person bought often inspired another to buy the same product, especially if the original purchaser said great things about the product. That's how human beings function; we're influenced and motivated by each other to do things. We're social beings, and sharing information about our experiences is all a part of social interaction.

Is influence bad? Of course not. More often than not, people *seek* that influence. People ask each other for advice; they share decision-making processes with friends and colleagues; they discuss their own experiences.

How much a person is influenced depends on multiple factors. The product itself is the most important one. When buying *low-consideration purchases* (those with a small amount of risk), people rarely seek influence, nor are they easily influenced by others. Buying toothpaste, for example, is a low-consideration purchase because each product may not be that different from the next one, and they're all fairly inexpensive — so you won't lose much money if you choose one that doesn't fit your needs. On the other hand, buying a new car is typically a *high-consideration purchase* (a purchase that includes a large risk).

The price of the car, the maintenance costs, and its reputation for its safety all contribute to making it a high-consideration purchase, not to mention the fact that you want to identify with a certain brand versus another one. Social influence plays a much bigger role in car purchases than in toothpaste decisions. Mercedes-Benz has used social media marketing time and again to leverage influencers in motivating consumers to purchase its cars. The Mercedes-Benz *Take The Wheel* campaign for which they hired five top Instagram photographers to each take the wheel of a new Mercedes CLA was a standout example. (Figure 1-2 shows the webpage for this campaign.) Whoever got the most likes on Instagram when publishing about the car and their roadtrips got to keep the car. So as you can imagine, the photographers really worked hard!

FIGURE 1-2:
The Mercedes-Benz Take The Wheel campaign.

TIP

Social influence matters with every purchase, but it matters more with high-consideration purchases than low-consideration ones. Most consumers realize that when they're making high-consideration purchases, they can make better and more confident purchasing decisions when they take into account the advice and experience of others who have made those decisions before them. That's how influence works.

Considering the types of influencers

When discussing social media marketing, people often ask us whether this means that they should add product review features to e-commerce websites or advertise on social networks. Yes, product reviews and advertising are important, but there's more to social influence than those two things. When you think about social influence in the context of your marketing objectives, you must separate social influencers online into three types: *referent, expert,* and *positional.* These categories come from thinking that social psychologists John French and Bertram Raven pioneered in 1959.

As a marketer seeking to deploy social media marketing techniques, the first question to answer is this: Which social influencers sway your consumers as they make purchasing decisions about your product? After you identify those social influencers, you can determine the best ways to market to them.

REMEMBER

Any major brand affinity or purchasing decision has referent, expert, and positional social influencers all playing distinct and important roles. Which one is most important may vary slightly based on the purchase, but the fact remains that you need to account for these three distinct types of social influencers in your marketing campaigns. If you're a marketer trying to positively affect a purchasing decision, you must market not just to the consumer, but also to these influencers.

Referent influencers

A *referent influencer* is someone who participates on the social platforms. These users are typically in a consumer's social graph and influence brand affinity and purchasing decisions through consumer reviews, by updating their own status and Twitter feeds, and by commenting on blogs and forums. In some cases, the social influencers know the consumers personally. *Social graph* is a term popularized by Marc Zuckerburg of Facebook and is used to describe the relationships that people may have on a social network and how they connect to one another.

Because the consumers know and trust their referent influencers, they feel confident that their advisers are also careful and punctilious. Because they're people they trust, they value their advice and guidance over most other people. Referent influencers influence purchasing decisions more than anyone else at the consideration phase of the marketing funnel, according to various studies.

For example, if Shiv decides to make a high-consideration purchase such as a car, he might start by going online and discussing different cars with a few friends on Facebook or via Twitter. And then that weekend, he might meet those friends over coffee and carry on that discussion in person. They tell him about the cars they like, their own purchasing experiences, and which dealerships they've had experience with. This influence is considered *referent influence* because these friends sway him by the strength of their charisma and interpersonal skills, and they have this sway because he respects them. What's worth pointing out, though, is that the friends whom he knows to be most informed about cars will probably influence him more than the others.

Expert influencers

A consumer who's mulling over a high-consideration purchase might also consult an expert influencer. An *expert influencer* is an authority on the product that the consumer is considering purchasing. Also called *key influencers,* they typically have their own blogs and huge Twitter followings, and rarely know their audiences personally.

When considering buying a car, suppose Shiv doesn't turn just to friends for advice, but also visits some car review websites like Edmunds (www.edmunds.com, shown in Figure 1-3). On these review websites, experts rate, rank, and pass judgment on cars. Because they put the cars through various tests and know the cars inside and out, their opinions matter. They're the expert social influencers — people whom Shiv may not know personally but are recognized as authorities in a certain field. Their influence is derived from the skills or expertise that they — or broadly speaking, their organization — possess based on training.

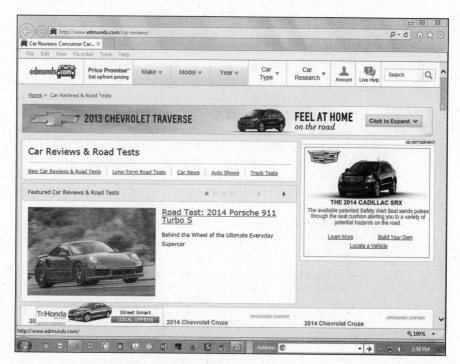

FIGURE 1-3:
The Edmunds car view website.

Positional influencers

A *positional influencer* is closest to both the purchasing decision and to the consumer. Called *peer influencers* sometimes, they are typically family members or part of the consumer's inner circle. They influence purchasing decisions most directly at the point of purchase and have to live with the results of their family member's or friend's decision as well.

As Shiv says, "I know that I can't make a high-consideration purchase like a car purchase without discussing it with my wife. Invariably, she'll drive the car, too, and sit in it as much as I will. It is as much her purchase as it is mine. Her opinion matters more than anyone else's in this case. After all, I need to discuss with her the relative pricing of the cars available and whether one is more suitable for our family versus another." This person derives her influence from her relative position and duties in relation to the actual consumer. She's closest to the purchasing decision and to the consumer and, therefore, has the most social influence.

Influencing on digital platforms

As we discuss earlier in the chapter, social influence impacts every purchasing decision and always has in some form or other. Each time people make purchasing decisions, they ask each other for advice. Sometimes they depend upon an expert's guidance, and in other cases, that advice comes from people they know.

So why is influence such a big deal today? This is because Internet consumption, and social media consumption specifically, have hit the mainstream. For example, as of June 2019, the social network platform Facebook had 2.41 billion users worldwide, giving it a population larger than any single country in the world, including China and India. That's a lot of people talking about a lot of things (including products) to a lot of people! But there's more to it than that. Social media traffic referrals have risen dramatically in the last few years. Facebook, Pinterest, Instagram, and Twitter have 18 percent, 7.5 percent, 0.73 percent, and 0.73 percent, respectively, of global referrals per Shareaholic (February 2018). These numbers show how much people are also acting on the influence of others — they're visiting the websites that they're being told to visit.

People are making more and more purchasing decisions online every day. It's as natural to buy a product online as it is to go into a physical store. People buy clothes and shoes online, not to mention high-consideration items such as computers, cars (yes, cars), and jewelry. But that's not all. Not only are consumers buying online, but thanks to social media, they're also conversing, socializing, and influencing each other online on a scale never seen before.

Call it a shift in web behavior, but the way people make decisions in the real world is finally moving to the Internet in a big way. The social media platforms such as Facebook, Instagram, Snapchat, LinkedIn, Twitter, and YouTube (shown in Figure 1-4), are just a few of the places where people are asking each other for advice and guidance as they make purchasing decisions. Smart companies are realizing that they should no longer design their e-commerce websites to convince buyers to make purchasing decisions in isolation. Rather, they need to design the websites to allow consumers to bring their social influencers into the decision-making process. As consumers, people expect and want that because that's how they're used to making their purchasing decisions. That's why social media marketing matters today. People are influencing and are being influenced by each other every day on the social network platforms, community websites, and destination sites.

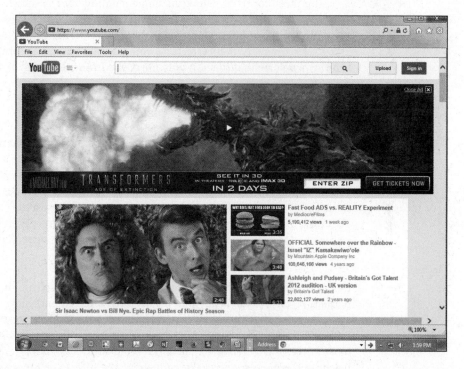

FIGURE 1-4:
YouTube.

TIP

You may need to put a lot of effort into convincing your managers how important the social media platforms are. The best way to communicate these ideas and techniques to your staff is by organizing lunch-and-learn sessions and bringing in external speakers who can walk your managers through the major social platforms and how best to market on them. Sharing case studies from other brands always resonates well and goes a long way to establishing credibility.

Comparing Social Media Marketing with Other Marketing Efforts

It isn't enough to deploy social media marketing in isolation of every other marketing effort. If you do, you're sure to fail. Your customers will notice that you have a disjointed, conflicted story — depending on where and how you're interacting with them. Therefore, it's important to understand how you can integrate your social media marketing within your other, more traditional marketing — direct mail, public relations, display advertising, and promotions.

WARNING

Some of the social media marketing philosophies are in conflict with traditional public relations, media buying, direct mail, and promotions tactics. It's no use damning those forms of marketing and alienating your peers who focus on those areas. Put extra effort in partnering with your fellow employees as you practice these marketing techniques. Explain what you're doing, why you're doing it, and how it complements their efforts. If you discredit the other forms of marketing and the people behind them, it only hurts you in the long run.

Direct mail

Direct mail is about managing an active customer database and marketing to members of that database via circulars, catalogs, credit card applications, and other merchandising materials delivered to homes and businesses. You've probably gotten a lot of direct mail over the years — perhaps mountains of it — and at some point, you've probably wished that these companies would stop mailing you. That's all direct mail, and whether you like it or not, direct mail has been a very successful form of marketing. The catalog industry has logged billions of dollars in sales because of it.

However, that has been impacted by social media marketing. Of all the areas of marketing, direct mail is one that will be most affected in the long run. Before you start worrying that your mail carrier will stuff your mailbox (or your email inbox through e-mail marketing) even more than usual, consider this: Direct mail is most successful when the mail is targeted and personalized. That means it's reaching the people who really care about the offers (or are most likely to take advantage of them), and it's personalized toward the recipients' needs in a voice and style that's appealing to them. Pretty straightforward, isn't it?

Direct mail is as successful as the marketer's customer database. The database should contain names and addresses of people who are open to receiving direct mail. But when people stop trusting the marketing efforts of large corporations and instead switch to each other for advice, that's when direct mail loses its power. Statistically, we know that consumers are now more likely to depend on each other for advice and information than they are on the corporations that are marketing to them.

With consumers who are even more connected to each other through social media than before, it has gotten easier for them to reach out to one another for that advice. That means that when they see a piece of direct mail, they're less likely to depend on it. They'd rather go online and ask a friend for advice or search for a product online than look at that flyer in the mail. And as marketers harness social media marketing tactics more, it could see further drops.

There's another side to the story, though. The more data that you can capture about your customers through social media marketing tactics, the more opportunities you have to feed your direct mail database. That's just a factor of consumers doing more online, sharing more of themselves, and opting into direct mail efforts in exchange for information or acceptance into an online community. Your database may get richer with social media marketing in the mix, but the value of it may decrease — although that doesn't mean that you can't use direct mail as a starting point to jump-start an online community, sustain interest in it, or reward participation through mailing coupons. The solution? Think about how you collect information about your consumers differently and, more important, how you share information back to them. It doesn't have to only be via mail or only via social media; knowing when to use what form of communication is key. More on this in later chapters.

Public relations

Among the earliest proponents of social media were digital-savvy public relations experts. Many of them entered this space by treating social media just as they have treated the mainstream media. These professionals equated *buzz* (how much people talk about a specific product or brand) in the social media realm with press mentions in the mainstream media. These PR experts identified the influential (*influence* defined as those having the most reach) bloggers and tweeters and started showering them with the same kind of attention that they had been bestowing on the mainstream media. They sent them press releases in advance, offered exclusive interviews, invited them to dinners, commented on their blogs, and carefully tracked how much their brands were mentioned and how positively.

For PR professionals, this approach made perfect sense. Arguably, they recognized early on how powerful social media could be and were among the first to track brand mentions and participate in conversations. In fact, many of the social media experts today are former public relations professionals who've taken the time to understand how social media works and how they can leverage it to support a company's or a brand's objectives. Many PR professionals also understand how bad press and traditional PR disasters can be amplified by social media if not addressed immediately.

But life isn't that simple, and the relationship between public relations and social media is a complex one — which is something that the savviest of PR professionals understand and have always understood. Public relations is fundamentally about managing the press (mainstream or alternative) and pushing a company's communications agenda out to the world as much as possible. Whether it's the mainstream or alternative media, it doesn't matter. From a public relations professional's perspective, the press is the press, and they're only as good as their ability to amplify a company's message. That's where the problem lies.

When we look at marketing and how it harnesses social media, some of its core tenets are in conflict with public relations. For example, social media marketing is about social influencers influencing each other through social media. The focus is on the social influencers influencing each other and not on the PR professionals influencing people in the social media realm. The difference is that as consumers, we're trusting and depending upon each other more for advice than on large corporations. The PR professionals, for all their sincerity and skill, will still push a company's message as forcefully as they can — and in that, it conflicts with social media marketing. But still, here's something extremely important to consider: The more forward-looking public relations experts approach PR from a broader communications perspective and have taken the time and energy to understand the space deeply. Those who do that are much better equipped to understand and market through social media than other professionals.

Is there a remedy for conflicts between departments? Not necessarily, but as you deploy social media marketing campaigns, be sensitive to the fact that your goals and aspirations may be in conflict with your PR organization if it hasn't embraced social media or social media marketing. Have a conversation with its staff early on, find ways to collaborate and delineate boundaries, too — who does what, who reaches out to whom, and how much space is given to authentic social influencers to do the influencing versus the PR professionals. And as you do this, keep in mind that for many PR professionals, social media marketing is an evolution of PR. That's a good thing, providing for even more opportunities to collaborate. And, of course, remember that you may have peers in the public relations department who could teach you a thing or two about social media marketing as well!

Online advertising

When it comes to buying online advertising (also referred to as digital *media planning and buying)* on websites where your customers spend time, social media marketing plays an important role. *Online advertising* is about identifying websites that your target customers visit, buying ad space on those websites, and then measuring how much those ads are viewed and clicked. It's as much an art as it is a science because knowing which sites your customers visit, where they're most likely to engage with an advertisement (where on the site as well), whether the site charges the appropriate amount for the advertisement, and how much that advertising affects purchasing is not always easy. We work with media buyers all the time, and their jobs are harder than you think, especially in the world of digital ad exchanges, data management platforms, and remnant inventory. (Books could be written on each of those terms alone.)

But the online advertising space is important even in an economic downturn. The reason is simple: It's one of the most measurable forms of advertising, especially in relation to print and television, along with search engine advertising. You can track those who view the advertisement, what they do with it, and in some cases, whether they eventually buy the product based on that advertisement. It's no surprise that the relationship to social media marketing is an important one as a result.

This relationship with social media marketing takes various forms. Here are some of those connection points:

>> **Market to the social influencers who surround the customer, as well as the customer.**

One of the ways in which you market to those influencers is using display advertising. So rather than just placing advertisements on websites that your customers visit, you place some advertisements (doesn't have to be a large percentage of your budget) on websites that their social influencers frequent, too. Is this as measurable as those advertisements targeting your customers directly? Maybe not, because these influencers are less likely to click the ads and make a purchase. But nevertheless, they remember the brand and influence your customers.

>> **Communicate and advertise on the social platforms — such as Facebook and YouTube — that your customers frequent.**

Most social platforms accept advertising in some form, and this serves as an important part of their revenue model. Figure 1-5 shows an eBay display advertisement on YouTube.

Granted, display advertising on social platforms used to produce bad results (users didn't notice the advertisements and didn't click them), but the ad formats for social platforms are evolving, and today Facebook is the second-largest advertising platform on the Internet after Google. One example of the evolution, is video-based advertising in the Facebook newsfeed itself. Another innovation that has been honed over the last two years is where consumers are asked to like the ads that they're viewing on Facebook, resulting in their action appearing more aggressively in the newsfeeds of their friends. This helps the platform target ads more appropriately to them in the future.

>> Use interactive social advertising.

Think about this scenario for a moment: You visit a major website like www.cnn.com and see a large advertisement on the right side. The advertisement asks you to sign up for suggestions about local deals in your neighborhood. That's an example of the ad unit becoming a platform for social interaction. There aren't too many examples of social ads online, but we're seeing more companies experiment in this space. Figure 1-6 shows how an ad appears on CNN's website.

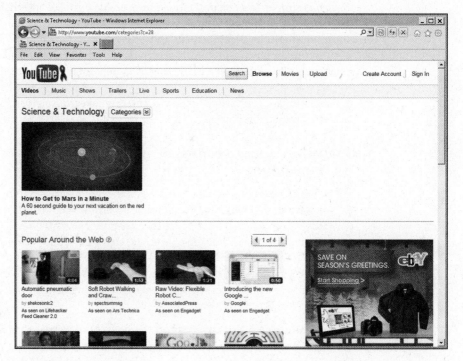

FIGURE 1-5:
An eBay placement ad on YouTube.

Promotions

Promotions are another important type of marketing activity that's affected by social influence marketing, owing to the fact that as people communicate with each other more, they have less time to participate in product promotions. But it also presents unique opportunities for marketers to put the potential of social influence marketing to good use.

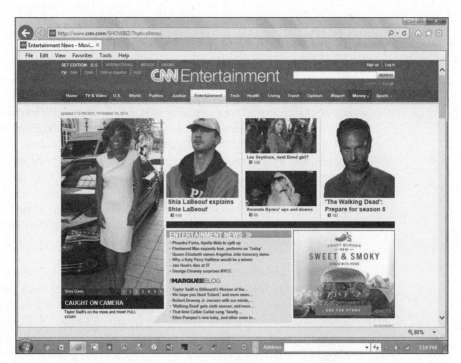

Consider this: Promotions are primarily about incentives that are designed to stimulate the purchase or sale of a product in a given period. Promotions usually take the form of coupons, sweepstakes, contests, product samples, rebates, and tie-ins. Most of these promotions are designed as one-off activities linking the marketer to specific customers. However, by deploying social media marketing concepts, you can design promotions that require customers to draw in their social influencers, whether it's to participate in the contest or sweepstakes with them or to play an advisory role. By designing the promotion to require social influencer participation (it needs to be positioned as friends participating), the specific promotion may get a lot more attention than it normally would have. What's more, you can now design promotions geared directly to driving social influence among people in a given network. We discuss promotions in Chapter 4.

Taking Social Influence Beyond Marketing

As we hint in the earlier sections, the benefits of social media marketing extend beyond the core domain of marketing. If you harness the power of social influence marketing to change other parts of your business, you stand to gain the most. You can use SMM to mobilize groups of people to take specific actions, make market-ers better corporate citizens, and further social change — and through those efforts, enhance a brand, too.

Using social influencers to mobilize

Social influencers obviously play an important role in getting people to do things. And this extends beyond the world of marketing. What makes social influence different on the web is that it's a lot easier to do now. Author Howard Rheingold was one of the first thinkers to identify this phenomenon in a book titled *Smart Mobs: The Next Social Revolution* (Basic Books). He discusses how the street protestors of the 1999 Seattle World Trade Organization (WTO) conference used websites, cellphones, and other "swarming" tactics to organize, motivate each other, and plan protests. The smart mobs (an intentionally contradictory term) could behave intelligently because of their exponentially increasing links to each other. Through those links, they influenced and motivated each other to perform tasks, form shared opinions, and act together. They used social influence marketing tactics on themselves to accomplish specific objectives.

In a seminal book, *Here Comes Everybody: The Power of Organizing without Organizations* (Penguin Press), Clay Shirky also focuses on the power of organizing and influencing using social technologies. As he explains, every web page can be considered a latent community waiting for people to interact, influence, and mobilize one another. People with shared interests visit the web page at various times and often seek out their peers' opinions — not just opinions from the web page's author. Shirky also discusses how Wikipedia, a user-contributed encyclopedia, can grow exponentially, publish efficiently, and self-correct using nontraditional corporate hierarchies.

We use the Seattle WTO protests and Wikipedia as examples to demonstrate how much social influence extends beyond the traditional realms of marketing into dramatically different domains. Driving the success of the Seattle WTO protests and the Wikipedia publishing model were two factors: social technologies that allowed people to contribute, participate, and converse easily, and technologies that allowed people to see what others were doing. The social influencers were at the heart of these efforts and many of the other "smart mob" initiatives over the years.

Twitter directly enabled protesters in Iran to organize in the wake of their 2009 elections, to such an extent that the U.S. State Department asked Twitter to delay a scheduled maintenance so that it wouldn't disrupt communications among the Iranian citizens as they protested the reelection of President Mahmoud Ahmadinejad. And arguably, one of the key factors that drove the Arab Spring and the fall of the Egyptian government in March of 2011, was the ability to use social media to organize on a mass scale quickly as well as share media about the protests around the world at a time when the official government channels of communication were blocking everything. In fact, many people believe that the simple Facebook status update "Advice to the youth of Egypt: Put vinegar or onion under your scarf for tear gas" significantly helped the protestors.

More recently, on March 20, 2014, the Turkish government blocked Twitter following the circulation of leaked recordings that implicated the Turkish prime minister and members of his inner circle in sweeping corruption allegations. Although people hadn't mobilized through Twitter, the Turkish government was worried that the leaked recordings would spread through the platform like wildfire and enable people to mobilize against the government. Just that fear was enough to make the prime minister order the blocking of Twitter.

In a similar fashion, social media became a battleground in Hong Kong's protests in late 2019. Pro-democracy protestors used social media as a way to galvanize, document, and organize large-scale protests. It was also used by both the government and the protestors as a tool to influence public opinion. From circulating images of protestors being injured while protesting to actual video clips of police brutality and campaign posters, Instagram was widely used by protestors to influence. The government used Instagram and Facebook to publish images and video clips of protestors disrupting traffic and vandalizing shops in the streets. With the protests being leaderless, social media's role as a connective tissue for the protestors was even more central to the protest than it had been in any other mobilization effort in the past.

But bringing the focus back to your company, this discussion of mobilization also demonstrates that you can harness those very same social media marketing philosophies to achieve other corporate objectives as well. We discuss those marketing philosophies further in Chapters 3 and 22.

REMEMBER

Social media marketing isn't just about how people influence each other by what they say on the social media platforms and on sites across the web. It also happens when people observe what others are doing online and offline. As a result, if you'd love others to mimic a certain type of customer behavior, make that behavior visible to everyone visiting the website. We don't just listen to people we admire; we also copy what they're doing.

Marketers as better corporate citizens

As has been the case in the last few years, marketers are increasingly supporting and furthering specific social causes that are in alignment with their brands. This win-win situation results in the marketers getting more favorable attention for their brands and the specific causes getting much needed sponsorship, too. One area where marketers are increasingly harnessing social media marketing tactics is in amplifying their efforts in the cause realm both to demonstrate that they have a business purpose that goes beyond profit and to better align with the values of their customers.

But why causes in particular? The causes have all the ingredients to make a successful social media marketing effort. They are usually time bound, have broad appeal, and are subjects that people like to discuss with each other. Marketers who tap into causes see their brands benefiting from the halo effect by being associated with important social concerns and by gaining visibility with much larger audiences than they normally would have. If you're a marketer, it bodes well to directly support a cause, encourage its supporters to harness social media marketing tactics, or sponsor it indirectly. Even better, it makes sense to market your own cause efforts using social media marketing tactics in a measurable fashion.

Procter & Gamble (one of the largest consumer-goods companies in the world) organized a social media education session for all its marketers. But instead of having a series of presentations by employees, P&G invited social media experts to visit its headquarters. The company divided the social media experts into teams and paired them with the company's own marketers. The teams were tasked with raising money for Tide's Loads of Hope disaster relief campaign using social media platforms to sell T-shirts. (The Loads of Hope website is shown in Figure 1-7.) The winning team raised $50,000, and Tide matched that team's contribution. Through this effort, P&G positioned itself as a better corporate citizen, raised money for a good cause, and was able to educate its marketers about the potential of social media by actually practicing social media marketing. Some detractors argued that this was just a one-day effort that got more attention than it deserved, but the fact that so much money was raised in so little time is admirable.

FIGURE 1-7: Tide's Loads of Hope.

WARNING

As you consider tapping into social media marketing to amplify your brand's efforts in the cause realm, keep in mind that consumers are increasingly skeptical of these efforts. Make sure that you're donating enough to make the effort genuine and meaningful for everyone involved.

Social graphs for social change

There's more to social causes than your ability to amplify your efforts around causes using social media marketing tactics. A larger change is afoot that demands attention, even if it doesn't directly relate to your objectives. The web allows individuals to financially support a cause at the very moment that they're inspired and then encourage their friends who reside in their social graphs to do the same.

When an individual provides monetary support for a cause, he can — in that very moment, using the social platforms and his own social media — broadcast his effort to his network of friends and associates. By doing so, he becomes a social media marketer, spreading the word about the cause and socially influencing his friends to contribute as well. This instant *viral effect* (the phrase comes from diseases and how they can spread rapidly from person to person) is collectively (and strongly) influencing how causes are promoted and funded — more so than the traditional strategies of backing by big corporations. This means that you, as a marketer, benefit from the halo effect of supporting a cause, but you can't just support it — you must be willing to participate in this viral affect the same way. Here are a few examples in this realm:

>> **The Pepsi Refresh Project:** In 2010 and 2011, Pepsi chose to give away millions and millions of dollars to people across America who had ideas for refreshing their communities in positive ways. But instead of making this a traditional charity program, the Pepsi Refresh Project enabled people across the country to submit ideas that deserved funding. Ideas were chosen by other consumers. Ideas with the most votes were then funded. This award-winning social media program, which Shiv was fortunate to be a part of running, was social at the core (with more than 80 million votes and millions of conversations about the ideas) and moved the brand's brand health metrics forward. In fact, The Pepsi Refresh Project has inspired many more cause-driven marketing efforts and is today a Harvard Business School case study used to inspire marketers of tomorrow.

>> **Causes:** This Facebook application (which is available at www.causes.com) was a perfect example of nonprofit organizations using social media as marketing and fundraising tools. (You can see the Causes application's home page in Figure 1-8.) It allowed you to choose a nonprofit, contribute funds to it, and track how many of your friends go on to support that cause after seeing your contributions or receiving your invitation to contribute. Within a year of its launch, the application had 12 million users supporting approximately 80,000 nonprofit causes

worldwide. Users raised $2.5 million for 19,445 different charitable organizations. Over its lifetime, more than a billion actions have been taken via Causes, with 186 million registered users in 156 countries. Since the success of Causes, Facebook has incorporated many of its features into the DNA of its platform directly allowing people to start supporting causes, raising money for others, and tracking the success of their efforts all via the newsfeed itself.

>> **MTV's Enough Campaign:** In the spring of 2018, and in response to the horrific Parkland tragedy where a gunman shot students in a school, MTV leveraged its various platforms to amplify the voices of young people who were taking action to stop gun violence. When it came to social media, MTV turned over its Facebook, Instagram, and Snapchat accounts to students who were taking action. MTV also supported the March for Our Lives protest in Washington DC by tapping celebrity influencers such as Lady Gaga, Jimmy Fallon, and Yara Shahidi to celebrate these young voices.

>> **Chase Community Giving:** Chase bank uses a simple but effective approach to cause marketing via its Chase Community Giving program. Since 2009, the bank has asked its Facebook fans to vote for their favorite charity or non-profit to receive a donation from them. In addition to the voting, Chase bank also promotes other charities on national holidays such as military related charities during National Military Appreciation Month and the Arbor Day Foundation on Arbor Day.

FIGURE 1-8:
Causes.com.

Chapter **2**

Discovering Your SMM Competitors

Which consumers are using the social web is no longer a subject of much debate. Rather, the debate has shifted to how consumers are using the social web. How many teens are using Facebook actively, what is the true reach of Twitter, and how aggressively are Instagram and Snapchat growing? These are the more common questions today. What's certain is that no one questions the scale or influence of the social web on culture, communications, and people's lives around the world.

The truth is that it's difficult to say who is using the social web and how. This is because the term *social web* is most commonly used to describe how people socialize and interact with each other across the web. With every passing day, many websites are becoming social platforms where visitors can interact and learn from one another. Even more critically, more and more websites allow you to log in with your Facebook or Twitter username and password. They then allow you to share your experience with the social network and, in some cases, customize the experience based on who you are and on your friends list. Those websites are becoming social, too. So how can you find out which consumers use the social web and in what way? The best way is to understand how your company fits into the big picture and how your competitors are using social media.

In this chapter, we explain how to do that. Having a firm grip on the lay of the land in the social web makes it easier to craft a marketing plan that works with it. Understanding what your competitors are doing helps you understand your customers' expectations.

Classifying Consumer Activities

Before you launch a social media marketing campaign, you need to have a feel for what activities consumers undertake on the social web. After all, your marketing campaign is far more likely to succeed if it is in harmony with what consumers are trying to accomplish on the social web. Consumer activity on the social web is classified into these eight categories:

>> **Information:** The Internet, with its academic roots, was conceived as a virtual library and an information-sharing tool. And to this day, consumers use the Internet for finding information more than anything else. In fact, it's no surprise that Google and Yahoo are two of the top five web destinations. (Facebook, YouTube, and Amazon are the other three.) Google and Yahoo are at the top because they're primary search engines, helping consumers find the information they're looking for. That hasn't changed, and even with the Internet going increasingly social, searching and finding information remains the number-one consumer activity online. If you're running a marketing campaign for a product or service that consumers seek, you're most likely to get strong results. When people are in "information seeker" mode, they're most apt to participate in campaigns.

>> **News:** One primary use for the Internet is news. More people read the news online than watch it on cable television. The instant, real-time nature of news makes it particularly suited for the Internet. Many cable television channels promote their websites to their TV audiences. But what's even more interesting is that practically all the major news websites integrate social media functionality into their user experience. When you go to www.cnn.com, www.nytimes.com, or www.washingtonpost.com, you notice that journalists have blogs and that the articles allow for commenting and ratings. Figure 2-1 shows the blogs offered by *The New York Times*. News sites often integrate video clips as well.

REMEMBER

With news, your marketing opportunity differs slightly. Consumers are more receptive to the campaigns if your product or service is either contextualized in some form to what they're reading or is directly targeted toward them. What's more, marketing programs that have cultural relevance or that are in the context of events in the broader world do better. People simply pay more attention to what is topical versus what distracts them from the stories of the day.

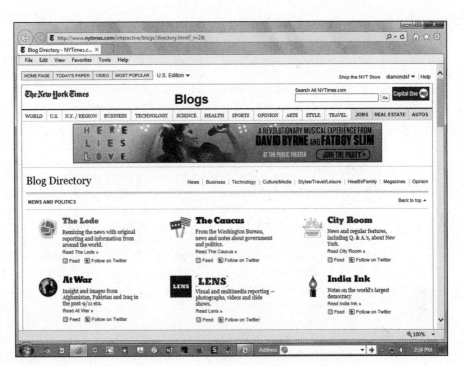

FIGURE 2-1:
Blogs on
*The New York
Times* website.

>> **Communication:** The Internet continues to be a core communication medium for most people. With the advent of social media, this communication takes place within social networks versus personal websites or via email and instant messenger programs. *Microcommunication* technologies such as Twitter, which let you communicate in short bursts of information, are very popular. The medium allows consumers to communicate with one another in new, dynamic ways, whether it be through microblogging, leaving notes on friends' Facebook profiles, commenting on personal blogs, or instant messaging from within websites. In fact, the explosive growth of WhatsApp and its subsequent purchase by Facebook for $19 billion dollars is testament to this trend around microcommunication on a huge scale. When consumers are communicating with each other, they're less receptive to marketing campaigns unless the campaigns incorporate their communications with their peers in a permissible fashion. This is why social media marketing campaigns that incorporate groups of people are so important. The trickiness of marketing in this context is also why at this point, WhatsApp has no intention of incorporating advertising into its mobile app. That could change in the future, of course.

>> **Community:** Online communities and social networks have seen explosive growth in the last few years. The amount of time that people spend on community websites is significantly higher than anywhere else on the web. Online communities include social platforms, such as Facebook and Twitter, and the more private online communities and forums that are often tied to company websites or niche interests.

For example, The Well (shown in Figure 2-2) is one of the most famous, early online communities, just as Facebook is the most popular social network in the United States as we write this. The reasons people participate in online communities are myriad. Suffice it to say, community participation is a key type of activity online. However, when people are engaging with each other, they participate less in marketing campaigns because engaging with one another captures all their attention. They have no time for advertising because they're busy hearing each other's opinions. When consumers are searching for information or looking to buy a product, they are more open to advertising. This is exactly why social media marketing, with its unique approach, is important.

FIGURE 2-2:
The Well.

>> **E-commerce:** Consumers across the country continue to choose to buy more goods online. The fact that the products have to be shipped has done little to hinder many consumers from using the Internet to make retail purchases. The largest online retailer continues to be Amazon (www.amazon.com), with

approximately 230 billion dollars in sales each year. E-commerce represents a growing portion of total retail sales. There are some very obvious marketing opportunities in this, especially when peers are asked to recommend products. Great social media marketing opportunities abound here.

>> **Entertainment:** No doubt about it — consumers look to the Internet for entertainment. The explosive growth of YouTube and the adoption of high-end video sites such as Hulu (shown in Figure 2-3) are testament to this trend. In fact, Millennials are more likely to turn to the Internet and YouTube in particular for entertainment than they are to look at a television screen. Social games like Fortnite and World of Warcraft, which are social by design, are just another example of this trend. Arguably, entertainment is becoming a driving reason for people to spend more time online, and this is in part thanks to the proliferation of high-bandwidth access in most countries. As long as the marketing is entertaining, consumers will respond to it. They don't care as much whether it's an advertisement in these instances.

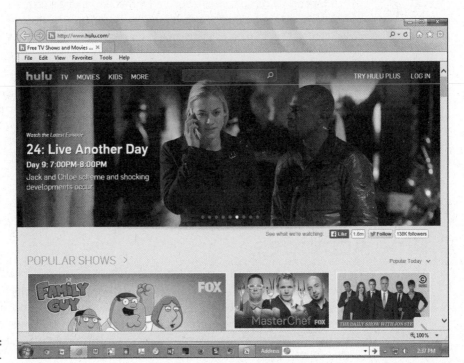

FIGURE 2-3:
Hulu.

>> **Services:** Another popular consumer activity online is the use of services to allow a person to lead a more efficient and productive life. Whether they're paying bills, checking bank balances, looking up phone numbers, finding jobs, or searching for apartments, consumers use the Internet as a tool to lead more productive lives. Most of today's businesses, such as banks and airlines, provide services on the Internet. In fact, consumers now expect today's businesses to provide their core services online or at least have a presence online. Consumers are typically very task-oriented when they're interacting with online services; as a result, they don't expect to participate in advertising campaigns, and especially not social media marketing campaigns, when they're in this mode.

>> **Business:** And of course, the Internet is used to conduct business. This may take the form of companies talking to each other and exchanging information, establishing online marketplaces, and initiating brand launches. Businesses engage with their customers online by marketing and selling products and services and providing customer service via the Internet. Consumers expect these online conveniences from brands that they interact with, and they increasingly engage with businesses on the Internet. They also use the Internet to start their own businesses. Depending on the business, social media marketing campaigns can certainly help here.

Critically, if there is any one significant change over the last decade, it is that consumers expect marketing to contribute to their sense of self and their personal needs (whether that's news, communication, e-commerce, entertainment, services, or business-driven tasks and goals). Marketing that distracts consumers from what they're trying to accomplish or how they want to feel has a much more difficult time succeeding.

Researching Your Customers' Online Activities

When developing a social media marketing campaign or a broader, continuing program, determining what your target customers are doing on the Internet is important. You can use several tools to find out where your target customers are going online. Without this information, you can't formulate a smart social marketing strategy. You're simply shooting in the dark.

Tools that help you research online activity fall into two basic categories: free and paid. You can simply register for and use the free tools. Tools and services for which you must pay can get expensive very quickly. In Chapter 4, we discuss the paid tools and services, which are more appropriate when you're planning a specific SMM campaign. In this section, we discuss some of the free tools:

» **Blog search engines:** These search engines *crawl* (sort through) just the blogosphere for the terms that you input. They search for those terms in the blog posts and the comments, and the searches generally include all publicly viewable blogs on the Internet. If you just want to get a sense of the conversations in the blogosphere about a specific topic or brand, these search engines can help you do that. The most popular one is Blog Search Engine (http://www.blogsearchengine.org), which is shown in Figure 2-4.

FIGURE 2-4:
Blog Search
Engine.

A discussion on blog search engines wouldn't be complete without mentioning the official Twitter search tool (http://search.twitter.com). Twitter is the most popular microblogging platform. *Microblogging* is similar to blogging except that you're restricted to a certain number of characters per post. In addition to the Twitter search functionality, several Twitter tools, such as TweetDeck (shown in Figure 2-5) and Hootsuite, integrate search functionality.

» **Buzz charting:** Similar to the blog search engines are the buzz charting tools. These tools focus on giving you a comparative perspective on how many different keywords, phrases, or links are discussed in the blogosphere. They search for the terms and then organize the responses into a chart, with the x-axis being time and the y-axis the number of posts. The most popular of these tools comes from Google and is called Google Trends (http://trends.google.com), as shown in Figure 2-6.

FIGURE 2-5:
TweetDeck.

FIGURE 2-6:
Google Trends.

>> **Forums and message boards:** To understand online behavior in the social web, you must be able to scan the conversations happening in forums and message boards as well. Boardreader (`http://boardreader.com`) shown in Figure 2-7, allows you to search multiple boards at one time. You can use it to find answers to questions that you may not find on a single board. Also, from a marketer's point of view, you can research people's opinions of brands or

products. Boardreader is so popular that it powers a lot of the forum searches that the fee-based brand-monitoring tools conduct. Another player worth mentioning in this space is Omgili (www.omgili.com), which similarly focuses on forums and message boards.

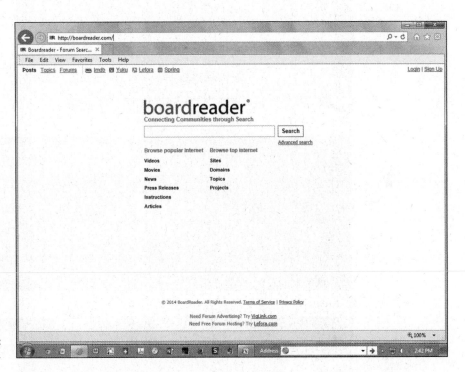

FIGURE 2-7: Boardreader.

>> **Video and image search:** Earlier in this chapter, we mention entertainment and the increasing number of people going online to watch videos — professionally created videos and personal ones, too. But how can you find the videos that are of interest to you or your brand? For video search, you have to depend on a couple of tools, because no single one truly captures all the videos created. All video searches must begin with YouTube (www.youtube.com) because it's the largest video website, but you should also look at 360 Daily (www.360daily.com); Viral Stats (www.viralstat.com), which also tells you how much the clip is being discussed; and AOL Video (http://video.aol.com/), another notable player, shown in Figure 2-8.

On the image side, you'd want to search Instagram on its mobile app, Pinterest (www.pinterest.com), Tumblr (www.tumblr.com), Flickr (www.flickr.com) and, to a lesser extent, Google Images (www.google.com/images). These tools, especially Tumblr, are valuable for understanding

WARNING

broader trends, your consumers, and conversations about your industry and potentially your company, too.

Google Images also searches professionally produced and published images, not just user-generated ones, so you might not get an accurate picture of what people are talking about.

FIGURE 2-8:
AOL Video.

Identifying Personas

After you understand what your customers do online, you can begin to define them more clearly. To do this, you can create what are known as *personas*. Personas are customer profiles that represent your actual buyers. Alan Cooper first wrote about personas in his book *The Inmates Are Running the Asylum* (Sams Publishing). He wrote, "We don't so much make up our personas as discover them as a byproduct of the investigation process." That is exactly what you need to do.

Some marketers swear by personas; others find it difficult to wrap their heads around the concept. We recommend the creation of personas because they help you stay focused on the buying strategies that matter. For example, suppose you identify your customer as a 45-year-old male who has an annual income of more than $90,000, a family with two children less than 12 years old, and deep interests in chess, gardening, and wine.

When you're developing your SMM campaign, you can stop your team from developing copy for a young woman of college age. This may sound obvious, but it's easy to get off track when the ideas are flying fast and furious. When a fun notion pops into someone's head, it can be helpful to look at your persona and think it through. You can remain focused and course-correct when you find you are getting away from the heart of the profile.

So what information goes into creating a good customer persona? Consider the following:

>> **Demographics:** Obviously, you want to know whether your customer is male or female, where she lives, what her estimated income is, and so on.

>> **Photo and name:** If you give your persona a name and choose a stock photo (or real customer photo), you bring life to it. When someone asks, "What would Alice want?" it makes a greater impact than visualizing a faceless and nameless customer.

>> **Online places where your customer hangs out:** This is important for your SMM efforts. Does he spend time on Facebook or a niche sports site?

>> **Online places where he looks for product information:** You need to know where he reads product reviews and what online bloggers influence him.

>> **Job level:** Is your customer a supervisor with staff to whom she can delegate? It's helpful to know the amount of responsibility she has at work.

>> **Children and pets:** Clearly, childcare responsibility, family pets, and other home care chores play a factor in his product choices.

>> **Hobbies and interests:** Learning about hobbies and special interests helps you speak to the customer's desire for specific products.

REMEMBER

Make sure that your team understands the value of personas. Start with one or two until your team gets used to using them. Also, task someone with keeping them updated. If something changes, you want your customer profiles to be current.

TIP

You may not have all the information you want to include when you start out, but you can fill in the blanks as you go along. Don't wait until you have every detail to create a persona. The value comes from the ongoing "investigation process," as Alan Cooper once wrote.

Analyzing Competitor Efforts

Just as it's important to understand where your consumers participate in the social web, it's also necessary to understand how your competitors engage in the social web. But where should you start? The following are some types of information to consider when you are planning your SMM investigation:

>> **Keywords being used by competitors.**

This is something you have probably heard again and again, but its importance can't be overemphasized. If you don't use the right keywords, you won't be found. Make sure to note which ones your competitors are using. They may not all be "home runs" for you, but evaluating them is important.

>> **Where their traffic is coming from.**

Using a host of tools (detailed in the three sections that follow: "Setting up Google Alerts," "Setting up Twitter alerts," and "Monitoring social networks"), you can learn more about the traffic to their website and other channels. It's worth noting that the strongest brands get significant traffic from social referrals (people coming in via Facebook and Twitter) along with the search engines.

>> **Rankings by important engines.**

You can do a quick look at major ranking engines such as Alexa (`www.alexa.com`) to see how their sites compare with yours. For very large competitors, sites like Quantcast (`www.quantcast.com`) can help you determine how many people are visiting your competitors' websites and whether they are visiting the desktop or mobile versions. Another important tool to look at is Google webmaster tools (`https://www.google.com/webmasters/tools`), which lets you see the approximate traffic of a website and the profiles of the people visiting, including the other sites they visit and their various interests.

>> **Which social media platforms they are on and which distribution channels they use.**

As we discuss earlier, if you don't know where your customers spend their time, you won't be able to market to them where they are most comfortable. You can't count on their going to your website. Most businesses are now using several channels besides their websites (such as a blog, Twitter, and so on), so be aware of their choices and see what could work for you. And as you look at this data, keep in mind that you may not have the resources to have strong social presences in all the places that your customers are — you'll have to make strategic choices on where to spend your time and money.

>> **Who they partner with.**

This is an often-overlooked source of competitive information. Businesses find synergy and partner with those who have similar audiences. Whom they partner with tells you a lot about how they view their audience. Those partnerships could also include where they advertise, people or organizations with whom they have comarketing agreements, and partners who serve as referral engines for them.

>> **Loyalty and other programs they employ.**

Find out what programs are keeping their customers loyal to them, and see how you can tap into the same vein with your own unique program. A recent trend is the creation of Social Loyalty programs, which reward consumers for social actions that they take on behalf of brands. This is something worth paying attention to as well.

>> **Their online customer service efforts.**

This one can be a secret weapon for you. If you see that your competitors aren't offering support through social media channels, you can distinguish your company with a solid effort here. According to Bain & Company, a customer is four times more likely to buy from a competitor if the problem is service related versus price or product related.

>> **What they do offline to connect with customers.**

Check out whether your competitors have special training programs or other educational sessions available locally. This might be a way they are increasing their customer base consistently.

TIP

If your competitors are already running marketing campaigns similar to what you plan to do, yours won't attract much attention. To prevent this from happening, a combination of sleuthing and the following third-party tools can help you.

Setting up Google Alerts

You can set up these free alerts for keywords related to your competitors. These keywords can include company names, brands, senior manager names, and partner names. Every day, you receive a Google Alert in your email Inbox with summaries of news stories and blog posts that include those keywords. It's a good starting point and completely free.

To set up a Google Alert, follow these simple steps:

1. **Go to** www.google.com/alerts.

   The Google Alerts page opens, as shown in Figure 2-9.

2. **Enter the search terms for which you want alerts.**

   Try to keep these to one word or a commonly used phrase.

3. **From the Sources drop-down list, choose the sources of content you want Google to search.**

   We generally choose Automatic so that we don't miss news items.

4. **From the How Often drop-down list, choose the frequency with which you want the alerts delivered to you.**

   We find At Most Once a Day to be the best frequency.

5. **Enter the email address where you want the alerts to be sent.**

   Remember that you can edit these alert settings at any time.

6. **Click the Create Alert button.**

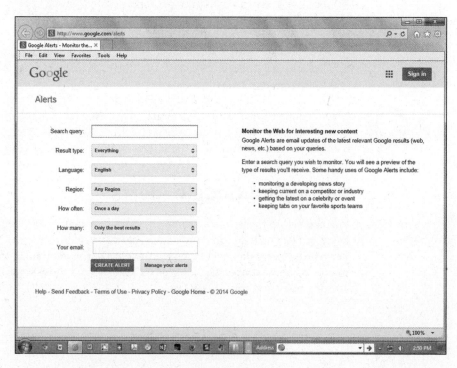

FIGURE 2-9:
Google Alerts.

Setting up Twitter alerts

Similarly, create Twitter alerts that track those same keywords in the Twitter world. Services such as Twilert (www.twilert.com) let you follow keywords and observe all the microblogging posts in which those words appear.

TIP

To set up a Twitter alert, follow these simple steps:

1. **Go to** www.twilert.com.

   The Twilert home page opens, as shown in Figure 2-10.

   To set up a Twitter alert, you have to be signed in to your Twitter account. If you don't have one, you can sign up at www.twitter.com.

2. **Type the keyword that you want the alert set up for.**

3. **Click the Create Twilert button.**

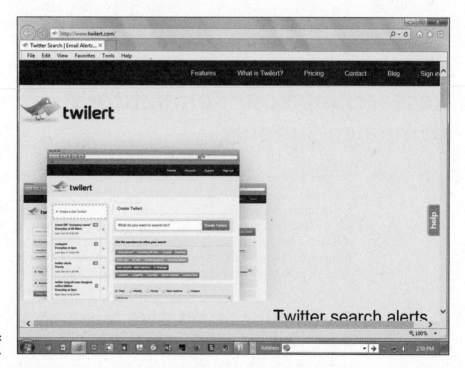

FIGURE 2-10:
Twilert.

CHAPTER 2 **Discovering Your SMM Competitors** 43

Monitoring social networks

You probably want to observe what your customers are doing on the various social networks. That's a little harder to do because most social networks are closed gardens, meaning that except for the public profile pages (a very small percentage of all the pages on the network), you can't search them with external tools, and typically, after you log in, you can't search the universe of activity on them. However, what you can do is search and follow the pages, profiles, groups, and applications created by your competitors. Keep in mind that some users hide their profiles, so you won't be able to track them. To search the Facebook public pages, log in to Facebook and type the search query in the search bar in the header.

Tracking competitor websites

REMEMBER

Look at the social media efforts that may reside on your competitors' websites. Often, those efforts are promoted or anchored in the company website or company-sponsored microsite through links. In fact, many of your competitors probably have (as they should) corporate blogs and Twitter accounts. (Start tracking those directly, too.)

Researching Your Competitors' Campaign Support

Practically every marketing campaign today has a social media component to it. As you see a competitor launch a major marketing campaign, scan the web and the competitor's website for that campaign's digital and social components. The social activity surrounding the campaign (elsewhere on the web) gives you a sense of how successful it is and how much it helps the brand. Also, watch prominent bloggers in that product category: They may be part of an outreach program and could be promoting the campaign.

Conducting qualitative research

Using the free tools and observing competitor activity is all well and good. But more often than not, you need to conduct qualitative research that doesn't just tell you what your consumers are doing, but also the goals, needs, and aspirations that drive their behavior. Here, there's good news and bad news.

First, the good news. Qualitative research, as you probably know it in the traditional marketing world, hasn't changed. You can still use interviews, focus groups, shadowing, and other ethnographic research techniques to understand your consumers. There are dozens of authoritative books on the subject — including a few excellent ones from the *For Dummies* series, such as *Marketing For Dummies,* by Alexander Hiam (John Wiley & Sons, Inc.) — on qualitative research, so we won't go into those research formats. All the same best practices of recruiting effectively, knowing your objectives, and having good interview guides and moderators apply.

And now for the bad news: The questions have changed, and you won't get all your answers from the qualitative research. Unlike qualitative research in the past, which focused on understanding a specific consumer's goals and needs, you must pay attention to the consumer's surrounding community and influencers within that community. For example, you need to ask who influences your consumers when they make specific purchasing decisions.

Running surveys and quantitative research

Similarly, quantitative research in the form of statistically significant surveys can be most helpful. Keep in mind that you must run surveys at regular intervals to get valuable, statistically significant results. The reason is that influence changes more rapidly in an online environment, and the social media platforms on which people participate change, too. Don't run extensive surveys irregularly. Run short, quick surveys about your audiences on a frequent basis to glean important insights.

Pay attention to where you run the surveys, too, because that can affect the results. A good strategy is to run the survey on your corporate website but simultaneously use a third-party survey vendor to run the same survey on the social media platforms. This way, you're gauging how people participate and socialize in their own contexts. Very often, the quantitative research can give statistically significant results about influence, with the qualitative research being used to explain the hows and whys of the responses. The two kinds of research go hand in hand.

Some of the survey vendors that you can use include

>> SurveyMonkey (www.surveymonkey.com); see Figure 2-11

>> Zoomerang (www.zoomerang.com)

>> SurveyGizmo (www.surveygizmo.com)

>> Key Survey (www.keysurvey.com)

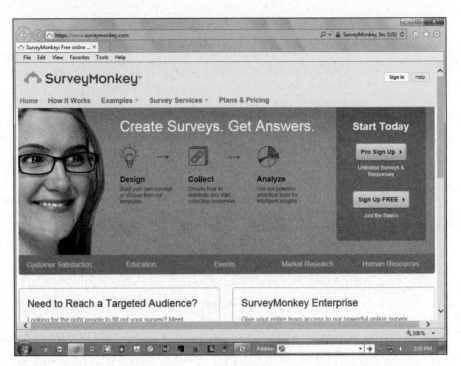

FIGURE 2-11:
SurveyMonkey.

TECHNICAL STUFF

As you may know, there are other important forms of research, such as content, discourse, and network analysis, which take on additional importance in the sphere of social media, but those can be relatively laborious. Generally, they're appropriate only when much deeper behavioral insights are required.

Seeing why all consumers are not created equal

A chapter on competition wouldn't be complete without addressing the fact that in discussions about social influence and social media marketing, all consumers aren't created equal. Social influence doesn't simply mean recognizing that every consumer may influence every other consumer; rather, in specific marketing contexts, specific consumers have an outsized influence on their peers around them. For example, on a social network, one of the authors' friends posts more comments than anyone else. Just by virtue of his volume of postings, we take his opinion into account more than that of our other friends who aren't commenting as much.

THE PSYCHOLOGY BEHIND SOCIAL INFLUENCE

Consumers have always been heavily influenced by each other when they make purchasing decisions. They ask each other for advice; they observe and mimic each other's decision making; and, frankly, they let peer pressure inform their decisions, whether they like to admit it or not. What's changed is that digital behavior has caught up with offline behavior, and that's why social media marketing matters to anyone who has a future in marketing.

Communication technologies such as social networks, prediction markets, microblogging solutions, location-based networked mobile phone applications, and even virtual worlds make it possible for consumers to influence each other more directly and dramatically than ever before. According to Harvard psychologist Herbert Kelman, this influence occurs in three ways:

- **Compliance:** Conforming publicly while keeping one's own private beliefs
- **Identification:** Conforming to someone who is liked and respected, such as a celebrity or a favorite uncle
- **Internalization:** Accepting the belief or behavior and conforming both publicly and privately

In addition to making for good copy in behavioral psychology textbooks, these concepts do translate into tactics for social media marketing.

In this regard, three steps help you gain a marketing advantage from influential consumers:

1. **Discover the influential consumers.**

   As you launch a social media marketing campaign and identify your consumers, pay extra attention to who is influencing your potential customers. Who are the consumers who are influencing your customers, and where is this influence taking place? (You can find out more about influencers in Chapter 18.)

2. **Activate the influential consumers.**

   After you identify the influential consumers, whether they're bloggers, forum leaders, or just conversationalists with lots of friends on the social networks, develop relationships with them and find ways to activate them to do the marketing on your behalf. In later chapters, we discuss exactly how you can do this.

3. Turn customers into brand advocates.

And finally, after a consumer becomes a customer, deepen your relationship with her so that the customer becomes a brand advocate. That's not a new strategy, except that now you can ask her to take specific actions within her social networks as a brand advocate. Rather than just ask her to talk about your product, you can have her actually reach out to her peers and then reward her for her participation.

Dipping into Hot SMM Concepts

One way to stay ahead of the competition is to keep abreast of the marketing trends that directly affect your customers. Several major trends have recently impacted the social media realm. You should determine whether those trends apply to your situation. Even if you do not immediately see a way to apply them, you'll want to monitor them closely. We mention them here and cover them more in depth in the chapters cited below.

Discovering gamification

There are basically two camps of people online — those who believe that online games are a complete waste of time and those who find them irresistible. But are social games actually games? They are, and again, they aren't. Social games incorporate game techniques in a social setting with the aim of encouraging you to interact with a business, a charity, or perhaps an educational entity, to name a few.

You're playing a social game if you are on one of the social media platforms and the game encourages you to take action that surrounds a brand. Where do these social gamers like to play?

Typically when you think of a "gamer," you might think of an adolescent with lots of time and energy to master ever higher levels of game play. But actually, according to the same study, the average social gamer is a 43-year-old woman. Businesses of all types are creating games that integrate the use of their products with the daily play. One example of this is Clarins, a French cosmetics company. Their game Spa Life on Facebook is about the challenges of running a spa. Their products are used at the spa and become part of the game solution.

But lest you think it's all for fun, gamification takes several different cuts at the online game experience. In September of 2011, a group of gamers who play at a site called Foldit was asked to help solve a complex protein folding puzzle that had stumped AIDS researchers for years. Surprisingly, the gamers were able to solve it within 10 days. It's reported that the competitive nature of the game drove the teams forward. CBS News reported that one researcher called it the value of "citizen science."

If your company is thinking about creating a social game, you'll want to make sure to take a broad approach and see what's being done online. These games can be short or long term. You don't have to commit yourself to something untried.

Choosing localized marketing

Many Internet marketers are excited about the opportunities they have to reach around the globe for new consumers. What many have overlooked is the opportunity to reach into their local communities to get more customers. As Adam Metz says in his book *The Social Customer* (McGraw-Hill), these customers "didn't exist at the turn of the twenty-first century."

Tools are now available to help small businesses and local sites of large businesses engage their fans. For example, Facebook has developed several types of advertising deals that help owners reward their customers for visiting the store often in the context of offers. (We cover these types of rewards in Chapter 8.)

Companies like BlitzLocal, shown in Figure 2-12, at (`https://localblitz.com/`), have sprung up to assist business owners in finding their local Facebook fans. Dennis Yu, co-founder and CEO of BlitzLocal, said, "It's quality, not quantity that counts" when it comes to fan numbers.

Creating an app for that

According to App Annie, the total number of mobile app downloads increased from 178 billion in 2017 to 194 billion in 2018. Furthermore, total app usage increased by 50 percent between 2016 and 2018 globally. Without a doubt, apps are big business and getting bigger every year. Social media marketers have an enormous opportunity to brand an app that is seen every day by their customers. Talk about product placement! Marketers can help their customers and proudly display their logo while they do it. But not all apps are a hit. It takes careful planning and research to create an app that resonates with customers. Apps can typically be categorized in one of the following eight categories:

>> Social networking

>> News

>> Lifestyle

» Games

» Entertainment

» Education

» Family and kids

» Music

If your company sells a product or service in one of those areas, you'll likely choose to create a consumer app in that area. But what if you run a manufacturing company or do field sales? Does this mean that you can't create an app? Not at all. In fact, you can create apps that provide a solution for your employees too. For example, if you are a manufacturing company, you could create an app that searches your catalog part numbers. Areas such as transaction processing, field sales, and competitive intelligence are all possible areas to create an app for. See Chapter 23 for more detailed information on mobile marketing and creating apps.

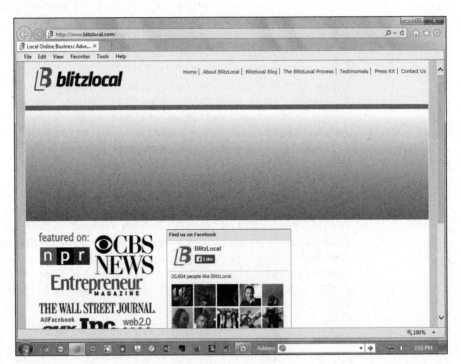

FIGURE 2-12:
BlitzLocal.

» Applying social media marketing to the marketing funnel

» Deploying specific tactics at each stage of the funnel

» Deepening customer relationships using SMM

» Complementing brand marketing

» Making direct-response and social media marketing work together

Chapter **3**

Getting in the Social Media Marketing Frame of Mind

The true power of social media marketing comes from applying its principles to all parts of your business in a rigorous fashion. This begins with examining social media marketing in relation to your marketing funnel. You then need to understand how it relates to brand marketing and direct response — the two traditional pillars of marketing that support the marketing funnel. Understanding the differences helps you to better know when to deploy social media marketing tactics versus when to depend upon brand or direct-response tactics.

In this chapter, we also discuss how big and little ideas relate to social media marketing. The marketing world has historically been driven by the big ideas. Whether it's been the glamorous advertising (Apple's iconic *1984* commercial comes to mind) or the clever in-store promotions that you see when you walk down the aisle at your local Whole Foods, ideas drive marketing. That changes with social media marketing. We explain how you need to think about the big idea a little differently as you deploy social media marketing to meet your marketing and business objectives.

Putting SMM in the Context of the Marketing Funnel

The marketing funnel is one of the most important metaphors in marketing today. It differentiates between prospects and customers, and maps out the journey from the point where a prospect learns about a product to when he becomes a loyal, repeat customer. Because practically every marketer uses some form of the marketing funnel, it serves an important framework through which to understand social media marketing.

The traditional marketing funnel typically has five stages, as defined by Forrester. These five stages are awareness, consideration, preference, action, and loyalty (as shown in Figure 3-1). The last stage (loyalty) has the fewest people. Those customers are the most loyal and, therefore, among the most valuable. For many marketers, marketing is fundamentally the act of moving people from having an awareness of a product, considering it along with other products, and establishing a preference for the product over the others, to eventually taking action such as purchasing it and developing loyalty toward it.

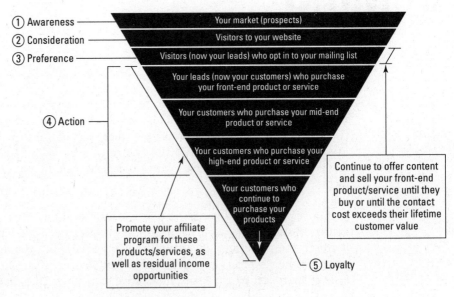

FIGURE 3-1:
A marketing funnel.

You employ different marketing strategies and tactics at every stage of the marketing funnel to move the prospects along. The movement of prospects and customers is measured precisely (especially when you do this online), and if there isn't enough movement, you need to devote more marketing dollars to pushing people through the funnel. How you spend these dollars and which investments do the most to move people through the marketing funnel is always a subject of much debate and varies by product category. Regardless, social media marketing and tapping into the social influencers with differing tactics can help with this journey.

The stages of the marketing funnel may vary from company to company. In some cases, it has changed significantly with the advent of everything digital; for others the fundamental marketing funnel is the same. Some link online funnel tracking with offline efforts, whereas others don't. You don't have to rigorously use the stages as we define them. It's more important that you look at SMM in the context of how your company builds its brand, drives awareness for its products, tracks leads, enables sales, and manages loyalty. In some cases, you need to consider how you can apply SMM at the different points in an advertising campaign. Regardless, the same principles apply whether you're looking at SMM in the context of the funnel for your entire marketing efforts or for just an online advertising campaign.

SMM at the awareness stage

The awareness stage of the marketing funnel is where you introduce potential customers to your brand. You build awareness and encourage prospective customers to remember your brand name so that when they do make a purchase in the future, they include your brand in their consideration mix.

Typically, marketers use television, radio, print, and direct mail to build awareness. They also sponsor events, conduct promotions, and invest in product placements to get further exposure. Marketers also use public relations professionals to influence editorial content in magazines and newspapers.

In the digital realm, you typically create awareness using display advertising on major websites, paid searches for category-related keywords, video advertising on YouTube and Facebook, and sponsorships across the web. Email marketing has also been successful at building awareness. Historically, creating awareness online is a lot cheaper but without the same mass scale effect of a 30-second television spot.

You can use social media marketing to build awareness of your brand, too. The reason is simple: As a marketer with a loyal customer base, you can encourage your customers to build your brand by talking about your product with their friends. Many a marketer has incentivized existing customers to tell their friends and families about their purchasing decisions. You aren't the first. In fact, you can also reach out to expert influencers to help you here. One important consideration with using social media marketing at the awareness stage is whether your SMM efforts can give you the type of scale that you can get with television, radio, or print. For a long time, marketers believed that social media marketing couldn't give that scale. That's changing fast, thanks to the likes of Facebook, YouTube, Google, and Twitter, which are now among the most trafficked websites on the Internet. In fact, marketers now recognize that you can get as much scale and often much more efficiently as TV could in the past. Some brands have moved toward a digital-only model for all their marketing efforts as a result.

REMEMBER

Expert influencers are the people who are experts in a field and have large audiences.

Here are some SMM tactics to consider for building awareness:

>> **Publish video advertisements to YouTube and tag them with category terms.**

For example, if you're publishing advertisements for orange juice on YouTube, use the tags *orange, orangejuice, beverage, vitamin,* and *drink* in addition to the brand name. Highlight these YouTube video clips on the corporate website, too. As you do this, first consider whether your advertisement is YouTube ready: Would people enjoy viewing it, would they share it, should it be longer, does it evoke strong emotion, and is it truly enjoyable? Figure 3-2 shows whether your orange juice video would be in good company on YouTube.

>> **Nurture relationships with expert influencers, such as YouTube and Instagram influencers, who publish content related to the specific product category you're marketing.**

Take the time to share product samples with these influencers, answer their questions, and invite them to special events. If required, sponsor a post on an influential blog. These expert influencers build awareness for your brand in ways that your customers may be more responsive to.

>> **Set up a Facebook fan page, a Twitter account, and a LinkedIn profile.**

Run polls, offer special discounts, publish games, promote coupons, and give members of these pages or accounts product sneak peeks. Share entertaining and educational information through them. Boost that content with paid advertising so that it reaches the right people.

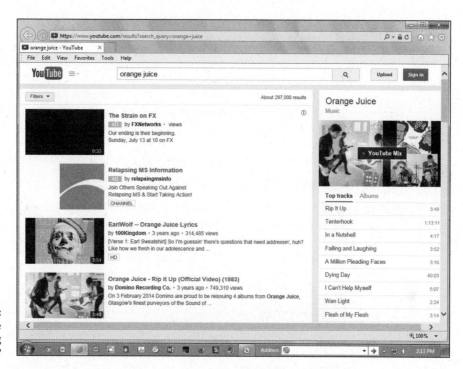

FIGURE 3-2:
Does your orange
juice video belong
here?

>> **Provide RSS feeds for content on the corporate website.**

An RSS feed is a content format that easily allows anyone to pluck the content from your site and place it on their website, application, or in an RSS reader. Feedly is probably the most popular RSS reader. Just visit http://feedly. com for instructions on how to set it up. Then each time you see the RSS icon on a website, you can click it and have that content fed into your RSS reader on an ongoing basis. Figure 3-3 shows how Apple has set up its RSS feeds.

Also allow for the easy sharing of information from your corporate website onto the social networks. Services from companies such as AddThis (www. addthis.com) and ShareThis (www.sharethis.com) allow you to make your content sharable.

>> **Allow new customers to broadcast their purchases to their social networks.**

Each time a customer makes a purchase, you can ask her whether she would like to announce the purchase on her favorite social network. Services such as StrongView and ShareThis, along with Facebook Connect, allow you to set up this capability on your website for your customers.

REMEMBER

If you're planning to broadcast customers' purchases, be sure to ask the customers for permission to do this before you do.

>> **Leverage social ads.**

Because social ads are highly engaging — by virtue of the fact that they tell the customer what his friends are doing — they're useful for building awareness and establishing consideration. For example, if a customer sees an endorsement from his friend in an ad unit for a movie, he is more likely to go for the movie. See Part 3 to find out how each social media platform approaches endorsements via ads. Also review the social ad options from Facebook at (www.Facebook.com/advertising), which give you awareness-building opportunities at scale.

>> **Support a cause via a social network.**

Promise to match the contributions of participants who encourage friends to participate in the cause as well. Companies such as Network for Good (http://www1.networkforgood.org/) help you run marketing campaigns that integrate cause marketing elements into them.

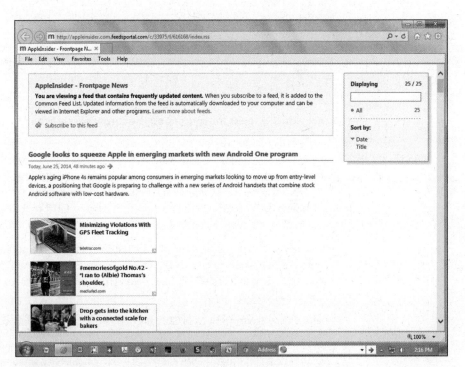

FIGURE 3-3:
One of Apple's RSS feeds.

SMM at the consideration stage

The consideration stage of the marketing funnel is where you make sure that as the prospective customer goes about making a purchasing decision, she considers your product.

To be included in the consideration stage, use tactics such as product comparisons, special promotions, sales discounts, decision tools, and calculators to convince prospects.

REMEMBER

The consideration stage is arguably the most important one because this is the point at which you can snag a loyal customer or forever lose one to a competitor.

Social media marketing plays the most important role at this stage. This is because the referent, expert, and positional influencers (which we define in Chapter 1) help a prospect determine whether he should make the purchasing decision. Increasingly, while making choices between different products, prospective customers look to each other for advice and guidance.

People ask their friends for advice, search the web for customer reviews, and read expert opinions from credible third-party sources. In fact, a study titled, "On Brands and Word of Mouth" that appeared in the *Journal of Marketing Research* in August 2013 showed that people spread the word on brands online for three reasons: social, functional, and emotional. No longer is it enough to know that people share product and brand opinions online; you need to pay attention to what sharing takes place in your product category and the motivations that drive it.

Your role at this stage is primarily connecting that prospective customer with these credible third-party sources of information. Now, you may feel that connecting a prospective customer to a bad review or to another customer who may not have liked the product is a bad idea, but it isn't necessarily so. Prospective customers are looking for the best information about a product, and they respect companies that help them research the product more thoroughly. This is important because as a Forbes 2018 study pointed out, 71 percent of consumers who have had a positive experience with a brand on social media are likely to recommend the brand to their friends and family. With that in mind, don't hesitate to use your existing customers to help you market to your prospective customers. It only helps.

TIP

You can't hide bad reviews on the web, and by pointing to all the reviews and not just the good ones, you establish credibility with your prospective customer. (Besides, we would hope that the positive reviews far outweigh the negative ones.) It is critical to note that reviews do make a big difference, and it is better to have some bad reviews than none at all. In fact, the number of reviews and average rating on a product correlate closely with conversion to purchase, according to a March 2014 Bazaarvoice study on Internet Retailers.

Here are some SMM tactics that you can use at the consideration stage:

>> **Publish customer ratings and reviews on the corporate website.**

Make sure that ratings and reviews appear for all products and that you do not censor them. Even if a product gets negative reviews, publish them. In all probability, customers will choose other products from your company. You won't lose the customer completely.

>> **Point to authoritative third-party reviews.**

It's important to point to credible third-party reviews from recognized experts so that you build trust. Doing so can make the consideration stage a shorter one.

>> **Encourage prospects to discuss the products.**

When you're designing your online catalog, encourage prospects to discuss the product with their friends and family. Make it easy for them to take the product into Facebook to solicit opinions from others using services such as ShareThis (`www.sharethis.com`), pointing users to the brand's business page on the social networks, and including email links, too.

>> **Connect prospective customers to each other.**

By setting up discussion forums, you can create spaces where prospective customers can exchange notes on the potential purchases that they're considering. Also point them to existing satisfied customers or real-world testimonials that visitors can rate and comment upon.

>> **Set up a Twitter account and respond to customer queries.**

It's important to watch the chatter about your products and brands across the social web. Where appropriate, respond in a thoughtful, helpful manner to the questions raised. Correct misrepresentations of your products in a similar way, especially those on Twitter.

REMEMBER

Twitter is useful for customer service. Companies such as Comcast have had great success in using it for responding to customer queries and concerns. But the tone you respond with is critical: You always run the risk of sounding defensive. You'll probably be doing more damage to your brand than good if you allow yourself to get defensive on Twitter.

>> **Track a list of websites, blogs, and discussion forums where the product's target customers spend their time.**

Track activity on these sites, and participate in conversations about the category, competitors, and customer needs in an authentic, productive, and useful manner.

SMM at the preference stage

At the preference stage, the prospective customer leans toward making a purchase. He has considered several products and established his favorites. He likes the product that you're pushing him toward. By this time, the prospective customer is concerned with confirming that he's getting good value for his money and that his purchase will be suitable for his needs. At this stage, you may offer free trials and 30-day money-back guarantees. Generally speaking, you hope your prospective customers have developed an emotional attachment to your brand that will push them to purchase your products.

By the time a prospective customer is at the preference stage in the marketing funnel, she has probably evaluated all the competitive alternatives to the product. She has found information about them through product brochures, the product websites, and customer reviews across the web. As she enters the preference stage, she's likely to talk to her friends some more and get their opinions. This may have less to do with whether one product is better than another from a feature standpoint, but the customer can get a feel for your brand as well. The prospective customer also views user-generated content about your brand at this stage.

You must be very careful at this stage. It's important that you establish a trusted relationship with the prospective customer. The prospective customer needs to feel that he will get good customer service after he makes the purchase. He wants to believe that his decision will be a good one over the long term, too. You can build that trust and allay those concerns by talking to the prospective customer in an authentic, personal, and genuine fashion.

TIP

This is when your product blogs play an important role. It reminds your prospective customers that actual people are behind your product or brand. Make sure to spend time answering questions, resolving product issues, and discussing how the product is evolving.

Consider these SMM tactics at this stage:

>> **A blog, or several blogs, that discuss the product:** Granted, blogs are valuable at the awareness and consideration phase as well, but they matter the most at the point of preference. Customers want to hear from you at this stage more than ever and it's important to frame the benefits of your product in ways that your customers will appreciate them the most.

>> **Podcasts with interviews and product explanations:** As a supplement to blogs, podcasts are an appealing way to explain the product to prospective customers in an engaging fashion when you're not in the room with them. Running your own podcasts, appearing as a guest on someone else's podcast, or advertising on a podcast network are all valuable strategies for marketing

at the preference phase. To learn all about *podcasts,* which are audio blogs that are easily distributed online, take a look at *Podcasting For Dummies,* by Tee Morris (John Wiley & Sons, Inc.).

>> **YouTube clips of product demonstrations:** With prospective customers establishing their preference for the brand, video clips demonstrating the product and explaining its benefits are helpful. Publish your videos to a site such as YouTube so that customers can easily find them. Posting on YouTube also gives people the opportunity to comment and rate the product videos.

SMM at the action stage

The action stage is when the prospective customer makes the purchase and becomes an actual customer. He goes through the process of buying the product, whether he does this online, via the phone, or in a store. During the action stage, focus on making the process as smooth, efficient, and hassle free as possible. You should put a lot of effort into making the purchasing experience a positive one because it is one of the first direct interactions that the customer has with your company.

Most marketers argue that at this point in the funnel, you should not play a role. Either the customer was positively influenced enough to make the purchasing decision or he wasn't. If he's at the point where he's taking action, he should be allowed to take that action without any distractions whatsoever because even a positive distraction is still a distraction. However, if the purchase is a high-consideration one, you can make the purchasing process social in a way that doesn't distract from the purchasing but enhances it instead.

At the point of purchase, the customer wants to know whether he is making a suitable purchasing decision and if his social influencers approve of his decision. Providing him with data points that he can share with those influencers and a means to broadcast the purchasing decision helps him. He can broadcast his purchasing decision and influence his friends to make similar purchasing decisions. And by providing valuable tidbits of information, he'll have valuable information to share.

The point of purchase also serves as an opportunity to upsell other products and services. This is a traditional marketing tactic that's been used in both the digital world and in physical stores as well. By highlighting other products that customers just like him purchased, social influence can play a role in encouraging that customer to make additional impulse purchases at the point of sale. For example, say you're buying a pair of Gap jeans from Gap.com (as shown in Figure 3-4) and as you're about to check out, you're told about a nice shirt to buy and that most people who bought the pair of jeans bought the shirt, too. You're more likely to add the shirt to your shopping cart. That's using social data to influence a purchasing decision.

FIGURE 3-4:
Gap.com recommends a shirt based on what's in the customer's shopping cart.

Consider these SMM tactics at this stage:

>> **Highlight related popular products.** As depicted with the Gap.com example, showcasing popular products relating to the ones already in the shopping carts often leads to impulse purchases.

>> **Provide tools to broadcast the purchase.** This is necessary to allow for the customer to do remarketing for you. The customer should have the tools to easily broadcast his purchase to his various social networks. (*Remarketing* refers to someone doing further marketing on your behalf after the person has already been a recipient of your marketing efforts.)

SMM at the loyalty stage

The last stage of the marketing funnel has the fewest people. These are the customers who have purchased your product and are consuming it now. At this stage, it's most important to encourage customers to spread the word about the product and encourage others to buy it. Loyal customers are often the best marketers for your company. With social media marketing, loyalty plays an even larger role.

You must first focus on making your customers loyal and repeat customers. It's no use encouraging a customer to talk about your product if she isn't loyal to or an advocate of the product. You can incentivize your loyal customers to encourage their peers to test the product and make a purchase as well. You can do this using social media marketing tactics.

The best way to encourage loyal customers to influence their peers is to start by encouraging them to talk about the product. Having them rate and review the products is the first step. You'll be surprised how many customers are happy to rate and review products. What's more, as they rate and review the products, they're also happy to broadcast the reviews to their social network. Allow them to do that. Provide the technological means for them to share their own reviews of the product with their friends and family.

Another way that social media marketing can help at the loyalty stage is by connecting prospective customers with loyal customers. In some cases, you can link prospective customers with loyal customers who they know in the real world. For example, if you're looking to buy a Ford Taurus, and you have a network of 350 people in LinkedIn, you may find that someone else in your network drives a Ford Taurus. Now, wouldn't it be valuable if Ford told you which friend drives the Ford Taurus so that you could ask that friend her opinion? That's increasingly possible to do in the social networks.

Regardless of whether you have any friends who own Fords, you might be interested in learning about Ford from other Ford customers. Social media marketing is about connecting customers to one another so that they can socially influence each other to make better decisions. In this instance, Ford should definitely try to connect all the prospective Ford Taurus owners with the current ones. One simple way to do this is to set up a Facebook page or a LinkedIn group for Ford Taurus owners in specific locations and then point prospective customers to that page, where they can ask existing owners questions. It can only help them make more purchases. Not surprisingly, Ford does exactly that, and in fact, it now goes a step further by offering Ford customers the opportunity to put a "badge" on their Facebook profiles showcasing the fact that they are Ford customers!

The loyalty stage of the marketing funnel is important because that's where the most remarketing happens by your own customers. Just because the customer has already bought the product doesn't mean you should care about her less. In fact, with her ability to spread the word (positively or negatively) about your product across her social network and the social web in an exponential fashion, you had better take good care of her. Otherwise, you may have a PR disaster on your hands.

Probably one of the most classic examples of a PR disaster at the loyalty stage has to do with Netflix. Without consulting its customers, Netflix made an attempt to divide its business into two, with one focusing on DVD rentals and the other online streaming. The pricing of each also increased with this announcement. Upon hearing the news, customers fled en masse, including those who had previously been among the most loyal. Management had to completely reverse the decision to split the company, and only now has gained back its lost customers.

On the bright side, when JetBlue suffered probably its most major PR disaster in its history, the chief executive officer decided to issue an apology via YouTube — using the very same social platform that was responsible for the propagation of the PR crisis. The runway fiasco, as it came to be known, was when passengers were kept in planes on the runway for hours on end during a winter storm. Using the social platforms to apologize made a difference, and it helped even more when the CEO announced a passenger bill of rights. These actions showed that he was engaging with his current and prospective customers on their own terms and on their social platforms of choice (he engaged with the angry customers on Twitter, too).

There are hundreds of examples of brands facing online firestorms, often due to something stupid that a company did. Table 3-1 highlights some of the more notable firestorms. Also listed are whether these online difficulties had offline ripples in the mainstream media.

TABLE 3-1   **Notable Online Firestorms**

Controversy	Online Noise Levels	Offline
Nivea's racially insensitive ad	High	High
American Airlines removes Alec Baldwin from plane for not turning off his phone when requested	High	High
Gilbert Gottfried's firing by AFLAC for insensitive remarks about the Japan earthquake	High	Moderate
Dunkin' Donuts/Rachael Ray wears keffiyeh	High	Moderate
Burger King employee bathes in sink	Moderate	Low
Motrin moms	High	Low
#amazonfail	High	None
SpongeBob SquareButt	Moderate	Low

Deepening Your SMM Relationship

After your customers are at the loyalty stage, can you do anything more to deepen the relationship? SMM gives you the opportunity to stay in contact with your customers and help them in ways they don't anticipate. Delight is a strong element in growing your bond. Following are some areas of SMM that help you extend that trust.

SMM for customer service

After customers found that they could quickly get a company's attention on social media platforms, the notion of customer service changed forever. Previously, the only option consumers had was to get on the phone and wait patiently until they could speak to a representative. Often, the outcome was less than satisfactory.

Presently, consumers make it a point to seek out companies that offer them a voice on social platforms. The SmartInsights study from 2017 found that:

>> Sixty-three percent of customers expect companies to offer customer service via their social media channels.

>> Ninety percent of social media users have already used social media as a way to communicate with a brand or a business.

>> Customers prefer social media 34.5 percent of the time for customer service compared to 24.7 percent for live chat, 19.4 percent for email, and 16.1 percent for toll-free phone service.

REMEMBER

If you are dissatisfied with a purchase or service, you can use social media to tweet, post, or otherwise rate your way onto the radar screen of the company in question.

Here are some post–sales SMM tactics that you can use to improve customer service:

>> **Demonstrate that you are really able to do something.**

It will be readily apparent if your employees on social media are not really empowered to actually help customers. It's great to listen, but if you don't take action, listening will prove to be a hollow exercise.

>> **Provide links on social platforms to information, discounts, and special promotions**.

It's all about the customer, so make sure that your response always has real, demonstrable value. Ask your management what options you have for rewarding the customer. How about a private briefing about your next product?

>> **Offer tips and video from customer service on FAQs.**

Don't wait for a hail of tweets to show up. If you know there's a problem, create content that speaks to it. Then go back and show the customer how your solution cut customer service calls in half. That will get management's attention and buy-in.

>> **Use different platforms for different kinds of customer service.**

Make sure that you have several levels of response available to the customer. For example, you can use a specific Twitter handle that's separate from your primary brand's Twitter handle for quick responses. For questions that require more investigation, you can direct them to your website or set up an outside service like Get Satisfaction, as shown in Figure 3-5, to answer questions.

» **Use photos to show that real people are doing interesting things.**

With a camera in every phone, it's hard not to take snapshots of events, celebrations, and charitable activities. At every event, pick someone as the designated picture taker. This serves to authenticate your staff.

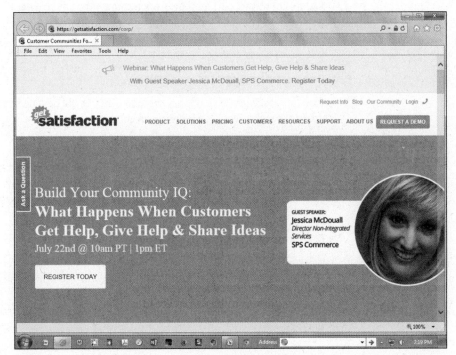

FIGURE 3-5:
The home page of Get Satisfaction.

SMM with offline marketing

When you see a heading that includes "offline marketing," your first thought might be, "Why are they including this as part of SMM?" There's a good reason. Marketing doesn't stop at the digital water's edge. People still spend a majority of their time offline. We think that's a good time to grab their attention and funnel them back to your social media platforms.

This means that you don't miss an opportunity to pair your social media venues with your offline ones. For example, if you send a postcard, you'd make sure to have all your "connections," such as your Facebook page and Twitter address, listed on the back of the card.

You should always be thinking about how your marketing universe ties together. When you look at each of the following tactics, think about how you can offer online tie-backs:

>> **Offer 30-minute training at a local venue.**

Give out the URL of the training notes online.

>> **Host an event for charity.**

Make sure to secure donations from a safe online environment.

>> **Send postcards.**

List your Twitter address on the back.

>> **Go to a conference or trade show.**

Have several types of handouts available. They could be a tip sheet with your web address or even a USB drive with company information.

>> **Call your customers.**

Most SM marketers encourage you to send online surveys. How about arranging a phone call to speak to a group of customers who have purchased your last product? Afterward, make sure to send them an online discount coupon or other bonus for sharing their ideas.

>> **Create a joint venture.**

Work with another online marketer who complements your offerings to hold a meeting or event. Then create a bundled product to buy online.

>> **Send an article to your local newspaper or trade magazine.**

Make sure that your LinkedIn URL is listed.

SMM in the world of real-time marketing

With the advent of social media platforms, the tools you need for real-time marketing campaigns are ready and waiting. For example, just search your Twitter feed or glance at Twitter trends if you want to see where the online attention is.

Earlier in this chapter, we discuss the marketing funnel. Your first goal is awareness. That's what you're aiming for with real-time marketing. If you can garner awareness with your real-time campaign, you have the chance to move customers through your funnel.

To make this information translate into traffic, leads, and revenue, you need an understanding of what goes into a real-time SMM campaign. The following are conditions that should be present to help you succeed:

>> **Determine your goals for this type of activity.**

You could do a plethora of things with your campaign. The key is to focus it on one major outcome. Ask yourself, "What action do I want the customer to take after engaging with the content?" (via tweet, video, link, and so on). This helps you choose the right first step.

>> **Invest in the right real-time marketing tools.**

Within the last two years, several technologies have been launched that allow you to truly understand what consumers are thinking, talking about, and doing on a real-time basis. Real-time tracking can be around your brands or around topics that matter to both them and you. Whether it be tools that help you identify real-time trends as they surface or technologies that let you observe how trends travel from one physical location to another, operating effectively in real time when your consumers most care about you requires investments in the right tools and technologies.

>> **Designate staff to monitor real-time activity.**

Make it someone's (or several people's) task to monitor the online activity in real time. That may sound obvious, but when you have very busy people on your staff, people think that the other person will do it or that they can get to it later.

>> **Have resources available to take action.**

If you agree that you are going all in on this campaign, make sure to let your creative people know that they may be required to create something in response to feedback. Of course, we're not suggesting that your campaign will have to be as elaborate as what a Fortune 10 company may do. But you can get great mileage by simply writing back to the comments made. The idea is that real people are listening and talking back.

>> **Monitor news in your topic area.**

When you are trying to decide how to make your campaign relevant, consider riffing off of some current event. This is an old PR trick. It's why when something of note happens, you see headlines like, "What X can learn about Y from the Old Spice Guy." When people Google "Old Spice," you show up in the results.

>> **Use the real words and phrases that customers use.**

Related to the item above is the idea that SEO (search engine optimization) should not be ignored. Pay close attention to the specific words and phrases that customers are using, and seed them in your campaign.

Treating SMM Differently from Brand Marketing

Because of the power of peer influence, social media marketing is increasingly approached differently from brand and direct-response marketing. The differences stem from the fact that the philosophical approaches, strategies, and execution tactics of SMM are more community and socially oriented.

Social media marketing is fundamentally about engaging with expert, referent, and positional influencers and strategically leveraging social media in all its forms to meet marketing and business objectives. As a result, you need to understand how social media marketing fits into the context of brand and direct response marketing.

SMM in the context of brand marketing

Brand marketing focuses on building equity around a brand, its personality, and attributes. Customers purchase products based on the brand promise. Through various forms of advertising and communications, the brand promise is brought alive to generate awareness, build excitement, and get specific products included in a consideration set. Mass media channels are typically used to build awareness for the brand, reposition it with more powerful attributes, or ultimately sell products. This will always be central to marketing efforts. All brands require significant effort to penetrate a market and generate desire.

SMM complements brand marketing in some key ways:

>> **SMM places extra emphasis on peer-to-peer marketing and allows for peer-to-peer decision-making in a digital context.**

The focus is on understanding how consumers are interacting with each other on social platforms versus how they're interacting with the brand. Consumers are asked to do the marketing for the brand by layering their own voices and perspectives on top. The result is the socialization of a message or story in a way that's meaningful and relevant to their world.

>> **SMM rarely uses mass media, whether television, print, or radio.**

Interactive channels that allow for the socialization and redistribution of a message are more important. But the brand cannot be simply pushed through the channels. Instead, invite consumers in the channels to experience the brand and make it their own.

>> **SMM is about becoming part of all media streams, across all channels, where consumers are responding to and discussing the brand messages.**

In many cases, they're self-organizing these conversations on the fly. In other instances, they gravitate toward existing community hubs where the conversations are already taking place. These conversations can also take place on your own corporate website.

TIP

Because of this, messaging, advertising campaigns, and even the products themselves don't define successful brands as much as the communities that surround them do. A brand supported by a large and influential community becomes more successful than one with a weak, disparate, and disjointed community. You have a huge opportunity to learn from their consumers as they listen in on these conversations. This is an opportunity you shouldn't miss.

SMM in the context of direct-response marketing

Direct-response marketing is designed to solicit a specific, measurable response from specific individuals. Unlike brand marketing, with direct response, for every dollar invested, you see a traceable return. The measurable relationship is established between you and the consumer.

Some of the core attributes around direct response include a *call to action* (which is when the brand asks the customer to do something like call a number or click a link), an offer and delivery of enough information to elicit a response, and guidance on how to respond. Television infomercials, which encourage consumers to call a number or visit a website, and direct mail offers, which invite consumers to purchase a product or send a reply, are the most common forms of direct-response marketing. Online advertising campaigns that are designed to drive clicks and purchases on brand websites are the most common online equivalent.

SMM complements direct response but historically has lacked some of the measurability found in direct response. Social media marketing isn't typically geared toward a specific individual with the goal of soliciting a specific, measurable response. With SMM, communities of consumers are targeted with the goal of enticing them to positively influence one another and other people within their networks of online relationships. The goals are to convert consumers into potential marketers for the brand and provide them with the tools and mechanisms to further influence others. While it's different from asking an isolated consumer to perform a specific task, increasingly the social media platforms are developing extremely powerful advertising formats that enable you to use their platforms for all your direct-response marketing needs.

More broadly speaking, SMM isn't as measurable as direct-response marketing is, although that is changing fast. Tracking how social influencers work is difficult; when a consumer shows brand affinity or makes a purchasing decision, it's hard to tell which factors or influencers impacted those choices most directly. In that sense, SMM is more akin to brand marketing, where the measurability is weak and needs to be based on feedback similar to that collected in attitudinal surveys. It's easy to track expert influencers online using social media measurement tools, but that's just part of the equation. Often, the social influencers who sway purchasing decisions aren't the most public and noticeable brand advocates.

Another factor to consider with SMM is that the call to action can't be too heavy-handed. As a result, some would argue that SMM is much more about social influence and much less about marketing. Social campaigns that blatantly push the call to action generally fail because they lack credibility, don't provide value to the consumer and appear calculated. For this reason, you can't always easily recognize or measure your successful SMM campaigns.

Tying SMM with brand marketing and direct response

Social media marketing, which is about harnessing and categorizing the local spheres of influence, complements brand marketing and direct response with its focus on reaching social influencers across a variety of channels and platforms at every stage of the marketing funnel. This is done so that influencers socialize the message in their own communities and conduct the marketing for the brand. Not all social influencers have platforms to project strong opinions; some are more anonymous, localized, and less recognizable. That's the bad news. The good news is that influencers obviously like to influence and have a meaningful and integral role to play in marketing online or offline.

Social media marketing resembles relationship marketing in that both focus on the relationship, not just the point of sale, and are more personal in nature. The difference is that relationship marketing focuses on establishing deeper, longer-term relationships with customers over a lifetime, whereas social media marketing relies on customers marketing the brand.

2

Practicing SMM on the Social Web

Learn about the nuts and bolts of SMM campaigns, including planning for them, managing participation, and responding to criticism.

Get to know why you need an SMM voice, how it differs from a brand voice or personality, where it gets manifested, and who can play that role.

Know the responsibilities you have as a marketer toward your customers, community, and company.

Chapter **4**

Launching SMM Campaigns

Launching a social media marketing campaign is, in some ways, similar to launching any other marketing campaign. But at the same time, you need to approach certain aspects of it very differently to maximize the results.

In this chapter, we discuss the components of a successful SMM campaign and how you can make it work in harmony with other marketing efforts. We also discuss how best to respond to criticism, how to turn a crisis to your advantage, and, finally, some tactics for turning the campaign into a long-term marketing asset.

Discovering the Types of SMM Campaigns

At this point, it's important to talk about the different types of campaigns. After that, we discuss the rules and guidelines that make SMM campaigns successful. In the realm of social media marketing, how you implement a campaign is nearly as important as what you implement.

REMEMBER

Before you launch your SMM campaign, make sure that you've done an inventory of all the other major campaigns going on at the same time that target your customers or are within your industry. The last thing you want is to launch a campaign in which you're asking your customers to do basically the same thing that they may have just done for a competitor.

WARNING

In 2017, the FTC (Federal Trade Commission) imposed guidelines on how pharmaceutical companies can market using the social web. Those regulations cover the promotion of FDA-regulated products. More information can be found on this FDA website: www.fda.gov/AboutFDA/CentersOffices/OfficeofMedical ProductsandTobacco/CDER/ucm397791.htm. If you're a pharmaceutical company or are operating in another regulated industry, be sure to check with your lawyers about what you're allowed and not allowed to do before launching an SMM campaign.

Influencer outreach

Among the most common form of an SMM campaign is the influencer outreach program. This campaign typically takes the form of identifying influencers on Instagram, Twitter, Snapchat, and elsewhere who your customers follow. They're the expert influencers who cover a topic or a passion point and have a following. The best way to think of them is as media that publish content, accept relationships with brands, and build fan bases. Many accept advertising but typically have day jobs that they're balancing unless they've done extraordinarily well as influencers.

Influencer outreach programs incentivize these influencers to publish about your brand or product. You can give them incentives by inviting them to the R&D labs of your company and treating them with the same deference that the mainstream press gets, to sending them sample products and providing them with prizes with which to run contests through their social media channels. Campaigns are sometimes built around these influencers.

It's important to note that the debate continues to rage online about influencer compensation. Some influencers absolutely refuse to accept compensation, whereas others are comfortable with it. Some companies, such as Aveda, a natural beauty products company, give influencers gift cards or spa treatments but no outright payments. Influencers typically accept these gifts with the understanding that their review will not be influenced by a gift of any kind. Companies want honest evaluations, and their readers demand it. You must know where your targeted influencer stands on this debate before reaching out to him.

** Knowing how to reach these influencers without coming across as heavy-handed, commercial, and ignorant is critical. Before you reach out to them, be sure to follow them in social media so that you know how they cover your brand or category; scan the comments on their channels so that you get a feel for the readers and how they participate; understand their policies with regard to brands engaging with them (some prefer to go through representatives, for example); and, ideally, try to develop a personal relationship based on the content that they publish and the topics that they cover before approaching them with an idea.

These are all common-sense ideas that would apply even if you were attempting to engage with traditional reporters who are doing a story for a print publication. But as the saying goes, common sense is often uncommon, and many a company has done exactly the opposite.

UGC contests

Contests in all their various forms have always been a big hit in the marketing campaign arena. But now contests structured around user-generated content (UGC) are all the rage. And with good reason: They are invariably extremely popular, engaging, and fun. You structure a contest built on participants who contribute something in return for rewards. This can be something as simple as crowdsourcing a TV advertisement, as General Motors did in the early days of social media with its Tahoe campaign in 2006, to asking users to contribute video clips of their funniest moment with a product. The best clip (by the predetermined criteria) gets a prize, with all the other participants getting some sort of recognition.

As *Wired* magazine reported, in the case of the Tahoe campaign, the microsite attracted 629,000 visitors, with each user spending more than nine minutes on the site and a third of them going on to visit the main Chevy.com website. Sales took off from that point, even though environmentalists tried to sabotage the UGC campaign by creating video clips that highlighted their views on the impact the vehicles had on the environment.

Another successful contest was run by Applebee's in the summer of 2014. Applebee's asked its customers to snap pics of their meals or themselves chowing. The best photos were then published by Applebee's on its Instagram feed using the hashtag #fantographer and were cross-promoted on Facebook and Twitter with posts and ads. When the campaign ended in the fall of 2014, engagement had risen 25 percent and tweets tagged with #fantographer appeared in 78 million users' timelines (users would submit their photos to Applebee's via Twitter and used the hashtag when doing so).

Brand utilities

The basic idea behind brand utilities is that instead of providing the consumer with some advertising, you build their trust (and get their dollars) by giving them a utility application that provides actual value. If the utility serves a purpose, users adopt the application and think more favorably of your brand. Dollars that would have normally gone toward buying media go toward building the application instead.

For example, Estee Lauder launched a Facebook brand utility called "Shine a Light on Breast Cancer." It lets breast cancer survivors and their families post "messages of hope." It also lets you know where breast cancer events are being held around the world. This connects people from all corners of the world to support one another in the fight against breast cancer.

An application doesn't always have to take the form of an application or a widget on a social network. The famous Nike+ solution, which is considered the world's largest running club, shown in Figure 4-1, is a virtual community that helps users improve their running via real-time coaching over audio, track the distances they've run, compare themselves to their peers, and share their running statistics in social media.

FIGURE 4-1:
Nike+ Running Monitor on Facebook.

The advertising industry moves between trends very quickly, and it seems that brand utilities are already out of the limelight. What's gaining favor now are apps that use *crowdsourcing*. For example, Lays potato chips used this type of application to solicit ideas from consumers for different chips flavors. In the program's first year, consumers submitted four million flavor ideas. Called "Do us a flavor," Lays designed the promotion so that an expert jury narrowed down the choices to four, which were put on the market. The winner was then chosen based on fan votes (through the application again) and made a permanent fixture on store shelves.

Podcasting

A *podcast* is a digital audio file that is made available via web syndication technologies such as RSS. Although it's not, strictly speaking, social media, it's often classified as such because it allows anybody to easily syndicate her own audio content. You can use podcasts as a way to share information with your audiences. Often, podcasts take the shape of celebrity interviews or discussions about your product or brand. A successful example of a podcast is the Butterball Turkey Talk podcast. It's a seasonal podcast including stories from Turkey Talk hotline workers. You can subscribe to it via iTunes and other online podcast directories.

Podcasts typically don't form a whole SMM campaign in and of themselves but work well with other parts of a campaign.

Sponsored conversations

Sometimes the most effective SMM campaigns are the simplest ones. These campaigns engage with consumers in a straightforward, authentic fashion on a social platform while also aggregating other conversations, pointing to new ones, and stoking the community. An early pioneering example was when Disney partnered with Savvy Auntie (www.savvyauntie.com), an online community focused on aunts without kids, for one such effort, which is shown in Figure 4-2. Melanie Notkin, who runs SavvyAuntie.com, tweeted about Disney's *Pinocchio* movie in March 2008 to coincide with its Disney anniversary release. She tweeted about themes in the movie, often in question form, encouraging others to respond. Her 8,000 followers on Twitter at the time (today, she has more than 24,000) knew that she was doing this for Disney (every tweet about Pinocchio had a special tag), but because the tweets were appropriate for the audience, entertaining, and authentic, the campaign was a success. Since that pioneering example, there have been many more scenarios in which brands have partnered with influencers around sponsored conversations.

A very different example comes from Casper, the direct-to-consumer mattress company, that used video to provide value to its consumers in thoughtful ways. While this example technically isn't a sponsored conversation, they treat it as such and it incorporates several different concepts that we've discussed in this chapter.

In 2019, Casper launched a sleep channel on Spotify, YouTube, and IGTV that helps people quite literally fall asleep. With soothing sounds and educational video clips, Casper launches new episodes on these channels each week and promotes them more widely on their other social media platform. Here Casper isn't promoting a specific mattress nor are they asking their customers to advocate on their behalf. However, by promoting sleep they're helping their customers as a branded utility would do. And in setting up a sleep channel, they're acting like an influencer themselves. Needless to say, Casper occasionally promotes its own mattresses and when it does so, its acting as if it is sponsoring a conversation elsewhere!

FIGURE 4-2:
Savvy Auntie.

Recognizing What Makes a Good SMM Campaign

A *social media marketing campaign* is one that specifically allows for social influence to take place digitally. A few years ago, marketing through social media was a niche activity, and the notion of targeting influencers was an obscure one. The closest comparison was word-of-mouth campaigns conducted in the offline world to build brand awareness for a product by incentivizing people to talk about it among themselves. Digital campaigns, for the most part, were about display advertising (those banner ads that appear at the top and side of a website) across large magazine and newspaper websites, complemented with paid search campaigns and maybe email campaigns. These campaigns were used to drive prospects to a *microsite* (a site devoted to that particular campaign) or a website, where they were encouraged to make purchases or engage with the brand.

REMEMBER

With an SMM campaign, you mustn't drag people away from the social platform on which they're communicating and interacting with each other. They don't want to be distracted, and you'll probably only waste precious marketing dollars trying to lure them to your website. Instead, it's more important to execute the campaign on those very platforms where your potential customers are in conversation. You have to engage your customers where *they* want to participate, not where you want them to be. And unlike in a digital marketing campaign of yesteryear, the customers of an SMM campaign ignore you unless your SMM campaign is aligned with their objectives and behavior patterns on those social platforms. In the following sections, we outline specific guidelines that you should follow when launching an SMM campaign.

A good example of a failed "build it and they will come" attempt was Bud.TV by Budweiser. They tried to create an entertainment destination bypassing YouTube. The effort failed miserably because Budweiser had to spend valuable advertising dollars to encourage consumers to do something that they had no interest in doing — moving away from YouTube, where they had the most entertaining content (and all their friends), to a corporate-sponsored website. What's more, the fact that users couldn't embed the video clips elsewhere (including YouTube) hurt the effort. Bud.TV launched in January 2007 and was shut down early in 2009. Fast forward to 2019, and you'll notice that very few advertisers launch social media marketing campaigns where they try to pull customers to their websites to engage with them (granted pulling customers to your website to purchase is different and appropriate if done with sensitivity).

Creating Your SMM Roadmap

As with any other good marketing campaign, you need to construct a roadmap that shows you where you are going and how you'll get there. In this section, we discuss seven steps that you can take to bulletproof your campaign structure. They are as follows:

>> Define your objectives.

>> Develop a powerful story/experience.

>> Create an action plan.

>> Craft the content path.

>> Execute for influence.

>> Create partnerships.

>> Track the results.

Define your objectives

This may seem obvious, but it is amazing how many of us forget about articulating the objectives when it comes to an SMM campaign. Your objectives need to be tightly defined, and they must be practical and actionable, too. The objectives must be specific to the stage of the marketing funnel that you're playing in as well. See Chapter 3 for more on the marketing funnel. Saying that the objective of the campaign is simply to take a TV advertisement and make it *go viral* is definitely not enough.

TIP

The objectives must also specify *where* you're planning to run the campaign, *whom* you're targeting (which customers and which influencers), the *duration* of the campaign, and *how it synchronizes* with other digital and offline marketing efforts. It's easy to forget that no SMM campaign happens in isolation. How you participate on the various social platforms is always a mirror of what you do and think in the physical world. If you ignore that fact, you'll lose your customers even before you've had a chance to meaningfully engage with them.

Develop a powerful story/experience

People's expectations about how they will learn about your business/products have changed completely. Because the Back button on the browser is ever-present, waiting to take users away from your website, you have a very short window to engage and educate. The days of posting a simple data sheet and a price are over. You have to work to communicate the intrinsic value of each offer.

Also, because people want to know whom they are dealing with, you need to inject the *why* into your business story. You need to let them know why you started your business and what you care about. The social aspect must be visible. The following are stories you should consider telling during your campaign:

>> **Why you are running this campaign:** Yes, you want to sell things, we understand that. But what is the larger picture? Are you contributing to charity, helping others be successful, providing a solution, or providing content that doesn't currently exist? You have to be specific.

>> **What value the customer will get from participating:** Customers want social proof that others you have dealt with have had a great experience. You need to gather testimonial stories to share. If you can provide video of previous customers speaking, you have a way to demonstrate authenticity. You also need to show how your brand will either specifically improve customers' lives or contribute to their sense of worth in relation to their friends (otherwise they won't share your content).

>> **People who are impacted; show visual stories:** Provide visuals that tell a story. Well-known screenwriter Robert McKee has said that stories "unite an idea with an emotion." Make sure that yours does. And with so much of social media being visually driven today, using rich, evocative photography has become all the more important.

>> **Who the hero is:** Have a story about the person or thing that is leading this effort. It can be a product that works, a founder who wants to do good, and so on. Show that hurdles have been overcome. The late Steve Jobs was a visionary who figured heavily in the promotion of Apple products because he was the heart and soul of the business.

>> **How internal staff feels about what they do:** A recently produced commercial by General Electric shows children talking about what their parents do at GE. The message comes through loud and clear that not only are the employees proud of what they produce but their children are, too.

Create an action plan

Obviously, the actions you take are dictated by the length and complexity of the campaign. Every campaign has special features and highlights that need showcasing. However, following are some things that are common to most SMM campaigns you'll want to consider creating:

>> **A clear call to action.**

Decide what action you want the user to take, and make sure that everything you do supports that. If the user has to sign up for something, display the sign-up process front and center at all times.

>> **Hashtags and other tools.**

Most SMM campaigns create a hashtag for Twitter and Instagram so that people can follow the conversation. A hashtag has the pound sign (#) and a word or phrase related to the project. For example, a 2011 campaign to feed people on Thanksgiving was started by Pepto-Bismol with the hashtag #HelpPeptoFeedAmerica. Whenever someone retweeted the message with that hashtag, the makers of Pepto-Bismol donated money to hunger relief.

Dyson, the vacuum cleaner brand, uses several hashtags when it posts to Instagram but chooses them carefully so that it doesn't come across as heavy-handed. Here's an example of the hashtags used in a single post on June 4th, 2019: #dyson #dysonhome #insidedyson #vacuum #instatech. Most brands limit themselves by only using one or two hashtags.

>> **A venue for crowdsourcing.**

Are you going to create your own web page for people to share and submit their comments, or will you use the current platforms? Decide whether you want to create a Facebook page or a community on your own website or another third-party one such as Tumblr. There are pluses and minuses to each choice. If it's important to own the content, by all means create your own. Just remember that getting people to participate is easier where they normally hang out. A new venue could be an impediment.

>> **Content that can be shared.**

The key to every great SMM campaign is the content you create to get attention. If you are a small business and can't afford to create something splashy, you can still do a video and create PDF posters, contests, and graphics. Look at all the content you have already created, and see what you can repurpose. If doing so makes sense, have your customers create content, and pick a winner.

Craft the content path

When creating SMM campaigns, people often forget to map where their actual touch points will be and how they will look. It's not enough to say, "We'll send a tweet with a link." You need to be specific about it. You need to document that you will send three tweets a day at 9 a.m., 5 p.m., and 9 p.m., say, with certain text and a link.

As a handy way to document your campaign, you can map each of your channels and the content that will go into it. One of the best ways to do this is to create a mind map that shows you the big picture of your campaign and all the moving parts on one sheet of paper. Mind maps start with a circle in the middle and radiate ideas that relate to it. For example, you can put your campaign name in the center circle and then radiate circles of the different platforms you are using. From each platform circle, you can note the content that will be sent. From those mind maps, you can then create specific content calendars that help you manage the content production process.

REMEMBER

Your preplanned content is only the first part of what you will be doing. You have to also organically create messages that respond to the ongoing campaign to make it real. When people post something about your campaign on Facebook or Twitter, make sure to respond to it in a reasonable amount of time, which should typically be no more than 12 hours later at the very most. The preplanned items are just the starting point. Social marketing means reacting to real-time events.

Execute for influence

Traditionally, most campaigns have focused on getting a potential customer to take a specific action or to view a specific brand message. The focus has always been on that individual engaging with the brand in some form. However, with an SMM campaign, you need to design for sharing, influencing, reciprocity, and social currency.

Unlike most other campaigns, an SMM campaign needs to accomplish two objectives concurrently:

TIP

>> **It needs to engage the individual who's being targeted via the campaign.**

This is similar to any other type of digital marketing campaign. You want to engage with your target audience in a specific fashion and solicit a specific response.

>> **You also need to design the campaign so that the target person shares or discusses it with someone else.**

Sharing is the social currency element. The person should feel that by sharing the campaign with someone else, he derives greater value from it. This greater value could be something as tangible as further discounts or something as intangible as status among his peers. The point is that the more people the person shares the campaign with (or discusses it with), the more value he generates from it. In this sense, the campaign takes on a network effect, with its value growing each time someone participates.

Create partnerships

Few SMM campaigns are successful in isolation. A more traditional digital campaign, which is based on display and search advertising, comes together through a series of partnerships between the agency, the advertiser, and the publisher, and the same is true of an SMM campaign. However, in this case, the participants vary slightly. Rather than have a regular publisher, you have the social platform to contend with. Your campaign must be in compliance with that platform's policies; otherwise, you can't run on that platform. For example, Facebook (https://www.facebook.com/terms.php) and YouTube (https://www.youtube.com/static?template=terms) have strict terms of service regarding the type of advertising that can appear on their platforms.

REMEMBER

The platform players aren't the only things you have to take into consideration. With most large brands, ad hoc user groups that have a sense of ownership over the brand or product category spring up on the social platform where you're planning to run the campaign.

For example, on Facebook, if you were to search for "Ford," you'd find not just the Ford Motor Company page (shown in Figure 4-3), but literally hundreds of pages created by and for people interested in the Ford Motor Company. If you're a marketer at Ford, when you're planning an SMM campaign on Facebook, it's not enough to talk to Facebook and your own agency about the campaign. For it to be a truly successful SMM campaign, you must engage with these ad hoc groups when the campaign is starting. They can be your biggest marketers, helping the campaign succeed. On the other hand, if you upset them, they can turn into saboteurs.

Irrespective of the social platform you're running an SMM campaign on, the ad hoc user groups are already there. Be sure to engage with them. An SMM campaign means new players and new partnerships that need to be forged early on for it to be a success. Finding and engaging with those communities of people becomes critical.

Track the results

There's a saying in the world of social media that only successful SMM campaigns can be measured; failures can't be. The point is that marketers often say that SMM can't be measured if in their heart of hearts they know that their campaign has failed. If the campaign is a success, you bet they'll be telling you about it and explaining exactly why it was a success.

You can measure an SMM campaign in a lot of different ways. The best method depends on the objectives, the targeted audience, and the social platform on which the campaign is running. But you must determine what you're going to measure and how *before* you run the campaign. Otherwise, you're never going to know whether it's a success. SMM campaigns often spiral out of control, and the law of unintended consequences starts applying.

That's not a bad thing, but it doesn't take away from the fact that the campaign you're running is being run for a purpose — and you'll know whether you've achieved that purpose only if you're measuring the results. It's also important to measure a baseline of online activity before you begin the SMM engagement and decide what to measure. The baseline helps you determine how successful your campaign is relative to the level of conversations and online activity before running it.

We get into measurement later in the book (see Chapter 25), but for now it's sufficient to say that you must measure not just how many people you reach or who is aware of your campaign but also the following: the influence generated; the *brand lifts* (increased awareness of the brand across key brand attributes); and, most important, whether any of this effort led to purchases. With the measurement tools in the marketplace (many of which are free or close to free), you can easily track your SMM campaign to the point of sale on the website or potentially even in a physical store. The measurement tools that exist on the social platforms are getting stronger and stronger by the day, too. Don't hesitate in trying to measure this.

Participating — Four Rules of the Game

Many different factors can make or break an SMM campaign, and sometimes it's even just a matter of luck. But four rules matter above all else when it comes to SMM campaigns.

These rules don't always apply to other forms of marketing. Pay attention to them, and make sure that your SMM campaign abides by these.

Be authentic

Authenticity is a tricky word. It's tricky because it's overused in the context of social media. Everybody talks about being authentic when marketing in the social media realm, but what that means is rarely explained. To spell it out, authenticity is being honest, transparent, and true to the values of the brand: It's as simple as that.

Here are some examples:

>> **When you set up a blog as part of your campaign, make sure that you're using your own voice.**

Don't outsource the publishing of content to a third party. If you have to, make sure that the writer accurately identifies himself as contributing on your behalf. George Colony's blog The Counterintuitive CEO is a great example (see Figure 4-4). The blog is written in the first person by Forrester's chief executive officer, George Colony. There's no doubt that he is the writer.

FIGURE 4-4:
George Colony's
Forrester blog.

>> **When you're publishing your thoughts and opinions or simply sharing information, don't do so anonymously.**

In the world of social media, your consumers don't relate to and care about brands as much as they care about the people behind them. People build relationships with each other, not with anonymous brands. Let your customers know who is behind the voice blogging, tweeting, or running the contest on Facebook. You're not authentic if your customers don't know who you are. Worse still, don't ever use a pseudonym the way the Whole Foods CEO did when responding to critical comments in a discussion forum about his company in 2007. Fortunately, companies learned from his mistake; fast forward to 2019 and it's rare for someone from a company to use a pseudonym to defend his or her company.

» Learn from the community and respond to its feedback.

A key part of being authentic is telling your customers the way it really is, hearing their feedback (both positive and negative), and being willing to respond to it. It's no use participating in the social realm if you don't respond to commentary or feedback. If you're worried about not having the time to respond, consider not participating at all.

» Be humane in your approach.

It's easy to forget that for every comment and every unique visitor, there's an actual person somewhere in the world. Make sure that you participate with consideration and with the same respect that you'd reserve for someone you're talking to face to face.

For more information on authenticity as it applies to word-of-mouth marketing and social media marketing, visit the Association of National Advertisers (ANA) at www.anao.org. Through their acquisition of the Word of Mouth Marketing Association in 2018, they have amassed a rich repository of research around word-of-mouth marketing that you can find at https://www.ana.net/content/show/id/womma.

For all the altruism associated with the social web, it's easy to forget that it operates on the premise of quid pro quo. We're all good human beings, but most people expect something in return if they're giving you their time. As you develop an SMM campaign in which you'll be demanding your customers' attention (and often a lot more than that), think about the possible quid pro quo. Are you giving enough back in exchange? If you're not giving something back, your customers won't participate. They'll simply ignore you. The social web is littered with marketing campaign failures. These campaigns assumed that just by putting a banner advertisement in front of customers, they would achieve their objectives.

Much better is the example of an SMM campaign that provided a strong quid pro quo for its audiences and was highlighted by Ad Age. Target ran a marketing campaign in the summer of 2014, through which it donated millions of dollars to the Kids In Need Foundation by contributing money for each Up & Up school supply purchased during a specific time period in the summer. The campaign was launched and promoted extensively through social media, which served as the anchor to the entire marketing campaign. This was an SMM campaign that encouraged the consumer to purchase a particular product by tying the purchase to a cause and then motivated him to share his experience and encourage others to participate in that fashion. Success of the campaign was defined as much by the amount of money raised as it was through any traditional measure.

In a similar fashion, Shiv's company Eargo, which has a high-end hearing loss solution, ran a 2019 summer campaign in which for every hearing aid sold, it donated a hearing aid to a person in need via charity. With the hearing aids costing approximately $2,750, this was a major cause marketing effort tying the purchase to people's belief that giving back is important. Customers were encouraged to share their purchase in social media and encourage others to purchase as well given the altruistic dimensions to the campaign.

Give participants equal status

Many marketing campaigns are designed to make the consumer feel special — more special than everyone else around them. That's a good thing. They feel special, and they end up having favorable feelings for your product and go out and buy it. Apple and Harley-Davidson are two brands that personify this philosophy: They make their customers feel special and different from everyone else.

That's wonderful, but it doesn't apply to the SMM realm in the same way. People across the social web like to believe that they're as special and as unique as the next person, as they should. If someone is doing something special, others want to do that as well. If a person does something interesting, others want access to it as well. That's human nature, and the social web encourages behavior through the voyeurism it allows for.

Let go of the campaign

By virtue of starting the campaign, you probably feel that it is your responsibility to moderate and shape it. That doesn't have to be the case. Successful SMM campaigns are the ones in which the brand advocates take the campaign in new directions. As you develop the campaign, think of yourself as a participant and not just the owner of the campaign. You make better decisions regarding its evolution that way, and by letting go, you allow others to take it in new and much amplified directions. And as always, remember that your consumers will be in control of the campaign. That's what makes social media marketing different. However, you will always be in control of your own response to the consumer participation, and that always presents exciting opportunities.

Killing the Campaign Expiry Date

You're probably used to thinking of campaigns as having a start date and an end date. And they usually need that. You have a finite marketing budget; the campaign is geared around a series of events (like Christmas sales); new products replace old ones several times a year, and that forces you to end campaigns and launch new ones. However, SMM campaigns are unique in that after they start, they may not stop when you want them to. It's like turning off the lights midway through a dinner party. If you have a conversation going and have brought a community of people together around your brand, product, or campaign, the last thing you want to do is to suddenly disown those people. It's very important that you plan for migrating that community of people to a broader purpose or goal.

Here are four ways to move people onward successfully:

>> **Give participants new reasons to engage with your brand.**

Your original SMM campaign has a set purpose and objectives. After those objectives are accomplished, don't turn off the lights. Instead, think of the next campaign that you have planned and how you can customize it to this community of people.

In fact, try to weave the campaigns together into a program that benefits these people. As you do this, remember the four rules of participation that we outlined previously: authenticity, quid pro quo, equal status, and disowning the campaign.

>> **Encourage participants to coalesce into communities.**

Often, the people who participate in your SMM campaign all share something in common. This may not always be the case, but depending upon the campaign type, they may indeed be interested in forming a community. If you believe that to be the case, encourage people to coalesce into self-supporting communities. It only helps you in the long run and gives new life to the campaign. Campaigns that have generated good will transform into customer communities that you can tap into for future marketing and business efforts.

A good example of this is the Walmart ElevenMoms campaign, which launched in 2008, and is still running today. Walmart tapped 11 mommy bloggers to go shopping at Walmart stores (they were given a budget) and then blog about their experiences. They did so successfully (at least from the perspective of Walmart) and are now organized into a social network. In fact, over time, they have added more moms and are now simply called Walmart Moms, as shown in Figure 4-5.

>> **Treat participants like existing customers.**

Someone who's participated in your SMM campaign may not have bought your product, but he has given you his time and probably has shared a bit of himself with you in the process. This may have taken the form of commenting on a blog post, participating in a contest, sharing your viral video clip with friends, or testing a product and writing a review about it. Because he has done more than someone who experienced a traditional marketing campaign, you owe him more.

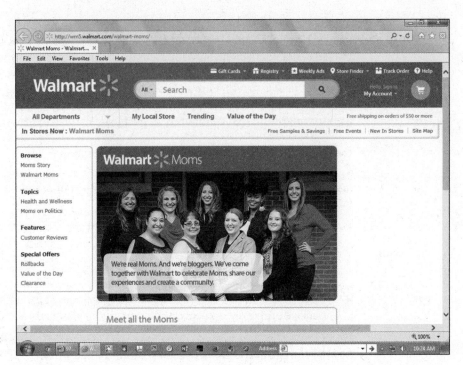

FIGURE 4-5:
Walmart Moms.

Treat him like an existing customer, whether that means sending him special offers, inviting him to participate in focus groups, or asking him to beta test new products. But always remember that when you send your customers a special offer, it must be on an opt-in basis. Don't spam them if you don't have their permission to communicate with them.

>> **Extend the campaign to the website.**

Many an SMM campaign has failed because it was kept separate from the company website. The campaign is traditionally built on a microsite with display advertising promoting the campaign. When the campaign has run its course, the microsite is shut down and the advertising is stopped. In the case of an SMM campaign, don't shut down the microsite. Instead, promote the SMM campaign on the company website, and when the campaign winds down, find a place on the company website for it. That way, your customers can always find it, and if they coalesced into communities during the course of the campaign, they always have a place to return to. In fact, it may be best to launch the campaign on the company website itself and move away from developing discrete microsites.

Often, your participants may know better than you how to create greater meaning from the SMM campaign in the form of a community. Ask them what you should be doing, if anything at all. You'll definitely get strong advice from the people who care the most.

Monitoring Brands and Conversations

It's no use running an SMM campaign if you can't measure it. You should always measure your SMM campaigns (see Chapter 25 for more detail on measurement). Depending on the SMM campaign, different measurements may matter more than others. The brand and conversation monitoring tools help you measure the success of your SMM campaign and your ROI (return on investment). But they do a lot more than that. These tools help you plan and design your SMM campaigns. They give you a peek into actual user behavior on social platforms, telling you what people are discussing, whether those conversations are positive or negative, and where they're taking place.

Any time you're planning to launch an SMM campaign, you must begin by knowing what your target audiences are doing across the social web. These tools help you do that. They can be classified into three groups:

>> **High-end tools and services** that use linguistic analysis and deep data mining to provide insights into the conversations, who is having them, and where. These tools can cost anywhere from $5,000 a month to $50,000 a month, based mostly on the number of topics mined and the frequency. Included in this category are Sysomis, NetBase, and Crimson Hexagon (since merged with Brandwatch).

>> **Low-end tools** that primarily focus on the volume of the conversation over a period of time and cover only positive and negative sentiment. Many of these tools are free or dirt cheap. Included here are HootSuite and Social Mention.

>> **Middle-of-the-road tools** that do some analysis but don't always have the breadth of sources or the depth of analysis that the high-end tools have. Tools in this category are Salesforce Radian6 and Sysomos. Cision, through its Viral Heat acquisition, is another player that straddles the high and low ends with different service levels and capabilities.

When choosing which tool to use, keep the following factors in mind:

>> **Your audience:** If you don't know your audience and aren't sure what their motivations are, where they are participating, and how, you want one of the high-end tools.

>> **The length of your SMM campaign:** If you're running a short campaign targeting a small population of users, you probably don't need to use one of the high-end tools. It won't be worth the money.

- >> **The size of the campaign:** If your campaign touches lots of people, you need a higher-end tool that can help you track the activity as well as manage responses.

- >> **Influencer identification:** If you're planning to focus on influencers rather than the mass population, choose a tool that's strongest at *influencer identification* (the ability to assist you in identifying people who influence customers about your brand). Not all tools do this equally well.

- >> **Regulatory considerations:** If you work in a highly regulated industry, you want a tool that lets you view commentary and glean insights anonymously. Higher- and mid-level tools have this capability.

- >> **Dashboard functionality:** Some marketers require interactive dashboards through which they can view the conversation in real time. If you're one of them, be sure to look for a tool that allows for that.

Lots of free tools for brand and conversation monitoring are out there. Regardless of the complexity of your SMM campaign and tracking needs, there's never any harm in beginning with the free tools. It'll cost you only the time in setting up the domain names. Also keep in mind that these tools are valuable to departments like public relations and customer research, too. They may be willing to share the costs of the tool or service with you.

Responding to Criticism

No SMM campaign is a complete success. It never is. Although you may reach many more people than you could have ever imagined, more likely than not, you're still bound to upset some people and even potentially spark an inflammatory response among a few others. From the outset, before you launch your SMM campaign, you need to plan for the potential criticism that may come your way. There's no perfect way to respond, and the answer usually depends on the type of criticism, how widespread it is, and where it is coming from. Your PR department is usually more versed in responding to criticism (and crisis management more broadly) than anyone else, so you should be sure to bring that department into the process early.

Regardless, here are some guidelines to keep at the back of your mind as you launch your campaign and prepare for the criticism that may come your way:

- >> **Respond early and often.**

  There's no greater insult to people criticizing your SMM campaign than to be ignored. Ignoring criticism results in greater anger and more vitriolic responses that can snowball into a full-fledged crisis as the anger percolates across the social web. Before you know it, your CEO — or maybe *The New York Times* — is calling your desk, so respond quickly.

>> **Respond honestly and clearly.**

Be sure to use your own name when you respond. Just as you have to be authentic with your campaign, so you have to be with your response. Be clear about your rationale for why the campaign is designed the way it is, admit mistakes when the fault is yours, and be inclusive in your responses.

>> **Be prepared to change based on the feedback.**

It's easier to be stubborn and not to change your SMM campaign. But if criticism about the campaign is valid, whether it's of the structure, the creative aspect, or the rules regarding the type of conversation, you should incorporate the feedback and make the appropriate changes. You'll win back trust quickly.

>> **Don't hesitate to bring humor to the situation.**

Some of the best responses have been those that included a touch of self-effacing humor. Brands aren't above people, and neither is yours. Humor goes a long way in the social web, and sometimes the response becomes the new SMM campaign.

>> **Use the same channels for the response.**

This may seem obvious, but it really isn't. Respond to people in the way they've criticized you. Don't go on national television to respond to a YouTube outburst. You'll become the laughingstock of the social web.

Chapter **5**

Developing Your SMM Voice

A social media marketing campaign, program, or strategic approach won't be successful if no observable people are behind it. Consumers want to know who the people behind the brand are. Being a trusted brand is not enough. Putting your chief executive officer's name on the About Us page of your website isn't, either. When consumers engage across the social web, they want to engage with real people who have personalities and opinions. In other words, the people representing the brand need to be SMM voices whom people can search on Google or Bing to find out more. That means that the consumer should be able to search the person representing the brand and see, via the search results, that the brand has put forth a real person to talk on its behalf. That's why you need an SMM voice.

Having voices that can be found through the search engines is instrumental to establishing credibility and being authentic. This chapter discusses why you need an SMM voice, how it differs from a brand voice or personality, where it is manifested, who can play that role, and how the two can come together over time. We then discuss using that person's relationships to help with *crowdsourcing* (asking people in a community to provide their content for a specific purpose).

Figuring Out Why You Need an SMM Voice

As we write this chapter, the United States, and indeed the entire world, is suffering from a breakdown in trust. Practically every major corporation is dealing with a trust issue. In this environment, does it make sense to introduce a new type of voice into your organization with potentially overlapping responsibilities confusing customers? On the surface, it may not appear so, but it's actually more important than ever. If the last economic downturn has taught us one thing, it's that consumers are tired of engaging with large, impersonal brands and often turn against them on the social web, trusting them less and less. They simply do not trust big brands as much as they once did. In fact, half of the respondents to a survey conducted by *The Economist* magazine said that the last economic crisis intensified their distrust of big business. The magazine went on to say that the downturn accelerated the use of social media because people began placing more value on the recommendations of their friends than they did in big business. According to the 2019 Edelman Trust Barometer, trust in business increased to 54 percent from 48 percent the previous year, showing that while trust in business is stabilizing, it's still quite low with nearly half of the American population not trusting big business. This is just another point on how trust in big business has not bounced back significantly from the downturn. The stock market gyrations in markets around the world should indicate to everyone that people are scared and confused.

If you run a business that tries to reach consumers in the social web, this distrust presents a problem. Those consumers don't want to listen to you as much. They'd much rather listen to their friends. This means that they're not paying attention to all the advertising that you're pushing at them and certainly aren't making product-purchasing decisions based on it. In fact, many consumers aren't even watching TV the way they once did. Compared to the past, they are either fast-forwarding through most of the advertising or are watching their favorite shows online via subscription services that may not support advertising. This means that you have to change your marketing strategy, and because you purchased this book, you've probably already realized that you need to.

It also means that if your consumers trust their friends more than big brands, you have to behave more like their friends to earn their trust. And at the heart of becoming more like their friends is developing an SMM voice that's associated with a single person in your company through whom you reach out to those consumers. It can't just be your brand name, your logo, or your witty copy that does it. It has to be a *real* person within your company who's reaching out to your consumers. And that real person can't be the CEO, either — unless, of course, that person can truly invest the time to talk to the consumers him- or herself.

TIP

Sometimes the best way to discover whether you need an SMM voice is by scanning the conversations about your brand across the social web. You'll probably find people talking about you or your product category, at the very least. That can give you a sense of how important it is, and the volume of conversations may serve as a guide to how quickly you need to establish your SMM voice.

Defining SMM Voice Characteristics

The SMM voice is fundamentally the voice through which you engage with your consumers in the social web. Every conversation touchpoint on any social platform from YouTube (www.youtube.com) and Facebook (www.facebook.com) to Twitter (www.twitter.com) and Instagram (www.instagram.com) and your own discussion forums needs to be in the SMM voice. This strategy can take the form of one voice, or it can be several employees who work closely together. But all SMM voices share certain characteristics that are in contrast to a traditional brand voice. In the next few sections, we look at some of those key characteristics.

Multiple and authentic

Most companies have multiple, authentic SMM voices. The reason is obvious. They are generally too large to have one person representing them digitally in all the conversations. Multiple people focus on different conversation areas, whether it's customer support, industry insights, product information, or awareness building. In some cases, each person represents the company on different social environments. Each person talks in her own voice and loosely follows centralized guidelines. Zappos (https://www.zappos.com/beyondthebox) is a good example of a company with multiple SMM voices. The company is proud of its multiple SMM voices and trusts those employees to represent the brand effectively without losing their own authenticity. Another example is the Virgin Atlantic blog called "Ruby" (https://blog.virginatlantic.com/), which uses multiple social media marketing voices that still conforms to general tone and voice guidelines while being deeply engaging.

Transparent and easy to find

Your SMM voices can't be anonymous voices. They have to be real people who are traceable; otherwise, they won't be taken seriously. Now, this may seem to be a bad strategy because so much is invested in the one person or very small group who's playing the role of the SMM voice, but it's necessary. When making these decisions, think about celebrity endorsements. People recognize that a celebrity may not be the permanent SMM voice, but people would much rather be talking to someone with whom they can form a relationship and relate to, even if it's only for a finite period, than to an anonymous brand voice. For an SMM voice to be real, it has to be someone people can find through Google: There's no question about that.

Engaging and conversational

Some people know how to have a conversation, and some *really* know how to. Your SMM voice, whoever she is, needs to be truly conversational. She needs to be a person who can start a conversation, build trust, and be responsive. The person needs to have more of a customer service mentality than an on-message marketing or PR mindset. This is not about marketing or PR but about more genuine, deeper conversations. The person or people who carry responsibility for the SMM voice can come out of PR but need to keep in mind that this isn't about PR.

Social web savvy

Your SMM voice needs to be someone who knows the social web intimately: the rules, social norms, acronyms, culture, and best practices of participating in the social web. This person ideally should have individual credibility that extends beyond the brand that he works for and must be easily accessible on all the major social platforms. Keep in mind that your SMM voices will make mistakes, and they will probably get flamed at times, too. You have to allow for that to happen. It's all part of the learning process.

Unique to the person

In contrast to a brand voice, this SMM voice must be unique to him and not unique to the company. This is incredibly important for the trust to develop. Otherwise, the whole effort is a waste of time. Furthermore, this voice should be irreplaceable. When the person goes on vacation, the voice cannot continue to participate and be responsive to customer queries. Someone else has to take over and introduce herself first. Think of it like a news anchor on a major television channel who takes the night off. The replacement is a different person, and that's not hidden from the viewer.

Distinguishing Between SMM Voices and Brand Voices

At this point, you're probably thinking that your SMM voice is similar to your brand voice or personality. You're probably already thinking of people — maybe representatives from public relations or corporate marketing in your organization — who can be your SMM voice. Before you jump into this decision too quickly, check out Table 5-1, which compares brand and SMM voices. Use this table to explain to team members why the two voices are different and why this effort may not be best relegated to the public relations department.

TABLE 5-1   **Brand versus SMM Voice**

Brand Voice	SMM Voice
Singular, anonymous company voice	Multiple, authentic individual voices
Reflects the brand personality and attributes perfectly	Transparent, easy to identify online, and only loosely on brand
Strictly followed by everybody	Engaging, conversational, and responsive
Designed to appear across all brand touchpoints	Mostly relevant only where the conversations are
Usually unique to the company	Usually unique to the person
Sometimes manifested in a person, but not always	Always manifested in a real person or many people
Used everywhere from signage to ad copy	Used only in real conversations by real people

REMEMBER

An SMM voice is very different from a brand voice. Someone who's spent a lifetime representing your brand and keeping everyone else around on brand message is probably not the best person to be the SMM voice.

As you compare the two voices, ask yourself whether you have an SMM voice and, if so, how it relates to your brand voice. It can be closely associated with your brand voice, but it doesn't have to be. In some cases, the SMM voice may be closer to the product brand than the corporate brand. That doesn't matter as long as it's driven by an individual or several individuals and is truly authentic.

REMEMBER

Establishing an SMM voice may appear in conflict with brand and public relations objectives. The best way to avoid this conflict is to include your brand marketers and your PR team in the early conversations about your SMM voices. It will prevent an adversarial relationship from developing because they will truly understand why you're creating it. They will also have a lot of valuable advice for you based on their experiences in dealing with the mainstream press and customers through other channels. It's worth noting that you can have multiple SMM voices, some of whom can be people who currently are your brand marketers and PR representatives. Their success, however, may require a change in how they're used to talking to the outside world, but that can be discovered only in time.

TIP

Over the last few years, some brands have been able to evolve their SMM voices into brand voices. This is where the brand voice and the SMM voice have become so similar that they can be combined. That's fine as long as the voice continues to be authentic, personally identifiable, conversational, and in tune with the ethos of the social web. It's important that the voice be personally identifiable because there will always be cases in which conversations with consumers in social media may need to be taken offline. In those cases, it helps for the consumer to know that the person he or she is talking to via phone is the same person who responded online. The Virgin Atlantic blog mentioned earlier is one example where the brand voice and the SMM voices are coming together.

Outlining SMM Voice Objectives

When you're defining your SMM voice, you need to consider what you'll be using the SMM voice for. Knowing the objectives that it serves and how it supports your marketing and business efforts more broadly is instrumental. If you haven't defined the objectives for the SMM voice, don't take up valuable time (and potentially resources, too) in identifying that voice and putting a program around it.

Some of the more common objectives served by having an SMM voice include the following:

>> **Providing industry and company insights to all stakeholders.**

A lot of people are probably talking about your brand on the social web. Many of them are probably forming strong opinions about your industry, your company, and your brand, too. Some of these people may be very influential. They could be key influencer bloggers, shareholders, customers, competitors, or market analysts. An important objective for having an SMM voice is to share your company's own take on industry and company issues with the broader world and negate any false or unfairly biased perspectives.

>> **Building awareness for your products and services.**

Every month there appears to be a new social platform on which your brand needs to have a presence. This may be Facebook, Tumblr (www.tumblr.com), Pinterest (www.pinterest.com), Snapchat (www.snapchat.com), CafeMom (www.cafemom.com), LiveJournal (www.livejournal.com), or Twitter (www.twitter.com). Your customers may be gravitating to that service and could be discussing your brand and forming opinions about your product there. Your SMM voice is needed to simply build awareness of your products and services, communicate accurately about the products, and dispel any myths about them on these social platforms.

» **Forging deeper, more trusted relationships with your customers.**

Sometimes your SMM voice is important to simply deepen your relationships with your customers. It may be focused on giving them category purchase advice, sharing tips and tricks about your product, and helping them through product purchase or upgrade decisions. In other instances, it may be about simply participating in conversations and being a helpful representative of your brand in ways that enhance your consumers' lifestyles or their sense of who they are.

» **Responding to customer service and product complaints.**

When customers are struggling with products, they often complain about them in conversations with their peers or other people who are facing similar challenges. You have a huge opportunity to listen in on these conversations, hear those concerns, provide customer support where you can, and learn from those complaints. Some of the most dynamic examples of companies embracing the social web successfully have been from companies hearing complaints on platforms such as Twitter, responding to them in real time, and providing superior customer service. The ROI (return on investment) of this strategy is easily measurable. The shoe company Zappos (www.zappos.com), acquired by Amazon in 2009, conducts this customer interaction successfully, as shown in Figure 5-1.

» **Providing discounts and promotional information.**

Most brands offer discounts and special promotions on a regular basis. What better way than to share these than via the social platforms as well? Increasingly, brands are forming micro-communities with passionate brand advocates for the purpose of offering them special discounts and promotions before extending them to the wider public. This strategy builds buzz for the brand on the social web and deepens the connection between the most loyal customers and the brand.

WARNING

If you do offer discounts and special promotions, you must be prepared to redeem them. Account for the promo to be successful; when it is, your company won't have trouble redeeming it.

FIGURE 5-1:
The Zappos customer service Twitter feed.

Choosing the Owner of Your Organization's SMM Voice

There's no question that you need an SMM voice for the social web. It's instrumental to forging relationships with prospects, customers, and expert, positional, and referential influencers in addition to the industry at large. But setting your objectives up front is as important as knowing the difference between your SMM voice and your brand voice. It's no use participating if you do so in a manner that's in conflict with the fundamental ethos of the social web. You invariably do more damage to your brand and credibility than you may realize. Remember that whatever mistake you make in the social web gets quickly amplified, so set your objectives carefully, recognize how different your SMM voice is from your brand, and choose the right people to play the roles.

REMEMBER

If you're a small company, either the CEO (chief executive officer) or the CMO (chief marketing officer) should always be your SMM voice or at least one of your SMM voices. Even Zappos, a mammoth shoe company, uses its CEO, Tony Hsieh, as its key SMM voice even after its acquisition by Amazon. The strategy works well, and given that it's building and establishing the brand primarily through social media marketing, the question of how the SMM voice conflicts with its brand voice doesn't really arise. The brand and SMM voices are perfectly aligned. That may not be the case for you, so as you wade into the social web, think carefully about your SMM voice and whether you're even comfortable having one before participating. It's also worth pointing out that there are inherent risks in having a person who isn't a trained marketing or communications professional as your SMM voice. Where possible, if you're going down that route, be sure to get the person basic media training first.

Richard Branson, chairman of the Virgin Group, has his own presence on Twitter (with more than 13 million followers) and represents himself and his company (`www.twitter.com/richardbranson`). The airline Virgin America (which is part of the Virgin Group) also has its own Twitter presence (`twitter.com/virginamerica`) that is used to interact with passengers, share special offers, and announce travel advisories. With 800,000 followers, arguably the Twitter activity makes a difference.

In the case of Marriot Hotels, its company blog "Marriot on the Move" (`https://www.blogs.marriott.com`) is written from the firsthand perspective of its CEO, Bill Marriot. His posts are a mix of business success tips, information, celebrations of how Marriot is doing, and stories from his personal life. What's most powerful about the blog is that it's easy to tell that Bill Marriot blogs from the heart in a very personal and authentic way.

Now that you know what an SMM voice is, how it differs from your brand voice, and what business objectives may drive the need for this voice, the only remaining question to answer is "Who exactly in your organization should serve in this role?"

In the next few sections, I look at the most common types of people who serve as the SMM voice and what they're typically best at doing.

CEO

A CEO can be an SMM voice. In many cases, he is already close to being an SMM voice anyway. He's representative of the brand but is recognized and noticed as an individual personality with independent opinions that happen to drive the business's direction. This person is best used as an SMM voice providing industry and company insights. After all, he has the credibility and experience to do so. In many cases, you can use the CEO SMM voice to forge deeper relationships with customers as well. The CEO of Forrester, George Colony, is actively blogging (`http://blogs.forrester.com/ceo_colony`), and you can tell that it's really him. The CEO participating in the social web and sharing his insights (and responding to blog comments) has done an immeasurable amount for the Forrester brand. If your CEO does not have time to truly commit to the online community, whether Twitter or a blog, do not ask him to. It's better that he have no presence than an abandoned one.

WARNING

Never let your CEO, or for that matter any employee, comment about your company on discussion forums anonymously. Although this may seem obvious, as mentioned earlier, the CEO of Whole Foods Market, John Mackey, was caught commenting on an investor forum about his competitors. He got into trouble for trying to influence the stock price of his competitors.

WARNING

When choosing SMM voices, be mindful of the PR disaster experienced by Domino's Pizza when two young employees at a franchise put up what they thought was a funny YouTube video about sanitation behind the scenes. The video went viral, and the CEO had to issue a major apology. The fallout was definitely not funny. Although more junior staff may know the social platforms the best, they probably also require greater supervision and education. This is because they may not know the culture of the company that they represent or be familiar with what's good practice versus bad practice when representing a company to its customers. This is why the SMM guidelines are so important. Those are discussed later in the chapter.

CMO

Along with the CEO, another good person to play the SMM voice for the company is the CMO (chief marketing officer). Often, she is closest to customers along with the actual retail outlet employees, talking to them most often, hearing their complaints, and feeding insights from them into new product development. The CMO, as a result, is also a natural choice to be the SMM voice. CMOs are typically useful for providing industry and company insights, building awareness for products and services, forging deeper relationships with customers, and in some cases (but rarely) sharing special discount and promotional information.

In 2014, Target faced a major reputational crisis when a letter from a disgruntled employee to the Target leadership leaked out. The CMO, Jeff Jones took it upon himself to issue a public response via the Target blog and a LinkedIn post, as shown in Figure 5-2 (https://www.linkedin.com/today/post/article/20140513221110-3501295-the-truth-hurts). Jones responded in his own voice, in a deeply authentic and transparent manner for which he won personal praise and helped redeem Target's reputation, too. It was especially powerful because the honest manner in which he responded was very different from the traditional Target culture.

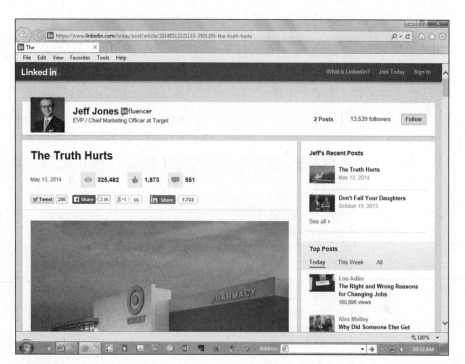

FIGURE 5-2:
LinkedIn post.

Social media lead

The social media lead is becoming a more common role within many large organizations. This person coordinates all social media activities across the company between all the different departments and to customers as well. She is, of course, the most natural choice to be an SMM voice or one of the key SMM voices. This person knows the social web well, often has independent credibility within it, and understands how to strike the right balance between representing the brand and speaking authentically as an individual. This person can accomplish practically any of the objectives with the exception of company and industry insights, which may need to come from the CEO or CMO to carry credibility. In some organizations, this person has the title of community manager, social media manager, community evangelist, or outreach coordinator. Ford Motor Company (with Scott Monty, who until 2014 was its social media lead) best exemplified this approach. Figure 5-3 shows Scott Monty's Twitter feed before he left Ford.

PR manager

The PR manager typically manages relationships with the mainstream press. Arguably, managing mainstream press relationships and being a brand voice can and does conflict with the SMM voice, but that doesn't mean that an enterprising PR manager can't play the role of the SMM voice. He may need to choose to take on the responsibility at the cost of being the brand voice to do this authentically, however. After he does, he, like a social media lead, can accomplish all the major SMM objectives with the exception of the industry and company insights.

FIGURE 5-3:
Scott Monty's
Twitter feed.

Agency

A social media, digital, or advertising agency can also represent you in the social web as your SMM voice. At the outset, having an SMM voice outside your company may seem inauthentic, but as long as the agency representative is transparent about it and is only building awareness for your product and sharing discount information, it's not a problem. Sometimes the agency can monitor conversations and provide recommendations on how and where to participate. But the actual participation with the objectives of deepening customer relationships, addressing customer complaints, and providing industry and customer insights must be conducted by someone within your business. The agency can also be used to help with training the internal representatives, monitoring conversations, creating reports for senior management, and providing strategy and insight.

Other external voices

Outside your agency, spokespeople for your company can serve as SMM voices. For example, if your company uses a celebrity or a series of celebrities to promote products and services, they too can serve as SMM voices. These celebrities can engage with your customers and build enthusiasm for your products and services. But each time you use an external SMM voice, keep in mind that they may not be as loyal to your brand as you may like them to be. They could be representing other brands as well as your own. If you have an independent expert serving as an SMM voice, keep in mind that she may not always be available to participate on your behalf when you need her to. Often when external SMM voices are used, they're used in conjunction with internal ones and not in isolation.

Crowdsourcing SMM Voices with Guidelines

For all the strategies that you may put into place to support your SMM voice, you need to do still more. If you're a large company with hundreds or thousands of employees, you can't stop your employees from participating in the social web. Just as you cannot stop an employee from talking about your company at a dinner party, you can't prevent him from talking about you online. That's not necessarily bad: The more people who know your brand and talk about it favorably, the more it can help you. But it's important to establish some guidelines so that your employees know how to talk about your company online.

Employees care about their companies, and they'll welcome the guidelines. They'll see it as a way for them to better represent the company in the public domain — that is, of course, as long as you don't make the guidelines too restrictive and incorporate feedback. If you develop the guidelines in isolation from your employees, ignoring how they typically participate online and want to represent your company, you're sure to face backlash. It is also important to design the guidelines to be adaptable based on how the social web is evolving and how behavior is changing on the different social platforms.

TIP

Before you write the guidelines, be sure to check whether your organization has any existing guidelines and policies that can serve as a starting point.

Here are elements that you can incorporate into your SMM policy:

>> **Purpose:** Start with the objectives. You need to explain why the guidelines are being established, what they hope to accomplish, and how they help the employees.

>> **Declaration of trust:** Just as important, you must establish that the goal of the guidelines isn't to restrict employees or to censor them, but to encourage them to be better ambassadors of the company. Similarly, it's important to establish that no one will monitor employees, nor will you ask them to edit or delete posts.

>> **Statement of responsibility:** Make clear that employees are personally responsible for all the content that they publish online, whether it is on a blog, a wiki, YouTube, or any other form of social media. They should do so in a manner befitting their identity as an employee of the company, recognizing that whatever they publish may be attributed to the company.

>> **An identification of themselves as employees:** Employees must know that although they do not have to always identify themselves as employees of a company, they must do so when discussing company or industry matters. In those instances, they should either speak as a representative of the company or include a disclaimer emphasizing that they are sharing their own personal opinions. Similarly, employees should declare any conflicts of interest when discussing professional matters.

>> **An SMM voice:** Employees should speak as an SMM voice by being engaging, conversational, and authentic but recognizing that they aren't the official brand voice of the company. And furthermore, it's important to do so in one's own name and not anonymously. The CEO of Whole Foods Market commented on discussion forums about his competitors anonymously. When he was caught, it hurt him and his company.

>> **Engagement principles:** Being a good SMM voice also means following certain engagement principles. These include responding to comments immediately, providing meaningful and respectful comments, being transparent in all social interactions online, and always looking to add value.

>> **No unauthorized sharing of business information:** Employees should not share client, company, partner, or supplier information without express approval from the appropriate owners. When referencing somebody, link back to the source.

>> **Respect for the audience:** As with any other form of communication, by virtue of being associated with the company, the employee is an ambassador and an SMM voice. He can easily tarnish the brand without meaning to do so and without even realizing it. It is, therefore, important to avoid personal insults, obscenity, or inappropriate behavior that is outside the company's

formal policies. This is especially important because when something is expressed in the social domain, it's easily amplified by others. Just ask Domino's about the crisis it faced when two employees published obscene videos online.

» **Respect for copyright, fair use, and financial disclosure laws:** Regardless of the media being published, employees should still respect all local, state, and federal laws, especially in the realms of copyright, fair use, and financial disclosure.

» **What to do when they make a mistake:** Regardless of what an employee publishes, at some point he is going to screw up. We're all human, after all. The guidelines must address what employees should do if they make a mistake. That means being up front about the mistakes, correcting the errors immediately, and accepting responsibility.

TIP

These guidelines are culled from an analysis of several social media guidelines, with the IBM guidelines, shown in Figure 5-4, serving as the primary source of inspiration because they represent the most complete set. If you'd like to see the complete set, go to www.ibm.com/blogs/zz/en/guidelines.html.

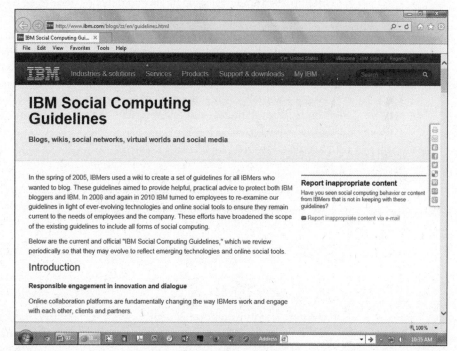

FIGURE 5-4:
IBM's social
media standards.

SMM guidelines can get long and unwieldy. You may not need every element mentioned in the preceding list. If you're a small company, these guidelines may fold into broader employee guidelines and may not need to be a standalone document. But you definitely need them in some form. They provide direction to your employees without hampering their enthusiasm for social influence marketing. And with the right excitement around SMM, you may find yourself turning every employee into a marketer who is representing the company in her own SMM voice, authentically and convincingly. You can't ask for more than that from your employees. Invariably, these spontaneous, natural grassroots efforts complement your more formal brand and SMM voices. They don't contradict but rather strengthen each other.

REMEMBER

Be sure to invite employees across your company to provide feedback on the guidelines. It's no use creating and publishing guidelines in isolation. Your employees provide you with valuable feedback. By being included in the creation process, they're more likely to follow the guidelines.

Chapter **6**

Understanding a Marketer's Responsibilities

O ver the last two decades marketing has changed dramatically. Without a doubt, the most significant change has been transformative technologies bringing new opportunities for ways in which we can engage and sell to our customers. These new technologies help us understand our customers much better, directly participate in conversations with them, encourage customers to do some of the marketing for us, and then sell to them in very different ways. For example, can you imagine spending $500 on a cellphone twenty-five years ago? Or having conversations with customers spread out around the world about their needs in real-time via those phones? Some of us didn't even have cellphones then.

With these new opportunities to market and engage with customers comes responsibilities that marketers didn't have to consider in the past. Responsibilities that you have to take very seriously if you want to continue earning the trust of your customers. In this chapter, we discuss what it means to be a marketer in the social media age, the new responsibilities that come with this change, and how marketers need to think about all their constituents moving forward.

Recognizing Who You Serve

Marketing used to be about identifying customers, building brands, and encouraging purchases of your product and services. The marketing funnel, which included taking the customers from awareness and consideration to purchase and loyalty, served as a foundational framework for all marketing. That still matters today and in fact, one can argue more than ever, even though how customers move through the funnel may have changed. But there is one fundamental difference today relative to the past. And that's about who marketers serve.

Marketing used to be just about serving customers and customers alone. However, what you do in marketing has significant ramifications for other constituents in society. As a result, you need to be sensitive to their needs and address them as well.

REMEMBER

You may think this is the responsibility of the CEO or the entire company, but a lot of this responsibility invariably falls on you as the face of the company.

Here are some of those other constituents and how you can play a more thoughtful role in serving them as well.

Employees

If you're a small business, you may take this for granted and assume treating employees well is the normal course of running a successful business. How you treat your employees is extremely important and with size and the complexities of a social media world, it only becomes more difficult in time.

When it comes to treating employees well, the first step is to compensate them fairly and provide them with important benefits. It also includes supporting them with training and education that helps them develop the new skills needed in the transforming world (and a world where every customer is on social media and one tap away from you). The training needs to include how to present themselves as employees in social media — how to identify themselves, what to talk about, and what topics to avoid.

TIP

Treating employees effectively also requires treating them with respect and fostering diversity and inclusion. As the saying goes, when you hire employees, you shouldn't just look for "culture fits" but also "culture adds," people who may be a little different but add something more to your culture.

Suppliers

Now suppliers are a constituent that are extremely easy to take advantage of. After all, they're providing you with a product or a service that serves as a component of what you go on to deliver to your customers. In the twenty-first century, that is not acceptable.

It's critical to deal fairly and ethically with suppliers. While they're not directly a part of your company, they're a part of your value chain. What they do or don't do can reflect badly on you as well. (Just think about the Nike sweat shop controversy from as recent as 2016 as an example of this.) The more you treat your suppliers fairly and ethically, the more they will treat their own employees and their own suppliers, in turn, the same way. When that happens, everyone wins. It's important to serve as a good partner to your suppliers.

Communities

Every company sits within a community. If you're a small business with a storefront, you feel this every single day. However, if you're a large multi-national corporation, you must remember that you have a responsibility when it comes to where your employees live and work and where you sell your products.

REMEMBER

It's important for you and your company to be sensitive to the communities in which they operate. This sensitivity translates into being good corporate citizens, adding more to the community than you take away from it, and supporting local community goals.

Shareholders

Without a doubt, shareholders are and always will be a very important constituent. They're the owners of the company and often are customers as well. Historically, their needs have been served at the cost of serving the employees, suppliers, and communities, but that's beginning to change. In fact, in August of 2019, the Business Roundtable, which is a group of CEOs representing some of the largest companies in America, issued a statement changing their purpose to account for employees, suppliers, customers, communities, and the environment as being equally important to shareholders.

Part of serving shareholders is focusing on delivering long-term value to them so that they continue to invest in the business. To do this effectively requires transparency, high ethical standards (just as it matters when engaging other stakeholders), and ongoing communication so that they know what the business is doing, what is working, and what the long-term plans are.

Practicing Socially Responsible Marketing

In addition to thinking about your commitment to different stakeholders beyond your customers, consider what it means to be a socially responsible marketer. Fundamentally, socially responsible marketing is defined as taking moral actions that encourage a positive impact on all the company's stakeholders from the customers and the employees to the suppliers, shareholders, and communities in which your company operates.

The American Marketing Association (AMA) has designed a statement of ethics that governs marketers' actions. The statement includes six ethical values that marketers are expected to uphold:

>> **Honesty:** Be forthright in dealings and offer value and integrity.

>> **Responsibility:** Accept consequences of marketing practices and serve the needs of customers of all types, while being good stewards of the environment.

>> **Fairness:** Balance buyer needs and seller interest fairly, and avoid manipulation in all forms while protecting the information of the consumers.

>> **Respect:** Acknowledge basic human dignity of all the people involved through efforts to communicate and understand and meet the needs and appreciate contributions of others.

>> **Transparency:** Create a spirit of openness in the practice of marketing through communication, constructive criticism, action, and disclosure.

>> **Citizenship:** Fulfill all legal, economic, philanthropic, and societal responsibilities to all stakeholders as well as give back to the community and protect the ecological environment.

For more details on the statement of ethics, visit the American Marketing Association Statement of Ethics at `https://www.ama.org/codes-of-conduct/`.

A commitment to the truth

If the last few years have taught us anything, it's that the truth can be highly controversial. Whether it's politics, business, or even within local communities, sometimes separating fact from fiction, truth from lies, and information from falsehood has gotten incredibly difficult. Finding the truth feels like searching for a needle in a haystack.

Sadly, these challenges exist across the business world. Put simply, companies aren't always truthful with their customers. It can be a CEO speaking about the company's future, a marketer talking about a product's benefits, or an engineer responding with data to a government ask. Companies, too, suffer from stretching the facts when it suits their interest. This is a problem and in a social media driven world where lies can spread like wildfire across the Internet, being true to the facts and honest at all times takes on even greater significance.

This puts a special responsibility on the marketers in a company or anyone practicing social media marketing. Marketers are in the persuasion business using stories to convince others to change their opinions and purchase specific products. Furthermore, through advertising budgets, the marketers also fuel other industries that depend on advertising revenue streams. Misinformation is rampant in our world, and by virtue of providing the revenue stream for social media platforms that may inadvertently allow for the spreading of the lies, marketers carry unique responsibilities.

As a marketer, you can easily fall prey to furthering falsehoods and misinformation when it supports a business's objectives or directly influences online sales. This is especially the case in social media where the way a product is positioned and marketed may not be visible to regulators or informed third parties who can call out misleading advertising. You may find yourself unintentionally marketing your own products in a way that may not be completely ethical and without the checks and balances that come with mass advertising, it may go unnoticed for a while.

Five ways to encourage truthfulness

Few marketers intentionally try to mislead or cheat their customers. And social media marketers are typically even more careful because they want to please their customers, being fully aware of the real-time feedback loops of social media. Those feedback loops serve as natural checks and balances. However, something can always go wrong when you're publishing a lot of content quickly. Here are five ways to encourage truthfulness from you and your team.

>> **Ask for facts.** When you have a team member reviewing their social media marketing plan with you, ask that person whether he or she has verified all the facts. Look for the facts and encourage the team member to keep opinions to a minimum.

>> **Use reflection to override bias.** You rarely mean to intentionally perpetuate lies. However, you're human and you may accept certain opinions as facts. One way to address this problem is by consciously choosing to delay arriving at your judgment. Let all the available information sink in and deliberately reflect on it before approving the direction.

>> **Engage openly with dissent.** When the facts are contested, one way to find what is the truth is to engage with those that disagree with you. Actively engage with all parties involved in a particular disagreement. Try to get as much of a 360-degree view of the issue as you can, before you form any judgments.

>> **Appoint people to play the "devil's advocate."** When tasked with making a major decision, set up an alternative team whose responsibility it is to justify the opposite conclusion. It leads you to better solutions.

>> **Be open to criticism.** Find trusted people who can provide you with feedback in a way where the message is heard without it feeling like an attack. It's important to have people surrounding you who don't always agree with everything you say.

REMEMBER

Marketers have unique and important responsibilities in any company. Knowing how to separate fact from fiction and truth from lies is supposed to be common sense — something that you learn as a child. However, in the social media world, it's hard to separate the two. Bad actors twist the truth, play at your weaknesses, and use psychology tricks to confuse you. As a marketer, you have to be extra careful both as a potential victim and as an unintentional endorser of those lies.

It may be retweeting a news headline that validates a product and not realizing that the headline isn't true, or it could be taking a fake endorsement of a product and putting it in a piece of advertisement, or anything in between. The point is, that in a social media driven world where information spreads like wildfire across the Internet, it's extremely important to only be a purveyor of truth and not lazy in what and how you communicate.

Accountability to Your Own Company

As a social media marketer, you're in a unique position within your own company. On the one hand, you're plugged into the outside world, listening and engaging with your customers in real-time. On the other, you're tasked with guiding your company on strategy and product roadmaps, based on what you're learning about your customers, any new developments, and what influencers are telling you. It's no wonder that social media marketing is an unenviable profession.

While the roles can be highly desirable, they do come with significant risks. As a social media marketer, it's key that you understand the risks that come with social media marketing and do everything you can to alleviate them. We have already discussed the risks around the truth, but there are others you need to consider. Here are six ideas for being a better corporate citizen:

» **Recognize the limits of your role.** When you're a marketer and one specifically tasked with social media marketing, it can be tempting to take your own role a bit too seriously. Be mindful that you're just one contributor among many that move your business forward. Work with humility, even though you may have a very dynamic role in your company.

» **Make the lawyers your best friends.** Social media can be dangerous, both for your company and for you as an individual. One way to mitigate against those risks is to get to know your corporoate lawyers well (if you're a large enough company to have some). It's imperative that you understand what the law allows you to say in social media and what it prevents you from doing. You don't want to cross that line.

» **Bring everyone along with you.** Just because you carry responsibilities for social media marketing doesn't mean you're the only person who's an expert in the area and can talk about the company publicly. Spend time educating your peers and encourage them to become voices for the company in social media. It takes the pressure off you and can only strengthen the company.

» **Understand social media marketing's role.** Social media has indeed had a broad, transformative influence on marketing and businesses. However, it has limits, and you must be careful not to oversell social media marketing. For example, for your business, it may be the perfect channel to drive interest in your product but terrible for closing sales. That's okay as long as you know the difference and manage expectations.

» **Learn from your peers.** If there's one constant in social media marketing, it's that it is perpetually changing! As a result, it can be difficult to keep pace with all facets of social media marketing. Don't be afraid to learn from others around you in your company. Some may have a much deeper knowledge in a particular platform or online community. Leverage them and highlight their expertise to others.

» **Let your customers influence your company.** Social media is unique in that it brings the relationship between a customer and a business so much closer together. While you may have responsibilities in social media marketing, be sure to use your responsibilities as a way to bring others closer to your customers.

3

Reaching Your Audience via Mainstream Social Platforms

Uncover how to choose the major social platforms on which to launch, sustain, and promote your brand.

Discover why Facebook is one of the "must-haves" for social media campaigns.

See the variety of tweet types that exist on Twitter and how you can exploit them in your advertising.

Lean how to incorporate YouTube, LinkedIn, Instagram, and Snapchat into your social media marketing strategy.

Look at using Pinterest for Business.

Learn how you can use Tumblr to create visuals to engage your audience.

Find out how to spread your content to new readers with Medium and other smaller platforms.

Chapter **7**

Finding the Right Platforms

I f you have been an Internet user since the mid-1990s, you probably know that the popular social platforms today are not the first to have been launched. Many came before Facebook, Twitter, YouTube, and Instagram. In some cases, those early social networks and online communities were extremely successful, too. For example, back in the mid-1990s, The Well was considered the most influential online community. It wasn't the largest, but it was the most influential.

GeoCities, which rose to fame in the late 1990s and was bought by Yahoo! for a whopping $3.57 billion at its peak, boasted millions of active accounts. Friendster, which was the darling of the social networking world in 2003 and 2004, fizzled when its technical infrastructure and lack of new features pushed people in America away from it. (Approximately 80 percent of its traffic came from Asia in its final years, until it was eventually shut down in June 2015.)

The point is that customarily, social platforms such as online communities, social networks, and loosely connected personal spaces online have periods of immense growth, plateaus, and then slow, painful declines. It appears hard for a social platform to avoid this evolution. We've seen this happen time and again. This poses a difficult challenge for marketers.

Where do you invest your marketing dollars if you don't know whether a specific social platform is going to be around in a year or two? Similarly, how do you know which up-and-coming social platform your users are going to gravitate toward after a major social platform starts fizzling? Knowing which social platform is going to have explosive growth next and where your customers will spend their time is not always easy. Nevertheless, you must try to answer those questions.

This chapter helps you identify the right combination of social platforms on which to launch, sustain, and promote your brand.

Before marketing on these social platforms, you need to figure out your social voice. See Chapter 5 for more information on how to do that.

Choosing Social Media Platforms

The first step in choosing the best platform for you is to recognize that no *single* social platform is going to be enough for your SMM activities. It's extremely unlikely that your potential customers use only one of the social platforms exclusively. In fact, research shows that a user is rarely on only one platform. Your customers are far more likely to have profiles on two or three social platforms and to use some of them more than others. Furthermore, you have to assume that your consumers will invariably gravitate from one social platform to another as time passes. For example, whereas Facebook may have the greatest scale, the sharp rise in usage of Instagram, Pinterest, Snapchat, TikTok, and WhatsApp shows how fickle consumers can be.

You've probably also noticed that marketing on several social platforms isn't that much more expensive than marketing on one, as long as your energies are focused. Choosing a few social platforms versus just one to do your marketing makes sense if you can reach different audiences in different ways at different points in the marketing funnel through each one.

Still, the question of where to focus remains. You can't be marketing on every social platform — Facebook, LinkedIn, YouTube, hi5, Flickr, Twitter, Instagram, Pinterest, Tumblr, LinkedIn, WhatsApp, Snapchat, Meetup — all at one time with the same amount of effort. Although SMM is considered relatively cheap, your efforts still take time and money when you're on many social platforms at one time. (You're probably going to confuse customers who are on several of the social platforms, to boot.)

The answer is to put a lot of effort into marketing on a few social platforms where your customers participate the most and to have lighter presences on the other platforms.

To pick the right platforms, you can start by looking at the audiences with which you interact, and at where they are most likely to make their purchasing decisions. For purposes of this discussion, you can break your audiences down into the following three groups:

» **Customers:** Obviously, this is your main target. You want to connect, interact, and prompt them to buy from you. You need to understand why they buy, where they buy, and what influences their purchasing process.

» **Industry:** These are the people who may be competitors, vendors, governing bodies, and so on. In the social media world, this group helps to support your visibility and influence with media outlets and customers directly.

» **Employees:** They can be either your greatest strength or weakness, depending on how you prepare them to participate in social media. If you don't have staff to dedicate to a project, you have a different kind of problem to solve.

Following is a look at how to work through the issues of picking platforms that support each group.

Learning about your customers

Choose where to practice SMM by researching and understanding where your customers are spending most of their time. This doesn't mean identifying where most of your customers have registered profiles, but instead researching where the customers have the highest levels of engagement. This means

» **Finding out what amount of time they spend on the social platform, what they specifically do, and how they use it to interact with each other.**

Tools such as Quantcast (www.quantcast.com) can help you understand engagement, but you may need to reach out to the social platforms themselves to understand the details of the engagement. Keep in mind that with Quantcast, only if the site has been Quantified (which means that the site owner has added Quantcast code to his site) are the statistics the most accurate. Comscore (www.comscore.com) is a paid solution that can provide more accurate numbers for non-Quantified sites. Figure 7-1 shows the Quantcast home page.

You may also want to survey your customers directly to understand their social media usage. There are several good survey tools, including SurveyMonkey and Zoho Survey.

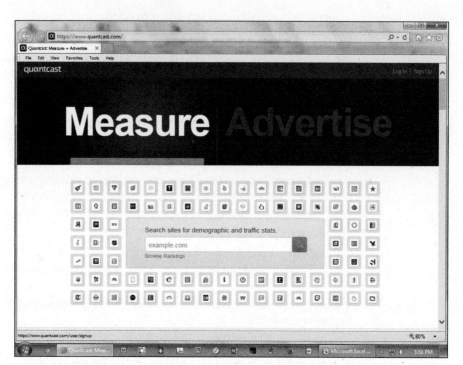

FIGURE 7-1:
Quantcast.

>> **Understanding the user behaviors on the social platform.**

For example, if you're a business-to-business (B2B) solutions provider, and your customers use LinkedIn to ask each other for advice when making business-related purchasing decisions but spend a lot more time on Facebook, LinkedIn may still be a better place to practice SMM. That's where they're making the purchasing decisions that matter to you. It doesn't matter if they're spending more cumulative minutes on Facebook.

TIP

In addition, consider monitoring mentions of your brand, competitors, product names, or industry keywords to determine how much activity there is across the platforms.

Invariably, you discover that three to four social platforms match your customers' demographics, have high engagement levels for them, and are what we loosely call *locations of influence* as far as your product category is concerned. That's where your customers make their decisions, get influenced by others, and observe how their peers are purchasing or discussing their own purchases. These factors together tell you where to practice SMM. And as you do so, recognize that you must also consider two broader aspects:

>> **Watching the macro trends of the social platform.**

For example, does the platform look like it's emerging, has it settled into a plateau, or is it fizzling? Accordingly, you may want to devote more or fewer dollars and effort to it.

>> **Determining whether the social platform is a place where your brand will have permission to participate and one in which you will want to participate.**

Participating in some social platforms may hurt your brand. For example, if you are a high-end, exclusive brand like Chanel, it may not be appropriate to engage in conversations in a casual, music-oriented social environment such as the relaunched version of MySpace.

REMEMBER

Your customers move between platforms as time passes. As a result, be prepared to adjust your social media marketing campaign significantly. Your customers may not always stay on the platforms that you're targeting them on currently. This potential migration matters, especially to small business marketers.

REMEMBER

Each social network has a reputation. Make sure that your brand is in alignment with that reputation. For example, Tumblr is known to be photo centric and has a reputation for attracting a young, creative user. Keep a platform's reputation in mind as you choose where and how to market.

Addressing your industry influence

A look at your industry yields a very long list of potential competitors, partners, vendors, and associations for you to connect with. The SMM goal is to make this group aware of your influence in the marketplace. We address the importance of influence and the role of influencers in Chapter 1 and discuss them in more detail in Chapter 18.

Here, we take a brief look at three free tools you can use right away to make a quick assessment of your overall business influence. Obviously, you want to take a much more thorough look, but the following can give you some feeling for your current state of influence:

>> **Kred** (www.kred.com): Kred measures your reach. You can evaluate your organization across such platforms as Twitter, Facebook, and LinkedIn at the same time. If you have an employee who has her own influence on these platforms, you can also check her out separately.

>> **Marketing Grader** (https://website.grader.com/): Evaluates the marketing on your website using HubSpot's tool for grading websites. It looks at a variety of measures, including your traffic rank, indexed pages, and linking domains.

» **Followerwonk** (www.followerwonk.com): You can evaluate your Twitter account by using Followerwonk, as shown in Figure 7-2, Followerwonk provides a visual depiction of your Twitter feed according to influence, popularity, engagement, and user habits.

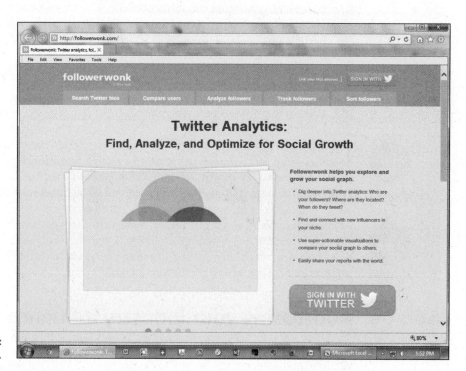

FIGURE 7-2:
Followerwonk.

Preparing Your Employees for Social Media Networking

A great social media campaign can be damaged if your employees are not given the information they need to support it. How often have you had a store employee say to you, "I don't know anything about that promotion. They never tell us anything"? It seems like it would be obvious, but in the whirl of planning and executing, managers often leave out the staff completely. If you're planning a social media campaign, you must make sure that everyone on staff supports the effort. Following are some important issues you must equip your employees to understand:

>> **The real value that consumers place on your products.**

Reality can sometimes be in limited supply when managers plan their SMM promotions. It's important to know the real value that customers place on your products, not the value you hope for. Social media tools allow you to get direct feedback and reviews from your customers. To plan effectively, your staff members need to know what they will encounter when customers talk back. Make sure that someone who has been on the front lines (such as a member of the customer service staff) is part of the team.

>> **The intellectual property hidden inside your business to create products and services.**

Some managers wonder why their employees are not more innovative. The answer may be simple. Innovation is not prized or rewarded in their company. Sometimes it's intentional. Most often it's not. Your staff has the opportunity to determine which website content your customers respond to. For example, if they find that customers are remarking about a multimedia video on a particular topic, they need to bring that up at meetings where creative solutions are welcomed. It could effect changes in your products and help build your social media influence.

>> **Who your real competitors are.**

It's easy to wear blinders when you're working on SMM campaigns. You are so focused on your own product that you can forget that the competition is everyone whom your customers can turn to for advice, training, education, and entertainment about the topic. When customers are not limited by geography or time zone, their choices open up. Develop a full list of competitors that everyone can monitor.

Evaluating Your Resources

It's often said that SMM takes a lot more time than money. This idea is proved false when you begin to factor in the amount of resources needed to implement a full-blown strategy. You can't overlook the fact that either you or your staff will have a variety of tasks to complete even before you start tweeting, blogging, and so on. Consider the following resource issues before you begin:

>> **Time:** Determine how much time your resources permit you or your staff to spend on SMM each day. How much employee time can be devoted to actually communicating with customers? This is the goal. You want to make authentic contact. This takes time. To make authentic contact first requires conducting rigorous social listening.

>> **Technical skills:** Examine the breadth of technical skills you have in-house. Who will do the technical work involved? Some of the platforms are plug-and-play, but more often than not, integrating them into your own sites can present problems. For example, if your website uses proprietary software, you might need to have technical staff write new code to connect the two applications without causing problems. This might be a quick fix or a long, involved project. You'll want to know that before you move forward.

>> **Design skills:** Understand the design skills needed to create visuals, charts, and so on. The quality of graphics and multimedia online continues to increase. You either need a designer on hand or you have to hire someone to create the graphics to match your own branding on one or several of the SMM platforms.

>> **Computing power:** Look at whether you're prepared to handle more traffic and sales. You've heard the warning, "Be careful what you wish for." What if you get more leads than you can presently handle — or if your site can't handle the traffic surge? It sounds like a great problem to have, and it is, unless you wind up disappointing potential customers who can't reach your site or get support.

For example, during the 2013 Super Bowl, Coca-Cola found itself in a spot of trouble when its Super Bowl microsite crashed after its advertisement aired on television. Coca-Cola had asked consumers to vote online for which ending to the ad was the best, and the voting made the site first slow down significantly and then crash completely. Coca-Cola had underestimated the amount of traffic the promotion on the Super Bowl would generate. See Figure 7-3 for the sign posted on Coca-Cola when the website crashed.

The Coca-Cola Company

**This site is undergoing scheduled maintenance.
Please come back soon!**

**Este sitio se encuentra bajo mantenimiento.
Por favor regrese más tarde y disculpe la molestia que esta actividad le haya causado.**

**Cet site n'est pas disponible pour le moment pour raison de maintenance.
S'il vous plaît, revenez vers le site plus tard. Merci pour votre patience.**

**Die Seite wird gerade planmäßig gewartet.
Bitte versuch es später noch einmal.**

**Este site está em manutenção programada.
Por favor volte mais tarde!**

**Sitemizde planlanmis bakim çalismasi yapilmaktadir.
Lütfen kisa bir sure sonra tekrar ziyaret edin!**

For information on The Coca-Cola Company, please visit www.thecoca-colacompany.com.

FIGURE 7-3:
Coca-Cola
website
crash sign.

Be realistic about the quality of your hosting and customer support. Prepare by evaluating how much traffic you can actually handle, and plan for a bit more than you estimate. That way, you won't look amateurish if your promotions succeed beyond your wildest dreams.

Assessing What Each Social Network Offers You

Now that you've looked at the factors that influence your choice of a platform, you can consider the platforms themselves to determine which ones are a good fit. In Chapters 8 through 16, we cover each of the major social media platforms in depth.

In this chapter, we look specifically at the user profile for the top four social media platforms. As of 2019, the statistics are as follows:

» **Facebook:** Facebook users are 43 percent women and 88 percent of 18–29 year olds are on Facebook. But Facebook isn't a youth platform alone, as 62 percent of online seniors are on the platform as well. The platform has 2.41 billion monthly active users. Users outside the United States and Canada make up 85 percent of its daily users. The average Facebook user has 155 friends. Users focus primarily on social interaction.

» **Twitter:** There are 330 million monthly active users on Twitter as of September 2019, sending 500 million tweets per day. The gender breakdown on Twitter is roughly 34 percent female to 66 percent male. Eighty percent of the users are mobile, with 79 percent of the accounts being outside the U.S. They focus primarily on world events, television shows, sports, and business-related topics.

» **LinkedIn:** There are 630 million users of LinkedIn around the world and approximately 303 million monthly active users. Seventy percent of the users are located outside the United States. Fifty-seven percent of users are men; the largest demographic on LinkedIn is 30–49 year olds. 87 million Millennials are on LinkedIn with 11 million in decision-making positions. Users focus on jobs, marketing themselves, and selling services.

» **YouTube:** This site has 1.9 billion users who log in to the site at least once a month, second only to Facebook. These users watch one billion videos every day. And more than 70 percent of that time is spent on mobile. Businesses are active on YouTube as well with 62 percent of businesses posting videos to a YouTube channel.

This gives you the broad strokes of the user demographics on these platforms. Next, you'll want to dig deeper.

Using platforms as audience research tools

You can use several tools to analyze demographics. In this section, we discuss the use of two platforms not usually used to do market research — YouTube and Instagram. Mining these platforms can bring you unexpected findings:

>> **Check out YouTube.**

If you have uploaded videos to YouTube, you can use YouTube Creator Studio to get a variety of analytics. But what about looking at YouTube as a large research lab? By using the home page search function, you can drill down on an almost unlimited number of topics. By using the Sort By drop-down list as shown in Figure 7-4, you can determine the following:

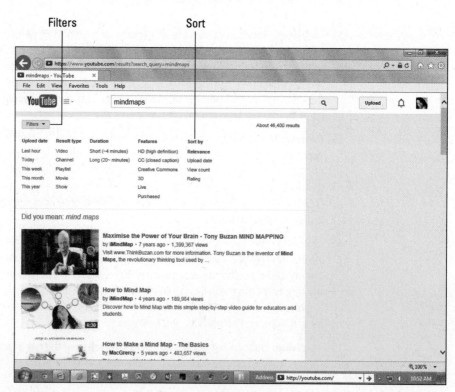

FIGURE 7-4: YouTube's sort function.

- **Relevance:** This is the default search. It brings you the videos most closely associated with the topic you requested.

- **Upload Date:** With this, you can see what's most viewed right now as opposed to something older. You can find out what's hot here.

- **View Count:** This shows you the general interest in a topic. With the millions of people on YouTube, you can see what's of interest to a big chunk of them.

- **Rating:** This is an interesting measure. YouTube used to use five-star ratings but found them to be ineffective. Most people would rate everything either a 1 or a 5. This didn't really give the viewer enough feedback. YouTube now relies on likes and dislikes, which gives you a quantitative measure.

- **Peruse Instagram.**

   When marketers look at Instagram, shown in Figure 7-5, their first instinct is to think about how they can display something — their products, conference photos, or staff pictures. Next, they think about how many people have viewed the photos they've posted. Those are both useful but are by no means the only way to use Instagram.

   You have to be very careful how much you push your products, conference photos, and staff photos on a social media platform like Instagram that's so consumer centric.

REMEMBER

FIGURE 7-5:
An example of Instagram's mobile app home page.

You can also use it as a research tool. For example, if you sell wedding invitations, you can use Instagram's search capability to find wedding photos that may include invitations. The idea is to use it as your doorway into customer's lives. Before the Internet, friends and neighbors would regale each other with stories, using slide carousels in their living rooms. Think of Instagram as a grand view into everyone's living room. If you want to see what kind of shoes people are wearing when they travel or millions of other things, you'll find that here. If you think creatively, you can get an enormous amount of information on Instagram.

Getting niche-savvy

In addition to picking the right major social networking platforms for your business, you should investigate niche platforms your customers may frequent. Convert with Content has a useful listing of niche social networking sites that can be found at `https://convertwithcontent.com/60-niche-social-networks-marketers/`. For more information on niche platforms, see Chapter 16.

See if you can find something directly related to your audience. The sites cover the following subjects:

>> Books

>> Business Networking Professionals

>> Family

>> Friends

>> Hobbies and Interests

>> Media

>> Music

>> Mobile

>> Shopping

>> Students

>> Travel and Locals

For example, if you sell eco-friendly baby toys, you may want to check out CafeMom, shown in Figure 7-6. It's listed in the Family category and can be found at `www.cafemom.com/`. Here, you can read about what types of toys moms are looking for and what they're currently buying. If you engage in a low-key, respect-ful way, you learn a lot without offending anyone. Any kind of "hype-y" sales pitch would not be appropriate here.

FIGURE 7-6:
CafeMom.

Chapter **8**

Exploring SMM Strategies for Facebook

When you perform your analysis to determine which social platforms are best for your SMM campaign, you'll likely discover that Facebook (www.facebook.com) is one of the platforms on which you have to engage. It has had explosive growth in recent years (Facebook now has more than 2 billion users) and is the largest social network in the United States. More than 66 percent of users log in to Facebook every day.

According to Statista.com (https://www.statista.com/statistics/247614/number-of-monthly-active-facebook-users-worldwide/), approximately 244 million North Americans are active on Facebook on a monthly basis, so it's fair to assume that at least some of your customers are going to be on Facebook.

According to Facebook Chief Operating Officer Sheryl Sandberg, you should be "social by design." By that she means that SMM should be a part of everything you do. With this idea in mind, in this chapter we spend a few minutes explaining how you can develop marketing strategies and use Facebook to grow your audience and engage your customers.

Looking at Facebook Basics

Deciding how to practice SMM on Facebook can seem intimidating because so much is going on at one time. The Facebook page for each business entity has a host of links, ads, posts, and so on. In addition, changes to the platform itself are being made continuously. You may feel that as soon as you understand how something works, it changes, and this can seem overwhelming. One way to overcome this sense of feeling overwhelmed is to remember the following:

>> **The key to SMM on Facebook is to understand that your network is the key.**

Together, you and your friends do things online that may affect each other's behavior. Marketers try to harness this activity to their own advantage. That's what you need to focus on. For example, if several customers like your business page, their friends will see that recommendation and perhaps buy it, too. By understanding the interconnectedness of SMM, you can build your business.

>> **The heart of Facebook is a user's newsfeed.**

It's easy to forget that the heart of Facebook is not your Facebook business page or a user's profile page; rather, it's the newsfeed. This is the page that a user sees when she logs into Facebook. It shows her friends' activities (including potentially your brand's activity). In 2013, Facebook redesigned the newsfeed so that users would have an easier way to show their friends what matters most to them. Some users have complained that the algorithm that supports this redesign (called Edgerank) actually makes it harder for their fans to see their daily content.

Because it's now harder to predict what your users will see, focusing your Facebook marketing efforts on the newsfeed is extremely important. A lot more users may learn about your company or your product through the newsfeed than by visiting your particular company page on Facebook or increasingly, your website.

>> **Using Facebook requires constant experimentation.**

No one right way to market on Facebook exists. Your audience and products are unique. You can follow some best practices, but for the most part, you have to determine what works for your specific audience. If you understand this idea going in, you won't have to feel as though you're failing because things are moving slowly at first. Try something and see how it works. Then use feedback and results to point you in the right direction.

>> **You have powerful tools at your disposal to enhance all your other channels.**

Facebook gives you tools to link to other channels to promote your company or products on. For example, you can link to your website, your Twitter account, your LinkedIn company page, and so on. Provide a link anywhere you have an opportunity. Don't forget to link all your email addresses and newsletters to your Facebook account.

>> **Facebook gives you an SEO (search engine optimization) advantage.**

The search engines regard Facebook as very important content. By publishing to your Facebook page, you can see a potential boost in your rankings.

>> **You can easily reach local customers.**

With Facebook, you can easily let customers know where you are, and you can choose to include a map. When customers are at your location, they can also choose to let their friends know. Furthermore, you can target specific posts in Facebook to certain customers in certain locations only. You can then use advertising to make sure that the posts reach the maximum number of people in that geography.

>> **Pay attention to the newsfeed.**

A newsfeed is the place where everyone goes to get their updates. With that in mind, publish content that is meaningful to your customers and drives them to like and share the content. It shouldn't just be occasional product-oriented content. You'll quickly lose the interest of your customers and worse still, if your posts don't get many likes, they won't get increased distribution. Make it a point to put a process in place, and use content calendars to manage the frequency and types of postings to the newsfeed. You want to be thoughtful in this endeavor.

>> **The number of likes you have should not be your only measure of success.**

The number of likes you have are only one indicator of interest at a particular point in time. You may have lots of likes and few engaged customers or buyers. Use several measures, including looking at Facebook's own Insights, to see how your actual published posts are doing. Pay particular attention to Facebook's Engagement metric, which tells you the number of times people have liked, commented, and shared your post. This is found in Facebook Insights.

REMEMBER

Facebook is always in the process of evolving its social platform. Besides the guidance we give in the sections that follow, we recommend visiting Facebook Business (https://www.facebook.com/business), which gives you advice on how to market on Facebook whether you're a small advertiser or a Fortune 500 company.

Starting with Search

"In the beginning, there was Search." Okay, we're paraphrasing, but just as you do with any good investigation into a subject, you may want to start with a search. When you're determining what's already on Facebook and how that relates to your own SMM plan, you want to use Facebook Search, which you can find in the header of Facebook after you're logged in.

You can narrow your search by clicking the options below the search bar:

>> All Results

>> Posts

>> People

>> Photos

>> Videos

>> Marketplace

>> Pages

>> Places

>> Groups

>> Apps

>> Events

>> Links

By starting with a search, you can get a good understanding of what exists in your product or service category. For example, if your category is productivity, you can enter that search term and get the results. You can also filter the results based on who published them, their type, location, and date that all appear down the left-hand column. Then you can use one of the search categories such as Apps, as shown in Figure 8-1.

The idea is to get an understanding of your customers, competition, and Facebook users' way of doing things. We recommend that whenever you want to investigate a question about the Facebook universe, start here.

TIP

Think of your consumer and the terms they would use to search in your product or category. Don't use terms that only people in your industry would know. It's important to put yourself in your consumer's shoes as you start searches in Facebook to determine who your real competiton is.

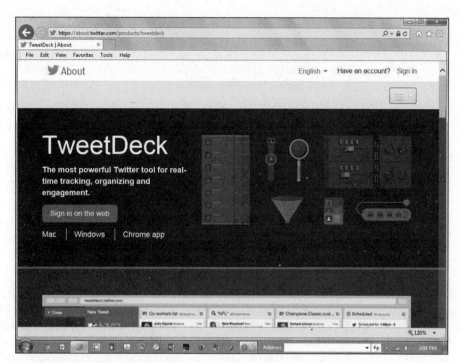

FIGURE 8-1:
Search in
Facebook for
productivity apps.

Facebook pages

Facebook has over 60 million active business pages. Think of Facebook pages as company profiles on Facebook. Everything starts here. You can set up a page for your brand and encourage others to Like it. It doesn't cost anything to create a business page, but it does take time and effort to make the page relevant and worthwhile.

TIP

Don't confuse a Facebook page with a personal profile. A personal profile has your name on it and is about you and your friends. A page is devoted to an entity such as a business, charity, or public figure.

The first thing you need to do is decide what type of page it will be — for a business or brand, or a community or public figure.

After you've selected your type, you need to decide what to add to your page to make it garner attention. If you begin to think like a social media marketer, you want to consider publishing media that includes the following:

>> **Posts, including location-based posts:** Ongoing posts that keep your community informed are necessities. Post as often as you can, but keep it relevant.

>> **Photo albums:** You can easily add a set of photos to Facebook in the form of an album. You can have an unlimited number of albums. Make sure to add any pertinent photos of your products, services, staff members, and anything else that will inspire your customers.

>> **Multimedia content:** To ensure that you provide a variety of formats, you can link to slides, video, and podcasts. Remember that your audience likes to be surprised.

>> **Twitter feeds and blog posts:** You can easily link your Twitter feed or blog to show up in your status updates using a plugin. For example, to link your Twitter feed to Facebook, go to www.facebook.com/twitter/.

>> **Event information:** The opportunity to alert your community to your events is worth taking advantage of. You can also show the location with a map. (See the section "Facebook events," later in this chapter, for more information.)

>> **Offers:** Using the Offers tab, you can create an offer for your customers on Facebook. This gets published like a post with a photograph, the details of the offer, and the mechanism to take advantage of it. Two things to remember here: First, make sure that you take down expired coupons and contest notices. If your original offer had been created using Facebook itself, you probably set an expiry date, which is good. Second, some people may un-like your page after they print the coupons or enter the contest. Therefore, make sure that you offer a prize that's relevant for the audience you want to attract and provide content that keeps them engaged when the contest is over.

PBS Kids, shown in Figure 8-2, has a popular Facebook page that sometimes offers coupons and giveaways.

TIP

Facebook constantly updates the designs and the features offered on its business pages. It's important to check back occasionally to see what new features have been made available for you to take advantage of as you find different ways to engage customers.

Facebook groups

Facebook groups are set up by users and are used to discuss topics of interest and express their points of view. To join a group, you have to be invited by another member unless it's a public group. Facebook groups had begun to wane in popularity with the rise of Facebook Pages until Facebook recommitted to them in the spring of 2019 and put them front and center in the app design. Groups is the third tab in the navigation bar across the bottom of the mobile app. Groups are mostly used because they can bring together people around common interests and offer the privacy that Pages cannot. As a brand, it's better for you to have a page than manage a group, which is really designed for user-to-user interaction only.

FIGURE 8-2:
PBS Kids offers a
giveaway on
Facebook.

Giveaway

You can't market directly in the Facebook groups, but you can certainly identify the ones in which your brand is being discussed extensively. In some cases, groups may be dedicated solely to the discussion of your brand. In those cases, you may want to observe the conversation, learn from it, and in a respectful manner, maybe participate as an SMM voice when and where appropriate.

Facebook events

If you're holding an event for your customers, employees, or business partners, you can promote it on Facebook by listing it as an event via your Facebook page. This can be a virtual or a physical event supporting your company, its products, special promotions, or milestones.

People can be invited to attend the event (you invite them from within Facebook either on your mobile device or computer), and the event page can include content about the event, your brand, and your products and services. (See Figure 8-3.)

FIGURE 8-3:
A Facebook event.

Conferences, product previews, and special promotions are popularly highlighted through Facebook events. After the event is complete, you can share photos and write-ups of the event on the event page.

If the event is a virtual one in real time, you can do a lot to encourage visitors by creating posts that tease about the event beforehand. You can have different types of events, such as a Q&A session with a guest, or questions about your latest product. People who use Facebook often appreciate the opportunity to stay there to get answers to their questions from their mobile device or computer. They don't have to make a phone call or log in to another online chat service. Also note, you can promote the event by running advertising against it so that it's visible to more people.

TIP

To stream video events in real time on Facebook, you may need to use a plugin. Facebook has teamed up with several external partners to make downloading and live streaming easy. You can find more information on live streaming on the Facebook Live Stream page (`https://www.facebook.com/live/create`).

Facebook applications

Creating pages and events that are supported by advertisements and sponsored stories may not be enough. Some companies choose to build applications that can be installed within Facebook. For a branded application to be a success, it must engage users in a meaningful fashion, whether its purpose is utility or entertainment. The most successful applications can take weeks to build and promote within Facebook, so don't expect this to be a simple endeavor.

Popular applications include games, quizzes, badges, calculators, and tools that analyze a person's *social graph,* which is a mapping of people and how they relate to each other. For example, TripAdvisor's Cities I've Visited application lets you show your friends which cities around the world you've visited. It has been an extremely popular application. For more information on building Facebook applications, visit the Facebook Developers page (`http://developers.facebook.com/`).

For a list of the top Facebook applications that can help your business, visit `https://blog.hootsuite.com/facebook-page-apps/` for guidance.

Login with Facebook

Facebook Connect continued to evolve since its introduction in 2008, and is now referred to as Login with Facebook. In a nutshell, when you use an application that allows you to use Login with Facebook, you have the ability to bring your Facebook social graph to a third-party website or simply use your Facebook credentials to log in to that website. In this case, the social graph is composed of your Facebook network. This means that when users log in to those sites with their Facebook credentials, they can see which of their friends have participated on that website in some fashion, whether by commenting, rating, or writing a product review. Whatever the users do is also sent to Facebook and appears in the newsfeeds of all their friends (if you have given the appropriate permissions). But the newsfeed has some lag time, whereas users can instantly see what their friends are up to by looking at the ticker on the right side of the page.

The ticker allows users to share their activity on third-party websites with their friends in Facebook, which inadvertently gives the site more exposure and greater power from a recommendation perspective. Figure 8-4 shows the home page.

For more information about Login with Facebook, visit the Facebook Developers page (`http://developers.facebook.com`) for general guidelines. Also check out the Facebook Login page for information on implementing the service (`https://developers.facebook.com/docs/facebook-login/`).

Using Ads on Facebook

To increase revenue using Facebook, you can do something as simple as a Facebook Ad. Facebook has continually tried to enhance its advertising. It has provided a very robust statistics engine, called Facebook Insights, and continues to improve the value of its ads. Facebook has a unique ad format in which demographics, user interests, and other keywords that are listed in profiles target the advertisements.

When you set up an advertisement, Facebook tells you how much you're narrowing your audience with each additional criterion you specify. You can also add social actions to those advertisements that include asking the viewer to rate the advertisement and become a fan of the brand directly through the advertisement.

Advertisements can be bought on a cost-per-click (CPC) or a cost-per-impression (CPM) basis and have been very popular with small businesses because of their low cost and the ability to pick a daily budget for how much to spend.

The following are ad formats that you should consider using.

Sponsored stories

As the name implies, sponsored stories appear with a title, body copy, and images, and they look and feel like stories. They appear on the right side of the page and may link to a Facebook page or even to an external site. (It's usually recommended that you link to a Facebook page and keep the user within Facebook itself.) The sponsored stories are targeted through profile data like the social advertisements and are popular because they're highly visible.

The newsfeed is what a user first sees when he logs into Facebook. The ads appear on the right side (not in the news stream) but are easily noticed.

TIP

A variation on the sponsored story is the sponsored video, which functions in a similar fashion. The sponsored videos are popular because they don't require the user to leave the newsfeed to view them. You can learn more about these at www.facebook.com/ads/stories.

Other advertising formats

When you're advertising on Facebook via your Facebook page, note that you're provided many different options. These include:

» Reach People Nearby

» Get More Page Likes

» Get More Signups

» Boost a Post

» Get More Online Sales

» Boost an Instagram Post

You also have the option to run automated ads that automatically adjust over time to help you get better results. To run these ads, you answer a few questions about your business. Facebook then recommends images, an audience to target, and a budget to help you get the results you want. Your ads start running and Facebook automatically adjusts them over time to keep getting strong performance.

Chapter **9**

Marketing on Twitter

Few social platforms have had more explosive growth in the last decade than Twitter, the microblogging service. Twitter (www.twitter.com) is similar to a blogging service, except that you're limited to 280 characters per message, or *tweet.* Also, only people who follow you on Twitter see your tweets in their Twitter stream. You reply to other people's tweets, forward their tweets, or send them direct messages. All your followers see anything that you tweet.

Today, Twitter has approximately 330 million monthly active users around the world, of whom 139 million are daily active users. Over 500 million tweets are sent each day. Unlike on Facebook, the largest social media platform, Twitter users are typically older. Although the total number of Twitter users is less than Facebook users, it's still quite large and has such an influential user base that marketing on Twitter requires a specific discussion.

You can market on Twitter using paid and unpaid methods. You can buy specific Twitter ad products that allow you to draw attention to your Twitter account, attach yourself to specific trends, and align with certain keyword searches. Third-party services let you also buy attention by associating with celebrities.

But in a similar fashion to Facebook, marketing on Twitter must start with the basic unpaid tactics. And as you do that, remember that Twitter is most powerful for building and nurturing relationships between people, even more so than Facebook. It's because you're limited to 280 characters (and in case you're a little confused, it was 140 characters until Twitter doubled the limit at the end of 2017.)

When marketing through Twitter, focus tightly on building the relationships, and everything else will follow. Don't worry too much about pushing messages to the community. But when you have to, there are smart ways to do that via the Twitter ad products that don't hurt your reputation in the community.

WARNING

If you do not take ownership of your company or brand name on Twitter, someone else may do so on your behalf. This could be a competitor, another business with a similar name, a customer, or a fan. If that happens, you'll probably have to spend a lot of time (and maybe money, too) to get back the username. Most Twitter users automatically associate your brand name on Twitter with your company. Many may not realize that the person behind the Twitter account is not from your company.

Figuring Out the Basics of Twitter

Twitter is fundamentally an asynchronous communication platform that drew inspiration from SMS (short message service, or texting) and Facebook when it was first designed. It allows you to publish 280-character tweets and view tweets from other Twitter users. To view other people's tweets in your feed, you simply have to follow them. In a direct contrast to Facebook friending, when you follow people on Twitter, they're not automatically made to reciprocate in return.

A second important contrast to Facebook is that on Twitter, your account is automatically set to public viewing by default. This means that anybody can view a tweet that you publish. This differs from Facebook, where posts by most people are private and viewable only by their friends. On Twitter, you can choose to make your account private, but most people don't. As a result, tweets by the millions of Twitter users around the world serve as a treasure trove for academics and marketers who want to learn how people talk online and what they talk about.

Following are some of the activities you can engage in on Twitter:

>> **Mentions:** As a user on Twitter, you can publish tweets as soon as you've signed up. Just enter your tweet in the message box with the question "What's happening?" and you're on your way. To draw attention to another user, you can mention her account in your tweet by preceding her account name with the @ symbol. For example, to use the Pepsi Twitter account in a tweet, you would need to type **@pepsi**. Then when a user clicks the Pepsi handle (@pepsi), she will automatically be taken to the Pepsi Twitter page.

>> **Retweets:** Another Twitter feature is the ability to resend (or retweet) someone else's tweet. Think of this as a Forward button. You can retweet by

clicking the Retweet icon that's below every tweet in your Twitter feed. It's the one with the arrows pointing towards each other in a circular fashion. If someone has tweeted something interesting, and you want to share it with your own followers, the Retweet icon is the one to use.

>> **Messages:** Through Twitter, you can also send direct messages to specific users. These messages are seen only by those Twitter users and not by anyone else. Direct messaging is useful when you want to communicate directly with a customer in response to something they may have tweeted. You cannot direct-message people who do not follow you. If you're in the Twitter app, just click the envelope icon to view and create messages. The envelope icon is in the left hand margin of the website.

>> **Hashtags:** The hashtag (pound sign) is used for spontaneous categories by people who want to participate in a conversation around a specific topic. For example, during the Super Bowl, people who want to tweet about the game include #superbowl in their tweet. Then, whenever people search for #superbowl, they see all the tweets related to the game even if they don't follow some of the people who are tweeting with the hashtag. Clicking a hashtag allows a user to see all the other tweets related to that category.

>> **Photos, videos, and more:** Twitter has made it easy to attach a photo that can be seen below your tweet. You just need to click the camera icon when typing your tweet. If you want to display a video, you can do so as well. Twitter also allows you to instantly run a poll with your followers or to share a GIF image or an emoji icon with them. All of these options are right below the "What's happening?" box.

A Twitter handle

Taking ownership of your brand on Twitter is very important. Sign up for Twitter with your brand or company's name as the Twitter handle. If you're lucky, no one has already taken it. Use this account to communicate company or brand news, special promotions, and product offers; respond to questions; and resolve customer service issues.

TIP

Should you follow every person who follows you? It's good Twitter protocol to do so if you're looking to build relationships with lots of people. But if your goal is just customer service, don't feel the need to follow everyone.

WARNING

However, when you do consider following someone, watch for spam, bots, and viruses. They've all made their way onto the Twitter platform, and probably the easiest way to put your account at risk is to follow another account that is then used to send you links to viruses. So when you choose to follow other people, make sure that they're legitimate people and not spambots or virus malware.

Searches

For anyone looking to market via Twitter, the first step is to monitor the conversations for your company, brand, and product mentions. You want to know how people are talking about you. You can set up these searches easily within Twitter itself or by using a separate application such as TweetDeck (www.tweetdeck.com), which is shown in Figure 9-1. Make sure to track not just your company's brand but also your competitors' brands. You'll probably learn more from people talking about your competitors than from their conversations about you. You can use the Twitter search engine (https://twitter.com/i/moments) or one of the real-time engines such as Social Searcher (https://www.social-searcher.com).

The reason for using a platform such as TweetDeck or Social Searcher is that you can find sorted information in real time. When you use Twitter search, you get a deluge of tweets that you have to sort through. The tweets may be current or a bit older. When you use the real-time search engines with the additional features, you get up-to-the-minute tweets that can be sorted by category. These are the best tweets to use for real-time marketing campaigns.

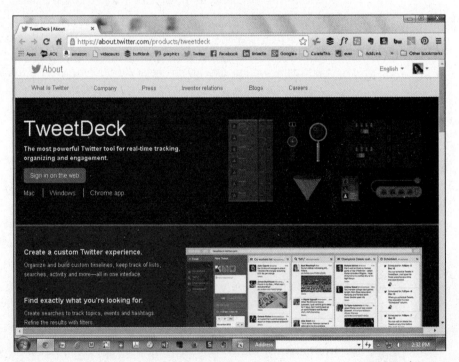

FIGURE 9-1:
The TweetDeck
website.

Responses

It's not enough to just listen in on the conversations. You have to participate in the conversations, too. This means responding to questions directly addressed to your Twitter username, whether the questions are customer service–related or more general. It also means watching your brand mentions and correcting misinformation (although you don't want to appear defensive when you do this because it can backfire), providing helpful advice when and where appropriate, and broadening relationships with the people who are talking about your company.

REMEMBER

Part of being a good social voice is allowing your own personality to shine through, which means opening up and being willing to talk about your own life and not just the brand you represent.

But there can be challenges in being personable and open. For example, if you're a mass brand with lots of followers on Twitter and lots of people talking about you, you may have a hard time responding to everyone. It can become cumbersome and resource-intensive, and worse still, it may make your Twitter account look like a series of individual responses versus being one that balances responses with fresh, original content.

Managing such a situation can be difficult. If your company receives lots of customer service queries, you may want to set up a separate Twitter handle to manage those. Similarly, if your brand has lots of consumers asking questions, you may want to create FAQ pages on your website and direct your consumers to those pages. Answering everything completely via Twitter may not be always possible, especially when you're restricted to 280 characters per tweet!

TIP

Keep in mind that when your customers talk about your brand, they may not always expect or demand a response from you. Knowing when to join Twitter conversations about your brand and, more important, how to do so is very much an art. Don't try to join every conversation, and at the same time, don't ignore all conversations. Apply common sense, try to understand the people behind the conversations, think about whether you can add value to it, and then choose to join or not.

Following and followers

The core of activity on Twitter is following other people, viewing their tweets, responding to them, publishing your own, and getting followed yourself. First and foremost, make sure that you consider following anyone who follows you. Second, consider following all the employees at your company who have Twitter accounts. You'll build goodwill with them, and they'll generate followers for you.

Next, identify, follow, and establish relationships with influential tweeters who have large followings. These people are similar to influential bloggers. They're the experts in a specific domain, with large audiences who can encourage people to follow you and who can influence others. In some cases, they may not be experts but rather celebrities of one kind or another. Friend Follower (`https://friendorfollow.com/twitter/most-followers/`) has a list of the most popular people on Twitter by follower count. Not surprisingly, many of them are celebrities, starting with President Barack Obama and Katy Perry. Next on the list are Justin Bieber, Rihanna, Taylor Swift, Cristiana Ronaldo, and Lady Gaga.

Different applications can help you identify these users, but one we like is Twiends (`https://twiends.com/`), which helps you browse Twitter users by category and country. It also gives you tips on how to grow your own follower base. You may want to also try the Who to Follow area in the lower-right hand corner of the desktop version of your Twitter timeline. It recommends people for you to follow based on your interests and who else you follow. When deciding whom to follow, think about it like a cocktail party. First, start with the people you know and the people that they know, and then people talking about subjects important to you, and finally random (or influential!) people and those who approach you.

Marketing via Twitter

Twitter can be used in any number of ways to market. But you can leverage the Twitter platform in a few critical ways to reach your customers. We list those ways here in order of priority:

» **Listening:** There's no doubt that Twitter is a powerful listening platform for you to learn how your customers think about your products, your company, and the category that your products fit into. Don't miss that opportunity to listen to your customers talk about you in real time. Comcast changed the way customers thought about it by listening seriously to customer concerns expressed via Twitter and by responding through the platform itself. As you listen on Twitter, be sure to also listen to conversations about your product category and industry versus just your own product.

» **Promoting product launches and events:** The real-time news element of Twitter has been fundamental in catapulting the platform into the mainstream. There are few faster ways for news to spread more quickly than via Twitter. In a similar fashion, marketers can use Twitter effectively to announce products and market events capitalizing on the newsworthiness of the announcements. In fact, marketing efforts can be announced this way. For example, Pepsi asked Snoop Dogg to announce its Pepsi Max commercial via his Twitter account to his followers first. It helped that he was in the ad itself.

>> **Making special offers, deals, and discounts:** Timely special offers, deals, and discounts are often communicated through Twitter. Customers respond quickly to these Twitter deals and often spread the word to their own followers. Some companies have set up special deal handles through which they tweet about deals. One example of a company setting up a special deals handle for tweeting about deals on a regular basis is @delloutlet. The Dell Outlet Twitter handle has approximately 1.2 million Twitter followers.

>> **Customer service:** Companies use Twitter as an alternative customer service option. They listen for customer complaints and respond to those customers via Twitter itself, or at the very least, they begin the response on Twitter before moving to a phone call or an email exchange. Comcast, JetBlue, and Home Depot are all examples of companies that have successfully used Twitter for customer service.

>> **Engaging meaningfully with customers:** Different companies take different approaches to engaging in a meaningful way with their customers via Twitter. Nike has a separate account, @NikeSupport, that encourages its community to support each other as well as provide customer support. Whole Foods provides healthful recipes. It also asks its customers what they like to read and watch and then recommends new food podcasts and invites the customers to upcoming company or in-store events.

Using Promoted Accounts

Twitter has several advertising products that enable marketers to reach their customers more effectively via Twitter. The first of these available to advertisers is Promoted Accounts, shown in Figure 9-2, which draws attention to your Twitter account. When you buy the Promoted Accounts offering, your Twitter account name appears in the Who to Follow area in the right side of the Twitter screen, with Promoted captioned below it. It may also appear in other places on Twitter encouraging people to follow you.

You can target who should see your Promoted Account via factors such as geography, interests, and profile descriptions. Promoted Accounts are priced on either an impression basis, which means that you pay for the number of people who see the Promoted Account listing, or by the number of people who choose to follow you. The latter can vary dramatically based on consumer interest levels.

Although having the most followers on Twitter isn't a true measure of success, it's valuable to build a base of followers who in turn can help you get others as they interact with you on the platform. Promoted Accounts helps you build this base and is especially valuable for when you're about to launch a new product or marketing program and want to have a large number of people to whom you can get the word out about the announcement.

Promoted Accounts help build that base with the additional benefit that after people become your followers, they typically stay your followers. This lasting value differs from display advertising, for which a dollar spent on an impression is lost after the ad campaign has run. You get no real long-term benefit from that investment. Keep in mind though, that Twitter changed its timeline at the end of 2018 to show tweets based on what they think you are most interested in seeing. You can switch back to the chronological view that shows all the tweets by recency but that is not the default view.

Promoted account

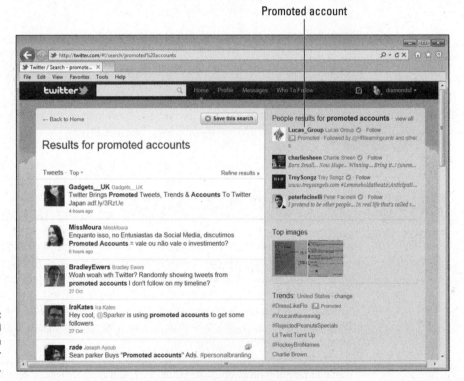

FIGURE 9-2: Promoted Accounts on the Twitter home page.

Making Use of Promoted Tweets

Promoted Tweets let you draw extra-special attention to a single tweet. Promoted tweets are primarily sold by being attached to a specific search term, although Twitter is currently testing it in a user's feed, too.

When you buy a promoted tweet, you are choosing to have a specific tweet of yours appear at the top of the search results page for certain Twitter terms. You can choose any number of terms. As with Promoted Accounts, you can add a layer of targeting to a promotion so that the tweets reach the people you really want to reach.

Following are the types of Promoted Tweets, also shown in Figure 9-3, and what they're best for:

» **Promoted Tweets in a search:** This product is best used to target users who do not follow your brand on Twitter. When using this product, you can reach users through a specific search term in a similar fashion to the way Google allows you to advertise based on searches on its website.

Bear in mind that only one advertiser can buy a search term at any given time. As a result, if you're looking to buy popular search terms such as those related to pop culture events, sports, or TV shows, you may need to spend a lot of money. Promoted Tweets are bought via an auction model. Whoever is willing to pay the most gets the rights to advertise. Often during the course of an evening, you can see different brands competing with one another in real time by buying Promoted Tweets using the same search term. In this way, they try to outbid each other for the customer's attention.

Promoted Tweets is popular because it allows brands to attach themselves most directly to consumer intent. For example, if you search tweets about holidays, airlines know that you'll probably be thinking about flights, too, and that it is valuable for them to advertise using that phrase so that they're visible as you look at tweets about holidays.

» **Targeting followers:** Promoted tweets can be used to target followers of your brand on Twitter as well. You may wonder why you should use advertising dollars to target followers when they're already following you. But the reality is that when you tweet to your followers, your tweet quickly drops below the fold and can be missed by your followers. As mentioned earlier, some of your Twitter users may not see the tweet at all if the Twitter algorithm deprioritizes it for them. When you use Promoted Tweets to target followers, the promoted tweet stays at the top of the feed. As a result, it becomes practically impossible for the follower to miss the tweet.

Promoted tweets are valuable when you want to promote something to your followers — the people who are typically your biggest brand advocates. This strategy works well when you have something to share that you believe will spread organically after it's seeded to a small group of brand loyalists.

>> **Geotargeting:** Promoted Tweets get even more powerful when you geotarget them at the country or even the DMA level (Nielsen-designated market areas). When you target a Promoted Tweet to just the people in specific locations that matter to you, your Promoted Tweet costs get much lower. This matters most for local businesses who care to advertise only in the actual locations where their businesses exist. Geotargeting can be applied as a layer over any kind of Promoted Tweet.

Promoted Tweets are bought on a cost-per-engagement (CPE) basis versus a cost-per-thousand-impressions (CPM) basis. CPE means that you pay only when a user retweets, replies, clicks, or favorites your tweet. You don't pay for the number of people who see the tweet but for those who take an action with it. (Paying for everyone who sees your tweet would be paying on a CPM basis.) This fee structure makes Promoted Tweets an extremely cost-effective, performance-based form of social media marketing and a nice complement to other forms of digital marketing.

FIGURE 9-3:
Promoted tweets in Twitter search results.

Promoted tweet

Using Promoted Trends

Twitter is an exciting social media platform for many reasons, but our favorite Twitter feature is how trending topics work. Every minute of every day, Twitter analyzes all the millions of conversations on its platform to determine what's trending in a particular moment.

The trending topics get featured next to the user's feed on the left side. They can be filtered by geography as well, so, for example, you can choose to see only the trending topics in the United States or even trending topics that are pertinent to certain cities. What's trending on Twitter serves as a barometer of how much something may be topical in the physical world in any given moment. Trending topics are definitely not to be missed.

Promoted Trends complement the organic trends and help brands build mass awareness, announce product launches, highlight events, and build the brand by association with other cultural events. They work in a similar fashion to trending topics except that Promoted Trends are defined by the advertiser. A user sees the Promoted Trend on the left side of the screen with the other trending topics but with the word *Promoted* below it. Note, that the Twitter design is always changing and what may have been on the left side at the time of publishing may now be on the right side!

As with Promoted Tweets, users can click Promoted Trends to view all the tweets containing the hashtag or trend terms associated with that Promoted Trend. Clicking the Promoted Trend takes a user to a search results page that has a Promoted Tweet from the advertiser at the top of it. Other tweets on the search results page will be unfiltered and open.

Promoted Trends, shown in Figure 9-4, are typically most valuable to buy on days when major pop culture events are happening and then best when aligned in some meaningful form around those pop culture events. For example, when the VMAs (Video Music Awards) air on TV, you might want to buy a Promoted Trend about music or, more specifically, about an award-winning artist from the VMAs because a lot of people will be on Twitter talking about the VMAs.

TIP

Promoted Trends are extremely popular with marketers, and it is worth buying the Promoted Trend in advance of the actual day that you want it to run. Because only one Promoted Trend can run on Twitter on a given day, marketers buy those terms well in advance of the actual day that they want the ad to run.

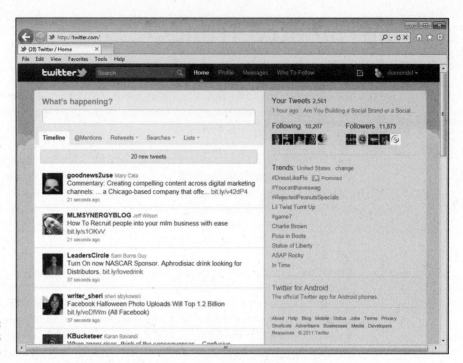

FIGURE 9-4:
Promoted Trends
on Twitter.

Working with Sponsored Tweets

One other current advertising opportunity that blends into the paid-tactics domain is sponsored tweets. In a similar fashion to sponsored posts on blogs, some Twitter users with very large followings are open to publishing sponsored tweets. Sponsored tweets are done by speaking directly to Twitter users and securing their interest in posting. You discuss the marketing campaign with willing users and they tweet about your campaign in their own language and style to their own audiences.

Typically, Twitter users publish sponsored tweets only if they can disclose the fact that they're sponsored, and if the marketing messages are in sync with their own personal brand and the type of information that they like to share with their followers. Sponsored tweeting is an emergent marketing tactic. An example of a company that helps you identify Twitter users who accept sponsorships and work with them is Sponsored Tweets at `http://sponsoredtweets.com/`.

Tips and Tricks

Twitter is a versatile platform, and marketers use it in many different ways to achieve their marketing and business objectives. In fact, the versatility of Twitter is what has made it such a valuable platform for marketers. Some use it primarily for customer research, some to promote specific marketing programs, some for outreach to influencers, and others for customer service.

Regardless of how you use it, you should keep in mind some key tips and tricks when using Twitter. Twitter helps you build a loyal, committed base of followers and drive up your digital engagement with them:

>> **Provide value to your customers.**

It's easy to forget that Twitter wasn't built as an engagement platform for marketers to use to connect with their customers. Rather, it was built for people to connect with each other, learn what their friends are doing, and broadcast their own activities. For brands to participate meaningfully, they must add value to the experience; otherwise, they will be ignored.

>> **Recognize that different strategies make sense for different marketing needs.**

It's important to remember that your Twitter strategy needs to align with your overall marketing strategy. If your business is all about customer service, use Twitter for customer service. If it is for providing exclusive access, use Twitter as a distribution engine for promoting how you provide exclusive access. Match the Twitter tactics to the marketing strategy.

>> **Prepare to adjust your Twitter approach.**

There's no better way to evolve your Twitter approach than by paying attention to how your customers respond to your participation in their social conversations. Learn from them, and adjust your Twitter approach based on what you see working effectively in real time. Are your customers responding to questions posed by you? Do they shy away from talking about your product? Are they more interested in learning about future marketing activities? Use their participation as a guide for how to market on Twitter.

>> **Use Twitter advertising to jump-start conversations.**

Nothing beats organic engagement on Twitter. To be able to hear from your customers in real time, participate in conversations with them, and watch them go about their lives through the conversations that they have on the platform is extremely powerful. However, there are times when you need to use the mass reach of paid advertising to jump-start those engagements or draw special attention to what you're doing. The Twitter advertising products help that process.

>> **Remember that knowing your customers is as important as ever.**

Some marketers make the mistake of believing that simply because this is a 280-character communication format, you don't need to know your customers as well. That's not true. Before you respond to a tweet from a customer, take a minute to understand who that customer is, what else she tweets about, and what matters to her.

>> **Listen, listen, and listen.**

It may be a cliché, but it's still very true: Listening to how your customers talk to each other, about culture, about your products' category, your products, and your company is critical to succeeding on Twitter. Listening is the first step in participating in conversations — a step that must not be skipped.

TIP

In recent years, Twitter has made it easier for marketers to identify the best ways to reach their customers on the platform. You can now choose an objective such as tweet engagement, promoted video views, awareness, website clicks, or conversions, in-stream video views (pre-roll), followers, app installs, or app re-engagement and then see recommendations based on that objective.

Chapter **10**

Creating a YouTube Strategy

YouTube (www.youtube.com) is another social platform that has had explosive growth in the last decade. Launched in 2005, it's now the number one website for online videos. Whenever marketers think of video-based marketing, they think in terms of YouTube first. You can't afford to overlook it as a marketing vehicle. In fact, today some marketers liken it to a TV network both in terms of its importance to consumers and its potential reach. (Not surprisingly, YouTube itself has noticed this and launched "premium channels" that function just like TV channels.) But what is probably even more interesting is that with 2 billion monthly visitors to YouTube from around the world and 300 hours of video being uploaded to YouTube every minute, if YouTube were a cable network, it would be the largest one.

What some marketers seem to forget is that developing an SMM strategy for YouTube is no less important than it is on Facebook or Twitter. You have to look at it strategically, in terms of both the community on YouTube and its potential reach. Although YouTube started out as a fun site, its marketing value has risen dramatically. In this chapter, we look at how YouTube fits into your SMM plan.

Looking at YouTube Basics

If you think that YouTube isn't a marketing goliath, consider the following facts, as of 2019:

>> It has approximately 2 billion unique users per month.

>> 35+ and 55+ age groups are the fastest growing YouTube demographics.

>> Approximately 80 percent of the traffic on YouTube is from outside the United States.

>> YouTube accounts for 28 percent of all Google searches and is the world's second largest search engine after Google.

>> Mobile views represent 70 percent of all YouTube video views globally.

Clearly, YouTube has all the muscle you need to drive your video SMM efforts.

Benefitting from SMM marketing on YouTube

The first thing you need to decide is the extent to which you will market on YouTube. You know that you want to participate, yet you're not sure how much time and effort to devote to it. To help you decide, here are some benefits you can derive from marketing on YouTube:

>> **Visibility:** First and foremost, being on YouTube puts you where the action is. People come to YouTube to search for videos, and you want your video nuggets to be found.

>> **Branding:** Extending your branding to your videos is pretty straightforward. Your logo and other design elements should be present, which assists in brand recognition. If you don't have these elements, you need to get them for all your SMM efforts!

>> **No cost to set up:** Unlike setting up a website, putting a video on YouTube and creating a channel is free. If you already have videos you've created, all you need to do is sign up. See the section later in this chapter called "Always create a customized channel."

TIP

The cost to create videos and all the work that goes into maintaining them should also be factored in. It's free to set up the YouTube channel, but everything else has a time or money cost associated with it.

>> **Fixed placement options:** You don't need to worry about how your video will be placed and viewed on the site. Yours will be displayed along with all the other videos. Your goal should be how to stand out, not how to fit in. If you have a developer who can use the YouTube API to help you stand out, that's an advantage.

>> **SEO done for you:** Thanks to the built-in SEO (search engine optimization) format of YouTube, Google displays your videos in its search results, along with everyone else. However, you should pay extra attention to the keywords you use to describe the videos so that they get the extra attention they deserve. How you name and describe your video is also very important.

Attracting subscribers

People on YouTube who choose to subscribe to your channel are known as You-Tube subscribers. Every time you upload a new clip, they're notified, and their names and icons are visible on your YouTube channel page.

Think of the subscribers as similar to followers on Twitter or fans on Facebook pages. Just as you'd nurture relationships on those other social platforms, you should do so here, too. So what's the best way to build a following of subscribers? Consider doing the following:

>> **Publish quality video clips.**

You've probably heard many times that online, "content is king." Think about your YouTube channel as you would a TV channel. If the content is weak, you won't build a community of subscribers who clamor for more. You don't have to have Spielberg-like quality, but you do need to project a certain profession-alism and consistency.

>> **Develop a smart video content strategy for your channel.**

Don't just think about your channel in the context of one video at a time but rather as a channel through which you'll publish specific pieces of content through the year — some educational, some more entertainment-driven, and some news-oriented videos that provide value to consumers and build your brand simultaneously.

>> **Encourage commenting on your clips.**

Comments on YouTube are not unlike the comments you find on blogs or other social media sites. Some have value; some are just silly, or worse. Your goal is to develop a community of people who appreciate and look forward to your new videos. If they post comments that indicate that you're meeting their needs, you've met your goal. One way to do this is to reference the comments in your videos and give shoutouts to subscribers who have been commenting.

>> **Subscribe to other people's videos.**

There is a twofold value in subscribing to other people's videos. The first is that you see what the experience is like. You want to understand how it feels to subscribe and how other channel owners engage with their subscribers. Second, it gives you an opportunity to meet and share with others on their turf. They're interested in getting subscribers as much as you are. Remember, this is a social platform.

>> **Share the clips on the other social platforms.**

You build goodwill, increase views, and get more subscribers by doing this. It also burnishes your image on those other platforms. But as you share your clips elsewhere, always put the video on YouTube first and embed from YouTube versus uploading directly to the site you're sharing on. The one exception may be Facebook, where you'll have higher engagement rates with your video if you upload the video directly to Facebook.

Promoting on YouTube

Knowing how to publish and promote your marketing video clips is essential to getting them the attention they deserve. The following are some recommendations for promoting your video clips on YouTube.

Always create a customized channel

Having a YouTube channel dedicated to your company or brand is important because it allows you to showcase all the related video clips in one place. A YouTube channel is your brand's account home, where clips that you have published can appear. Setting up a channel is very easy, so don't hesitate to do so.

A channel also allows you to create a profile for yourself and have a place to link your website. Make sure that you customize the channel to match your company's or your brand's visual identity. You don't need to manually create a YouTube channel. As soon as you sign up for an account (using the Create Account link in the top-right corner of the home page) and upload a video clip, a channel is created for you. To reach your YouTube channel, just click your username after you log in. Figure 10-1 shows one such channel.

FIGURE 10-1:
Khan Academy is a customized YouTube channel.

REMEMBER

Don't forget to provide a link to and from your website to your custom channel. Also, make sure that your other channels, such as your Facebook page and blogs, also have links to your YouTube channel. Reciprocal links are very important to a cohesive SMM campaign.

Creating custom content for YouTube

It's not good enough to simply add your TV advertising spots to YouTube. Create custom content that matches the style and format of YouTube. Keep the running time to five minutes or less, and stay within the 100MB limit on file sizes. The average length of a video on YouTube is 11 minutes and 7 seconds, though some videos that are considerably longer or shorter do very well. Group the video clips into themed playlists for increased viewing. It also helps your users find the video clips they need quickly. For example, some companies categorize their videos into playlists with names such as advertising, customer stories, support, and demonstrations.

Often, a clip that lasts a minute or two can have great impact. You're trying to get your audience to share your video with others. Don't expect viewers to devote a lot of time to one video. As you know, the site has millions of users and tons of clips to watch. The worst thing you can do is bore your audience.

Tagging and categorizing all your clips

Choose the category for your video clip carefully. Start by looking at how popular video clips in your category have been tagged (see Figure 10-2), and consider using some of the same tags. Those tags have probably worked for the popular clips, and they'll work for you, too.

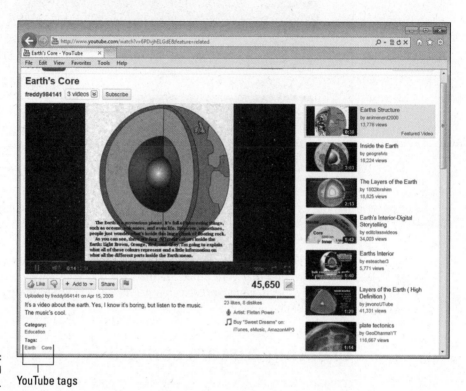

YouTube tags

REMEMBER

Your content may not fit into a category neatly. Choose your category based on the number of similar video clips that reside in it.

Use tags to make up for the limits of categorization. YouTube doesn't limit the number of tags that you can add. These tags also make unsearchable data (such as photos and video) searchable by adding metadata to them. Video titles and descriptions can also help with this.

Leaving video responses

Don't forget that you can build goodwill with other users by leaving video responses to their clips. This matters, especially with the extremely popular clips in your category. Don't hesitate to create YouTube video responses. When you do, make sure that your responses are civil and relevant.

Procter & Gamble used this technique to great effect with its very popular Old Spice guy campaign with Isaiah Mustafa, shown in Figure 10-3. First, the company created a funny video promoting the product. Then it followed up by creating video responses by Mustafa to the comments made online. This captured even more attention and doubled the company's sales. The great news about this technique is that although it's inexpensive, it can pack a punch. Imagine the surprise of your viewers when you respond to their comments with a video personalized for them.

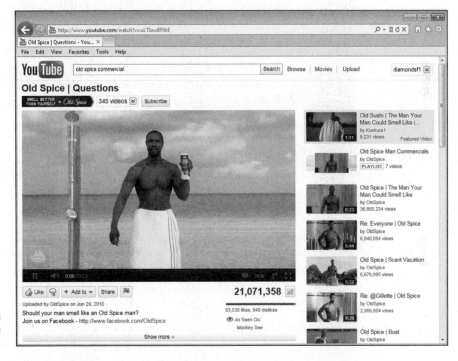

FIGURE 10-3:
The Old Spice
guy video.

Including a call to action

In every good commercial you've ever seen on TV, you are asked to buy or do something after watching. That's called a *call to action*. Promotional videos are no different. Just lose the hard sell. If you create a how-to video, it should include a link back to your site for more how-tos. If you discuss a customer problem, give an email address that customers can contact for the solution. Make these videos pay off by engaging your customers. When they're gone, they're gone. Don't miss an opportunity to generate a lead or a sale.

When considering calls to action for YouTube, don't feel that you have to wait till the end for the call to action, especially for longer videos. You can use clickable annotations that appear in the first few seconds of the video to drive people to where you want them to go.

Have some fun, too

Your customers are typically looking to be entertained when they're on YouTube. Have some fun with the videos that you post. Even if they're educational in nature (which can be very valuable and popular on YouTube), don't shy away from injecting a bit of humor into them (as Procter & Gamble did with Old Spice). Keep in mind that the clips should be engaging enough that they encourage the user to share the clip with others.

When you're producing your videos, remember that the first few seconds are the most critical. You want to start off energized; otherwise, you run the risk of losing your viewers as the video progresses. On average, you should expect to lose 20–30 percent of your viewers over the length of your video.

Seeding a Viral Campaign

Viral videos are of two types, and it's important to know both:

>> **Organic:** This is a video that creates a national frenzy, and people rush to see it and share it with their friends (like Psy's Gangnam Style, which is one of the most viewed videos of all time, with more than 2 billion views). Usually, it just happens organically without planning. It captures the imagination of viewers, and off it goes.

>> **Seeded:** This video has a carefully planned viral seeding campaign with lots of thought and advertising dollars behind it. It may go viral, but there's no guarantee. Some companies specialize in viral seeding, or you can go through a general social media agency to get assistance. Companies such as Medianeedle (www.medianeedle.com) and Video Viral Views (www.videoviralviews.com) can help you in this regard. Others like Sharethrough (www.sharethrough.com), TubeMogul (www.tubemogul.com) that was bought by Adobe, and Tubular (www.tubularlabs.com) focus more on the paid distribution and the measurement of the video views across all platforms on the Internet. Can you make a video go viral? Decidedly not. If you could, marketers would be launching them by the armload. However, these few tips and tricks may improve your chances of creating a viral video:

>> **Keep the content fresh:** Nothing beats fresh content when it comes to creating viral video clips. The content needs to be so engaging and unique that people can't help but want to share it with everyone they know. Always start by focusing on the content.

>> **Use celebrities if possible:** If you're representing a large brand and can afford to use celebrities, don't hesitate to do so. Adding celebrities to the mix typically makes the videos more viral. We're a celebrity-obsessed pop culture, and celebrities drive views. It is as simple as that. Some of the most popular videos during the World Cup from advertisers all used celebrities.

>> **Make it surreal:** A video that you want to watch many times over and share with your friends is often a video that has a surreal element to it. Someone is doing something in the video that is so out of the ordinary or so crazy that you can't help watching it several times or talk to others about it. Better still is if a celebrity is doing something surreal.

>> **Arouse emotions:** More broadly speaking, studies by psychologists have shown that the videos that get the most attention and are shared most frequently are the ones that arouse emotions in the viewer, whether they be emotions of awe, anger, amusement, or disgust. Although surreal videos are often the ones that get shared the most, don't ignore the other ways in which you can arouse the emotions of your potential viewers. And keep in mind that videos that elicit a range of emotions are typically the ones that perform the best because they're more multidimensional.

>> **Make it short:** People online have no time at all. You must keep the viral clip short. Sometimes clips as short as 10 seconds are long enough for a video to go viral. Focus on quality versus quantity more than anything else. But also remember that there are no hard and fast rules for what the appropriate length of a YouTube video should be.

>> **Don't make it an ad:** Sometimes marketers can't resist the temptation to turn everything into an advertisement. Don't let that happen. The content needs to be thought of as entertainment, and in fact, the more it is in a user's casual language (both in terms of words and shooting quality), the more likely it is to do well. The best way to appeal to your target users is to look at everything else they are probably viewing on YouTube and then use that as a baseline to understand what style of content they'd be most interested in.

TIP

You can also do a viral seeding campaign on the cheap. Someone in your organization can be in charge of developing a campaign. You need to decide how high the stakes are and what your overall goal is.

Viral seeding involves sharing your video in a very targeted way to increase its shareability (if that's a word). Those elements can include the following:

>> **Targeting influencers:** People who are influential in that category may comment to their audience about the video content, either online or off. These can be YouTube influencers or other types of social media influencers.

>> **Creating resonance:** Anchoring the videos in deep, global, human truths that everyone can relate to increases the video's chances of going viral. This matters especially if the human truths are powerful ones that your customers subscribe to and want to endorse.

>> **Placing it on social networks:** Links to the video start showing up in tweets, Facebook posts, and other venues. Don't forget Twitter and Instagram either, which have evolved into strong platforms for video distribution.

>> **Emailing it to popular lists:** Popular newsletters may include a link to the video.

>> **Advertising:** Video owners buy different types of advertising — Google, YouTube, Facebook, and so on — to encourage sharing.

>> **Blogging:** Well-known bloggers include a link to the video in one of their posts. Most of these have a strong presence on the social media platforms as well.

>> **Partnerships:** Collaborating with YouTube stars who are celebrities on YouTube with large channels to help promote the videos can help.

>> **Doing giveaways:** Links to the video mentioning free prizes start showing up online.

One example of viral seeding is the campaign Unilever created for its Dove brand, as shown in Figure 10-4. In April of 2013, Unilever launched a video on YouTube in which several women described themselves to a forensic sketch artist who couldn't see his subjects. The same women were then described by strangers whom they met the previous day. The sketches were compared with the strangers' sketches. Interestingly, it was the strangers' sketches that were more flattering and accurate. In a single week, the video had more than 15 million views globally. An article on Mashable about the video was shared more than 500,000 times in just 24 hours. One overriding reason that the video performed so well was because it was based on a surprising universal human truth that every woman could relate to and understand. The content was fresh, deeply emotional, and did not feel like an ad for the beauty product at all.

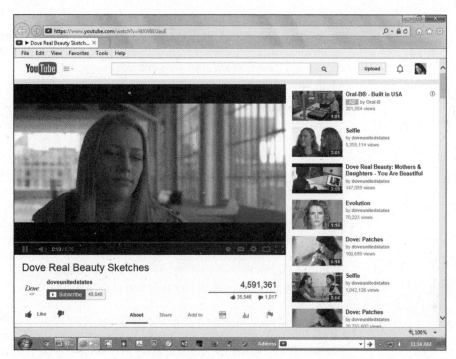

FIGURE 10-4:
The Dove
Portraits video.

Advertising on YouTube

If you're a marketer at a large brand, you may have the dollars to invest in some paid advertising tactics. YouTube provides several options based on your objectives. They categorize the objectives as Build Awareness and Ad Recall, Grow Consideration and Interest, and Drive Action. For each objective, YouTube recommends different ad formats, specifications, and pricing structures all available at https://www.youtube.com/ads/running-a-video-ad/.

After you've determined your objective, you're offered ad formats including the following:

>> **Home-page ads:** This provides the advertiser with a premiere spot on the YouTube home page in the masthead, as shown in Figure 10-5. More than 60 million unique users go there every day. It's prime advertising real estate and can cost upwards of $500,000 depending on the day!

>> **TrueView Videos ads:** YouTube introduced this ad format a few years ago that allows users to click a Skip This Ad Now button after the user has viewed the ad for five seconds. With this popular format, advertisers are motivated to make the first five seconds of their videos particularly interesting.

>> **Brand channel:** This category offers several levels of customization for a channel dedicated to your brand. The customizations include how the page looks, what videos are promoted, and how users are drawn to it. This is different from a user channel, which is free when you sign up.

>> **Mobile:** Video ads are served up on your customer's mobile devices — iPhone, Android, and BlackBerry. Comscore lists YouTube as the number one destination for mobile video.

With these paid tactics, YouTube provides all the standard media metrics with YouTube Insights. These include impressions, click to play, click-through rate, and quartile viewed in addition to the community metrics (likes, views, and comments). A *quartile view* shows the data segmented in equal quarters so that you can determine how well each is doing. Also included in the metrics, are demographics, locations of viewership, viewer sources (where the users came from to view the video), and how much of the video they viewed. These metrics are so illuminating that they're now forcing advertisers to rethink how they create videos.

You can also target these advertisements to run next to select partner content, if you prefer. This placement matters to many marketers who worry about what their own advertisements (video or otherwise) may appear next to.

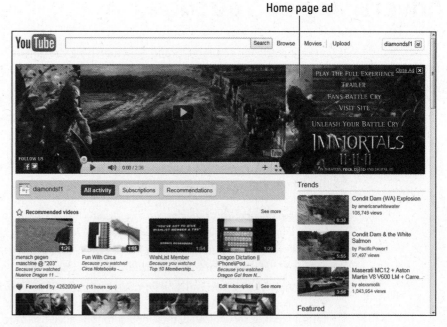

Home page ad

FIGURE 10-5:
A home page ad on YouTube.

IN THIS CHAPTER

» **Exploring ways to enhance your career with LinkedIn**

» **Promoting your company**

» **Harnessing the use of content**

» **Using LinkedIn groups to connect more effectively**

Chapter **11**

Considering LinkedIn

The old adage "It's not what you know, but who you know" is even more true with the growth of the web. People used to be limited in their ability to stay in touch and nurture their small cadre of relationships. With the advent of new web tools, you can connect with people in ways never before possible. An outgrowth of this capability is the ability to identify people who are connected to you by virtue of their proximity to your contacts — or "degrees of separation." You now have the ability to identify and request an introduction to the connections of your connections!

LinkedIn is different from the other major social media platforms like Facebook or Twitter in that it focuses specifically on the world of work. Information about your favorite restaurant or new shopping acquisition is best shared elsewhere. The tone is serious and the social media marketing potential is vast because people join to network. If you sell to a business audience of any kind as a business to business marketer (B2B), LinkedIn can provide you with a great focus group of interested members. According to 99firms, LinkedIn has over 90 million senior level influencers and 63 million decision makers on the platform. And what's more is that these influencers and decision makers are thinking business when they log in and are, therefore, more likely to respond to a B2B marketer's message than elsewhere.

When LinkedIn (www.linkedin.com) launched in May of 2003, many questioned whether it truly fit the mold of a social media network. With the addition of more than 3 billion worldwide users, that question is answered. As of February 2019,

LinkedIn was the fifth-most popular social media site after YouTube, Facebook, Instagram, and Pinterest in the United States. It has 660 million users globally of which 150 million are in the United States alone. That's growth!

Why did LinkedIn grow so robustly? Like all the other popular social networks, it met a need. It provided a way for like-minded business people from around the globe to find each other, share information, and give advice. It legitimized a way for professionals to communicate in an environment that had guidelines and accountability.

The key to success is remembering that LinkedIn is just one channel of your social media strategy. You need to pay attention to how your connections here can drive traffic to other channels. For example, you may want to provide a link to a discount on your website. By integrating selling with everything else you're doing, you won't seem like a crass self-promoter. In this chapter, we look at LinkedIn's varied uses for social marketing of both yourself and your company.

Getting Started

To understand the potential marketing value of LinkedIn, as shown in Figure 11-1, you can view it in two distinct ways: as a marketing vehicle for your own career and as a marketing tool to understand and connect with the audience to which you market.

It's safe to assume that everyone on LinkedIn is sold on the idea of networking. LinkedIn members know the value of a connection that can take you where you need to go. This means that you can connect with people knowing that you don't need to convince them that sharing contacts or advice is valuable.

On the other hand, the fact that they understand this value means that you can't use connections frivolously. At no time should you connect with someone without the understanding that you or your contacts could also be of value to them. It's also important to remember that a lot of salesmen aggressively try to connect on LinkedIn without explaining why they want to connect and how the connection can be mutually beneficial. This has led to some people being more hesitant to accept connections.

LinkedIn gives you the option to start with a free account. This account has lots of great features. If you're just getting started, you may want to join without making any additional financial commitment. You can decide whether you need additional premium features after you get the lay of the land.

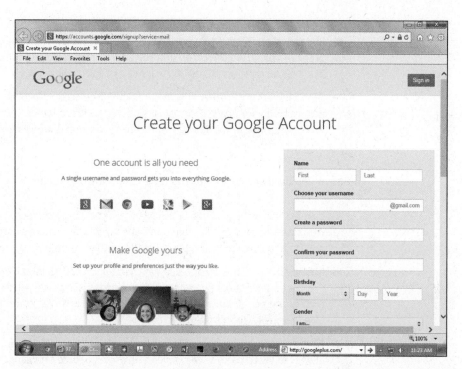

FIGURE 11-1:
The LinkedIn
home page.

If you have used LinkedIn for a while or know that you will be using your account for something specific such as an immediate job search, you may want to consider joining at a premium level. (See the section called "Finding a Job," later in this chapter.)

You have a series of sales-oriented account tools at your disposal as well. The lines between marketing and sales blur here but these tools are most helpful when you're attempting to reach a smaller set of people who are closer to buying your product or service:

>> **Access to more profiles when you search:** A premium account allows you to see more profiles than you would if you had a free account. This access to more profiles increases the likelihood that you will find the right person to connect with.

>> **Search filters:** You can apply a variety of filters to your search so that you can zero in on the right target. For example, you can search for people who work for a certain size company or target only the Fortune 1000. Search filters are especially helpful to find the exact types of people you need to reach.

>> **Expanded profiles:** When you see profiles, you see a more expanded profile of the people in which you are interested. You also see everyone on LinkedIn who fits the criteria, not just those limited to your own network.

>> **Who Viewed My Profile:** This feature of the free account allows you to see who viewed your profile. The list is restricted to a few names and profiles. With a premium account, you can see everyone who is interested in you and how each person found you.

How much do these cost you? You have the following payment options:

>> **Career:** This is the first tier, which lets you direct message recruiters, see who's viewed your profile, gain applicant insights, and stand out as a featured applicant to recruiters. You pay $29.99/month for the service.

>> **Business:** This is the second tier, which lets you send 15 InMail messages to profiles you're not connected to, gain business insights, see who's viewed your profile, and get unlimited people browsing. You pay $47.99/month when billed annually for this plan.

>> **Sales:** This tier offers you 20 InMail messages, specific sales insights, advanced search with a lead builder, unlimited people browsing, and lead recommendations, all for $64.99/month when billed annually.

>> **Hiring**: This final tier gives you 30 InMail messages, Smart suggestions, unlimited people browsing, an integrated hiring management process, and recruiting specific design, all for $99.95/month when billed annually.

TIP

To view the specific benefits for each service tier of LinkedIn Premium, visit the products page at https://www.linkedin.com/premium/products/. And note, that pricing for these LinkedIn products can change periodically so be sure to double check before putting together your marketing and sales plans.

Creating a New Profile

Whether you're planning to use LinkedIn for personal career networking or consumer research, you're talking to a group of people who are focused almost solely on professional activities. Therefore, the most important first step is to look at your overall business strategy to see which social media marketing goals can be met by LinkedIn.

After you know your goals, you need to determine how to present yourself. This presentation is done by setting up a profile. You can set up only one profile on LinkedIn, so it needs to work for you in a variety of ways.

TIP

You also have the option of setting up a company page, but we recommend that unless you're specifically setting up a company page with several employees, wait until you're more familiar with LinkedIn to do it. You want to be familiar with how things are done on LinkedIn before you promote yourself. If you have several employees who will be active online and need to get started right away, by all means do it.

Setting up your profile is deceptively easy. The quality of your LinkedIn profile is highly important. As with any career-related activity, you are judged on a variety of measures, including the description of your previous successes and your willingness to help others achieve their goals.

We recommend that you start with a profile to support the main goals you have and then revise as you go along. For example, if you're looking for a job, your profile contains very different content from that of a business owner doing market research. We cover these differences in the rest of the chapter.

Preparing a content strategy

You've probably heard a good deal about the concept of content strategy. It boils down to evaluating what content you have and what you need to meet a specific marketing goal. Content can be articles, product descriptions, videos, audio interviews, or any material that informs people about you or your business.

To illustrate, one of your LinkedIn goals might be to find new consulting clients. If this is the case, you want to review all the content you have created that shows off your consulting expertise. Then you can start to share it on your profile. You can then use this newly repurposed content in other channels, such as your newsletter or blog.

Begin by doing an inventory of your e-books, posts, proposals, and so on, and determine what content you can use to let colleagues learn about you on LinkedIn. Then make an editorial schedule for yourself so that you can create in a timely manner any new items you need. Usually if you don't schedule a specific time to do it, you won't. For inspiration, look at other people's profiles and see what they have posted.

Covering what matters first

Your profile continues to evolve as you meet new people, join more groups, and attend events. You can't do everything all at one time in the beginning. Consider the following tips when you're starting out:

>> **Keywords matter.**

We put keywords at the top of the list because as you put together your profile, you want to make sure that you include keywords that can be used to find you. You probably have some keywords that you already use for your websites and other channels. Make sure to include some of those, but also think through the goal of this profile and include any new keywords that will move you toward the top of the search results. Be sure to think about keywords from the perspective of other people. What terms would they use to search to find someone like you?

>> **List the professional name by which you wish to be known.**

This is the name you use in your industry. You want colleagues and potential connections to find you. Don't use a nickname unless you use it professionally. It's best if your professional name matches the name of your company in the physical world.

REMEMBER

LinkedIn lets you create only one profile, so if you own a business, decide ahead of time whether you intend to use your own name or your business name. We recommend that you use your own name in case you close your business or want to change direction.

>> **Use a real headline, not just a title.**

This section introduces your brand. If someone were to give you a wonderful introduction, it would include this content. If you're a best-selling author or award-winning salesperson, or have some special designation, this is the place to use it (for example, Jane Smith, Award-Winning Salesperson).

>> **Provide a summary that highlights your uniqueness.**

Here you detail the contents of your headline. Think of this as the follow-up to the headline. Imagine that you're speaking right after the person who introduced you. Explain who you are and what makes you different among a sea of other members. Don't be modest.

>> **Think carefully about how you list your positions — current and past.**

Display what you're doing now and any significant positions you previously held. This is not a detailed résumé. If you are seeking a new job, see the section later in this chapter called "Finding a Job."

>> **Supply a professional photo.**

This is a key item. People don't like to admit it, but they like to be able to picture the person which whom they're connecting. It's not a beauty contest. Get a professional photo with appropriate attire. Save the pose with your favorite pooch for Facebook.

>> **Use links other than just websites.**

Don't be too literal. You can put in any link that you want to send people to. It doesn't have to be your main website. Just make sure that any links you provide are relevant and polish your brand.

REMEMBER

Check your links periodically. The last thing you want is for a recruiter or a potential business partner being taken to dead links off your profile page.

>> **Look at the ways in which you can list your achievements.**

The possible sections available include Education, Certifications, Patents, Languages, Honors and Awards, Organizations, Projects, Publications, and Test Scores. Use any of these that are pertinent. You have wide latitude here to really showcase your talents.

>> **Ask for recommendations.**

LinkedIn provides a recommendations tool that you can use to solicit comments from people who have been impressed by you. This could include a coworker, manager, or client. Obviously, you want to have great recommendations, but don't go crazy at the start. Perfunctory recommendations from your friends aren't all that valuable. If someone has some real value to add, ask for their recommendation when you get started. This section will grow organically because your colleagues want to commend you (and have you commend them) for a job well done.

>> **Start making connections.**

Connections are at the heart of LinkedIn's success. You are here to build your network. Remember that these connections are people who will help you reach your goals, so make them meaningful. Don't be in a race to see how many connections you can get. After you reach 500 connections, LinkedIn lists your connections as *500+*. See more details in "Finding connections," later in this chapter.

TIP

To make it easier for other LinkedIn members to endorse you, make sure to add a list of skills that you want to highlight in the Skills section of your profile. When other members look at the list, they can pick from skills that you want them to endorse instead of inventing them.

>> **Show work samples.**

LinkedIn has added the ability for you to add your work samples to your profile. Content types include video, images, podcasts, and so on. You should definitely take advantage of this feature when you get started. This way you can highlight your best work up front. You can add samples in the Summary, Education, and Experience sections. This function replaces the built-in app section.

Accessing LinkedIn from your mobile devices

Of course, you'll want to stay connected when you're on the go if you're searching for a job using LinkedIn. LinkedIn makes it easy to access your connections from your mobile devices. You'll find free apps for the following:

>> iPhone

>> iPad (iPad 2 and higher)

>> Android

For more detailed information about marketing with mobile, see Chapter 23.

Finding connections

LinkedIn helps you easily get started in finding new connections. One way to start is to click the Connections navigation item in the My Network section. You have several options to choose from. You can find colleagues from your various email programs such as Outlook, classmates from your educational institutions, or people you may know from nonprofits or clubs all by using the Search with filters functionality.

As you're presented with lists of these contacts, go through and choose the ones you want. Be certain to deselect the Share All check box so that you do not send invitations to people who don't belong in your network but are on your email lists.

Choosing to advertise

In contrast to some other social media platforms, advertising on LinkedIn involves little controversy. Perhaps LinkedIn's business orientation keeps the idea of advertising from seeming intrusive. When you're on the site, you can create ads of the following type:

- » **LinkedIn page:** Think of this as a brand page on LinkedIn similar to how you may have a Facebook page. Use it to attract followers and build awareness for your brand and communicate about your business. Most companies with successful brand pages use them to share news about the company, awards, product announcements, and recruit employees. Many also promote special offers through them as well.

- » **Sponsored content:** These are native ads that appear in a user's LinkedIn feed when he/she logs into the website. It comes in different formats namely single image ads, video ads, and carousel ads. You can run these on desktop or mobile. Depending on the content, how much explanation is required, and what you're trying to accomplish (build awareness versus educate, for example), you should use a different format. The benefit of sponsored content comapigns is that you can use sponsored content to personalize and test the ads for specific audiences without having to publish all the versions on your own LinkedIn brand page. Visit the Sponsored Content page (also refered to as native advertising in some places) for more information at `https://business.linkedin.com/marketing-solutions/native-advertising`.

- » **Message ads:** This premium feature allows you to email anyone on LinkedIn regardless of whether that person is in your network, although you're restricted to a certain number of emails. You can communicate with your prospects without having to worry about character limits. You can also add a lead generation form to your message and collect leads on LinkedIn that way. LinkedIn has a high open rate for these messages with 1 in 2 prospects opening a message on average. You can also see which roles at a company are taking action on your message ad with demographic reporting. It also allows you to track conversions from people who viewed and clicked your message with the LinkedIn Conversion tracking. You can build your campaign objective, build your message based on your objective, and measure the results as you normally would with any other campaign. Visit the Message Ads page (also refered to as Sponsored InMail in some places) for more information at `https://business.linkedin.com/marketing-solutions/message-ads`.

- » **LinkedIn text ads:** In addition to message ads and sponsored content, you can also run LinkedIn text ads via a self-service pay-per-click (PPC) or cost-per-impression (CPM) advertising platform. If you advertise on Google or Bing, you are familiar with pay-per-click platforms. These are ideal to drive traffic to your website and to optimize for leads. Be sure to visit the LinkedIn text ads page at `https://business.linkedin.com/marketing-solutions/ppc-advertising` and view the Text Ads resources for ideas on how best to run these campaigns. After you have, you can trigger campaigns in a matter of minutes.

- » **Dynamic ads:** This ad format allows you to engage prospects with ads that are automatically personalized to them based on everything they've published on LinkedIn. They can include their profile data such as their photo, company name, job title, and more. It allows you to have automated campaigns on a huge scale that appears as if they've been personalized for each user individually. Depending on what content you're using for the ads, these can be effective for building brand awareness, driving traffic, and converting prospects.

In a similar fashion to Facebook and Twitter, LinkedIn helps you identify the right ad formats based on your objective. Objectives are categorized as Awareness (Brand Awareness), Consideration (Website Visits, Engagement, Video Views), and Conversions (Lead Generation, Website Conversions, and Job Applicants).

LinkedIn does a good job of helping you segment your ad targets, so knowing who you're targeting is important. In addition to the kind of segmentation you have probably gotten used to expecting on most social media platforms, LinkedIn offers some unique filters that are more professional oriented. Some of these include:

- » **Industry:** There is a large list of worldwide industries to choose from. The LinkedIn report shows that the top five industries represented are Higher Ed at 18.7 percent, Information Technology and Services at 13.9 percent, Financial Services at 11.6 percent, Retail at 10.9 percent, and Computer Software at 8.9 percent.

- » **Seniority:** This segment pertains to job seniority, with 2 million members identifying themselves as holding C-suite jobs. (A *C-suite job* refers to a job with a *C* in the title, such as CEO, CFO, or COO.)

- » **Job titles:** While a little similar to seniority, this filter lets you narrow your audience by specific job titles such as Director, Engineer, Manager, and Sales (to name just a few).

- » **Geography:** The entire world is represented. The United States is the largest group, with more than 27 percent of LinkedIn members residing there.

- » **Job function:** The top five job functions reported are Sales, Management, Business Development, Information Technology, and Marketing.

- » **Gender:** LinkedIn skews — 57 percent male and 43 percent female.

Carefully go over the details of ad spending. The ad itself is not unlike the one you might create for Google. If you decide to try advertising on LinkedIn, look at several ads and see what's possible. As with any other ad platforms, the costs can mount, so you need to set goals and limits.

Participating in Groups

LinkedIn members sometimes overlook the value of joining groups. They focus on one specific activity, such as finding a job, and forget that LinkedIn has the added value of connecting them with second- and third-degree contacts (people who are separated from you by one or two other people). The most powerful use of groups is to find people who you would never have the chance to meet in person. Joining a group they're in makes the introduction easier.

Benefitting from joining groups

You have several choices about how you want to participate in groups. One option is to join several groups right away to get introduced to those with similar interests. If you prefer, you can join one group and see how you like it. You are allowed to join a total of 50 groups. That sounds like a lot, but remember that you may have several goals for joining. Some benefits of joining groups are

>> **Finding members with similar experiences:** You can join a group of those who have worked at the same company you have or are alumni of the same school.

>> **Extending your knowledge of a company in which you are interested:** If you're thinking about working for a particular company, you can find other employees to connect with.

>> **Connecting with members who are interested in the same charitable activities:** Nonprofit and charitable groups are in abundance. You can find like-minded members easily.

>> **Establishing yourself as an expert in your field:** You can choose to take a leadership role in a group or make your feelings known.

>> **Understanding the trends in your industry:** You can stay informed about important issues and developments.

>> **Determining who the industry leaders are:** By virtue of their popularity and activities, you can learn from industry leaders who are active.

>> **Connecting with and participating in discussions:** You can do a lot of consumer research in these groups if you take the time to read and listen.

>> **Finding partners for joint venture activities:** If you're looking for investors, you may want to extend your feelers out in the group without having to give away too much information.

>> **Discovering new clients:** People who are impressed with your breadth of knowledge on a topic can seek you out for consultation.

One great benefit of joining a LinkedIn group is that you can directly connect with members of the group without having to use InMail.

Starting your own group

If you have determined that starting your own group will help you meet your business goals, you'll be happy to know that LinkedIn provides a great framework to do so. The most important thing to consider before starting is whether you have the time and enthusiasm to be the leader. Managing a group takes work. If you start a group and then let it falter, it reflects badly on your professionalism. With more than 640 million people as potential members, you can develop a solid group fairly quickly, but it's your responsibility to keep it lively and active.

Imagine yourself as the host of a party that needs your attention to be a success. This is particularly true for small business owners who wear all the hats in their organization. Picture yourself running this group a year from now and see how that fits into your plans.

Rather than hope that everyone will police their own groups, LinkedIn has set some guidelines that can be accessed from `https://www.linkedin.com/help/linkedin/answer/61178/linkedin-groups-best-practice`. Some of the guidelines include the following:

>> **You can send only one email a week to members of your group.**

You can envision the amount of email that could be generated by a group leader eager to connect (and sell things) to his members. Limiting email communications helps everyone control the information flow.

>> **The group must either be open or closed (by invitation only).**

You can choose to have an invitation-only group or an open one, as shown in Figure 11-2. If you choose a closed group, members must be approved by the group leader and are the only ones who can see and participate in discussions.

If you choose to have an open group, anyone can join. You should be aware that the discussions generated in an open group can be seen by anyone on LinkedIn, not just group members. In addition, the content can be shared on Facebook and Twitter.

Leaders of open groups can decide whether everyone on LinkedIn can participate in discussions or just be able to view them.

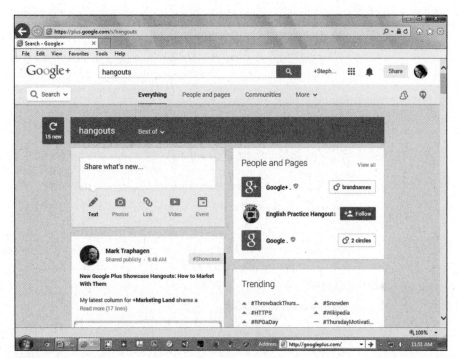

FIGURE 11-2:
Choosing an open or closed group.

>> **The group leader can allow members to invite people to join the group.**

As the group leader, you can allow members to seek out new members for the group by sending them invitations. If they accept an invitation from another member, they're instantly accepted.

Leading a successful group

What constitutes a successful group on LinkedIn? It's one that has value for both you and your members. You may hope to build a personal empire from your LinkedIn group, but the real success comes when your members act like a community. The value of the group comes from the power of the network. As members bring in others from their own network, the power grows. Here are some tactics that will help your group be a success:

>> **Use your weekly email.**

You are allowed to send only one email a week, so make it count. Think of it as the newsletter you might send to your website mailing list. Provide value and help members discover each other.

>> **Hold the line on promotions.**

As the leader, you're responsible for making sure that other members aren't overpromoting and ruining the experience. Nothing is worse than feeling like you're being taken advantage of by other group members. The best way to do this is to set a strong example yourself.

>> **Encourage comments and discussions.**

The shared discussions are part of the valuable content your group builds. If you choose an open group, it can be shared on Facebook and LinkedIn. Monitor the groups and stir up some lively discussions.

>> **Use events.**

As mentioned previously, LinkedIn has a great event tool. Create some virtual events and have members speak. Get everyone talking about new events. If enough people are interested in the idea, you can hold an in-person conference.

>> **Interest the media.**

One of your goals for the group should be to help the media find you. Publicity benefits the entire group. Think about having your members create an e-book or manifesto about your topic and let the media know about it. Some social media press releases could also do the trick.

Using LinkedIn to Answer Questions

To become a stand-out thought leader on LinkedIn, you'll want to share your advice. LinkedIn users post questions that require a level of expertise to answer. If you provide that answer, you can be perceived as an expert. Demonstrating your expertise is a great way to provide value and get noticed.

One of the best ways to provide expertise used to be LinkedIn Answers, but that function has been discontinued. According to LinkedIn, the best way to do that now is to share your expertise from the following locations:

>> Your LinkedIn home page

>> An article you publish on LinkedIn

>> LinkedIn discussion groups

>> Partner sites

>> LinkedIn Pulse

LinkedIn Pulse is a news feed gathered by LinkedIn that can be accessed by going to Interests ⇨ Pulse in the main menu of your profile. Here you will find news based on your interests as determined by your LinkedIn preferences. In addition, you will see a link to Top Posts on the service and a Discover link that displays suggested people you may want to follow.

» Any webpage to your LinkedIn account

» Someone else's update on LinkedIn by liking, commenting, or sharing

Answering questions also has additional value to a social media marketer. For example, you can get the following benefits:

» **Discovering content for blog posts, e-books, and slideshows:** The best way to create content is to answer questions. Not only will you develop material that people are interested in, but you can also see how helpful your answers really are. If they are not understood or require more information, that's great feedback for you. Then you can turn them into posts or other media with the knowledge that they have value.

» **Uncovering trends by mining the questions people are asking:** If you start to notice a new concept cropping up, you may have uncovered a new trend. Keep your eyes open and read widely in your area of interest.

» **Locating potential joint venture partners:** If you are looking for an expert in a particular area, you can ask questions to find other thought leaders who may want to partner with you (or invest).

» **Finding a technical expert:** Locating a technical expert whom you under-stand and trust can be a risky business online. If you find someone who answers your technical questions and can act as a freelancer or consultant, you have saved yourself a lot of time and money.

» **Letting new clients find you:** A great by-product of showing off your skills is that someone with a budget to buy your products or hire you could be listening. Be generous with your expertise and let people get to know you. They'll be more likely to consider working with you.

Finding a Job

For job seekers, checking out LinkedIn is must. The basics are free, and employers are actively looking. If you have diligently read and acted on the preceding sections, you should be ready to hit the ground running for your job search. You have a great profile, lots of important contacts, and an understanding of the various groups dedicated to your industry. So what else should you do to market yourself? Following are some ideas that you can try when you are actively looking for a job:

>> **Look at your profile as an employer would.**

If you have been on LinkedIn for a while and you are starting a job search, you want to evaluate your profile as an employer would. Review it carefully to make sure that the chronological order is accurate and matches your profile. If you seek a design job, make sure that you upload PDFs, images, presentations, and anything else you want to show off. This ability to upload almost any format makes it easy to show off multimedia content you have created.

>> **Create a unique presentation.**

In addition to anything you have done with your résumé to make it look better, think about showcasing a presentation that you've done. Programs such as Prezi can be used to develop something unique. You can also link to SlideShare (`http://www.slideshare.net`), which is now owned by LinkedIn, or post a video. It's worth repurposing your best work and showing it off. You need a way to stand out, and this will help.

>> **Reexamine your keywords.**

You may have chosen general keywords when you first signed up. Now that you know specifically what type of job you are searching for, add keywords that will help you get found by your preferred employers.

>> **Create a list of companies you would like to work for.**

Even if you aren't targeting a specific company, making a list of potential companies will help you. Do some research on what jobs they have open and where you might fit in. It will give you ideas about how to improve your profile. If you do have a target list, look for someone in the company whom you might be able to approach to discuss the company.

>> **Target your recommendations.**

If you've been reticent about asking for recommendations, now is the time to actively seek out people whose endorsement speaks directly to the job you want. LinkedIn makes adding a recommendation easy, so it's not an onerous request.

>> **Mine your network.**

Look at the second- and third-degree contacts in your network and see whether you want to ask for introductions. That's where the power of LinkedIn is really demonstrated. Get started immediately because this could take some time. Not everyone has the same sense of urgency that you do.

>> **Include other channel links.**

Don't forget that there is a whole wide world of other online channels that you are connected to. Make sure to showcase a website or show that you have an active Twitter following.

>> **Consider purchasing Premium Career services.**

LinkedIn provides special subscription premium services for job hunters. If you are considering this, you may want to start with a month-to-month subscription to see whether it works for you. If you find that the job hunt is slow, you can always move to an annual subscription.

Chapter **12**

Delving into Instagram

I f you're already an Instagram user, you might approach this chapter with happy anticipation about what more you can learn about it. On the other hand, if you're not, you may feel some pressure to finally try this social platform that has made such a great splash since its launch in 2010.

By July of 2012, Instagram was purchased by Facebook, and the explosive growth continues. Key to this social platform, like Pinterest and Tumblr, is the incredible ease with which users can share visuals. It also has filters that you can apply to make your images as though a professional took them. The key difference between Instagram and a site like Pinterest is that users and marketers alike are creating new original content and posting it. Pinterest pins are made up mostly by images already online that are shared.

In this chapter, we look at how Instagram is deployed by both personal users and marketers to develop a relationship with their community. So relax and enjoy finding out about the ultimate platform for image sharing online. In this chapter, you see how to edit your photos, develop unique story lines, and discover photos posted by other users.

Recognizing the Basics

First and foremost, Instagram is a mobile application. You get started by downloading the app to your mobile device. There is an app for iOS, Android, and the Windows phone. You can also view your pictures from your computer, but only after you have set up an account. We look at websites that help you manage your account in the section "Using tools to manage your account from your computer."

But before you do download Instagram, you want to determine whether Instagram users match your target demographic. So who uses Instagram? While you can find the official statistics on the Instagram Press page (https://instagram-press.com/our-story/), it's worth noting the following:

>> Instagram has 1 billion monthly active users.

>> The average user spends 53 minutes a day on the site.

>> Thirty-seven percent of U.S adults use Instagram.

>> Seventy-one percent of U.S businesses are on Instagram.

In its report called "Social Media 2013 Update," Pew Research says that

>> Sixty-three percent of Instagram users visit the site at least once a day.

>> Fifty-two percent of Instagram users are females and 42% are male.

>> Seventy-two percent of teens use Instagram.

Does this sound like your audience? If so, you need to get on Instagram right along with the 71 percent of U.S businesses who consider this user group valuable because of their high interaction with brands.

According to a study by L2-Intelligence (http://L2ThinkTank.com), 93 percent of prestige brands such as Chanel, Estée Lauder, and Cartier can be found on Instagram. If you are wondering why, just look at an image from one of these brands. For example, Cartier gold jewelry, shown in Figure 12-1, requires no explanation. The images say it all.

Signing up

To sign up, first download the app from your device store — iTunes (https://itunes.apple.com/us/app/instagram/id389801252?mt=8), Google Play (https://play.google.com/store/apps/details?id=com.instagram.android), or the

Windows Phone store (http://www.windowsphone.com/en-us/store/app/instagram-beta/3222a126-7f20-4273-ab4a-161120b21aea). After you launch the app, you can register with either your email or Facebook account, add some profile information, and you're in!

TIP

You can make your account public or private. We assume that because this is a business account, it will be public. All our descriptions will use a public account as our model.

FIGURE 12-1:
Cartier on Instagram.

Sharing photos or videos for the first time

When you open Instagram on your mobile device, you see, aside from your feed, icons at the bottom of the screen, as shown in Figure 12-2.

Following are the icons from left to right:

>> **Home:** This is where you see your stream of the latest photos by the people you follow.

>> **Explore:** Here you can search for topics of interest and see a stream of photos that may be of interest to you.

>> **Camera:** When you click the camera icon, your camera comes up ready to take a photo.

>> **Following:** This is where you see your followers' activity.

>> **Your photos:** Photos you have taken and uploaded to Instagram.

FIGURE 12-2:
Icons at the
bottom of the
mobile device's
screen.

Home   Camera   Your Instagram feed

Explore   Following

REMEMBER

Don't forget to put a location tag on your image so that viewers who search for that location will find you. For local brick-and-mortar merchants, this is critical.

You also want to make sure to use video on Instagram when appropriate — you have up to 60 seconds to record. It's as easy as taking your photo. Here's how:

1. Choose the camera icon (refer to Figure 12-2) and tap again to change it to video.

2. **Hold down the red button to start recording and tap it again when you want to stop recording.**

3. **Pick your filter if you want, add a caption and a tag, and send the video on its way.**

REMEMBER

You can like and comment on others' videos (you can't add a tag), just as you can with photos, so remember to do that to get in on the conversation.

Using filters

When you first post images, you may feel that you must use one of the filters that Instagram provides. That's entirely up to you. Actually, 50 percent of users use the normal (no) filter on their photos. So snap some shots just to experience the process.

Currently the filters are as follows:

>> Normal

>> Clarendon

>> Gingham

>> Moon

>> Lark

>> Reyes

>> Juno

>> Slumber

>> Crema

>> Ludwig

>> Aden

>> Perpetua

>> Amaro

>> Mayfair

>> Rise

>> Hudson

>> Valencia

>> X-Pro II

>> Sierra

>> Willow

>> Lo-Fi

>> Inkwell

>> Hefe

>> Nashville

When you select one of these filters, the image is given a specific effect; for example, Inkwell renders your photo in black and white.

The top five filters used on Instagram as of this writing are Normal, EarlyBird, X-Pro II, Valencia, and Rise.

TIP

In its quest to enhance and upgrade its editing tools, Instagram provided several in June of 2014. For example:

>> **Filters:** The filters now have a slider switch that allows you to see how much of the effect you want to apply.

>> **Vignette:** In addition to the Tilt-Shift tool, you can now use the Vignette tool to create a black border around the photo, thus making it easier to see the way the photo is positioned.

>> **Cropping and Straightening:** These tools have been combined to make it easier for you to fix a photo that is out of square and then crop it.

Getting Found on Instagram

Who doesn't love a good hashtag? It helps you get found. But we can all agree that hashtags can sometimes get out of hand. Every social media platform has its own etiquette when it comes to these tags. Some feel that less is more when it comes to the number of hashtags. However, Instagram culture embraces hashtags, so you can use them to your heart's content. Just remember that as a business you don't want to seem frivolous, so choose your hashtags wisely.

One of the key things you use hashtags for are marketing campaigns. They help you track how well you are doing and enable you to find your engaged users.

TIP

Because of their importance, it is wise for you to look at what hashtags are currently being used and what new ones you should create. One way to find out this information is to look at search tools for hashtags. Some of these hashtag tools include:

>> **Talkwalker** (`http://talkwalker.com`): Free/Fee versions. This tool has lots of value. You can see the performance of a hashtag and much more; for example, you can see the influencers who use it and whether the sentiment about it is positive or negative.

>> **Rite Tag** (`http://ritetag.com`): Free. One of the great features of this tool is that it will go over the hashtags you have used in Twitter and tell you whether they are overused or unlikely to be seen. Obviously, you won't use this tool for a new Instagram campaign.

>> **Tagboard** (`https://tagboard.com`): Free/Fee versions. What's so useful about this tool is that you can build tagboards that display specific hashtags, making it easy to see what's happening.

Check these out to see how helpful it can be to analyze and evaluate your hashtags.

Structuring Instagram for Business Goals

As you can see, Instagram is a sleeping giant that has enormous potential for almost every business. (One obvious clue to its value is that it was purchased by Facebook.) Many small and medium-sized marketers have yet to take advantage of it. One reason is that they are already overwhelmed by the number of social media platforms that they feel required to use.

Don't be one of these marketers. Look carefully at which platforms you choose to devote your time and budget to. If a platform is large but not right for your user base, don't get pulled into using it because everyone else is.

TIP

The Instagram blog, shown in Figure 12-3, is really helpful and provides both tips and case studies to help you optimize your use of the service. You can find it at `https://business.instagram.com/blog`.

Creating content for your business

As with any social platform you choose, you want to develop relationships with a community of like-minded people who can become your customers. On Instagram, your tool is images and the stories they tell.

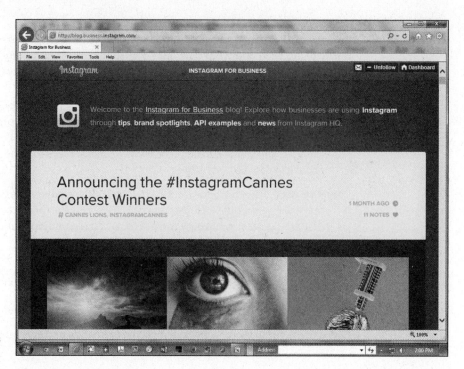

FIGURE 12-3:
Instagram blog.

To help your team focus on uploading the right images for the company, it's helpful to create a list of category stories to which your staff can refer. You want your staff to easily generate new photos and videos and not miss the great moments to capture.

For example, some story categories could be the following:

>> **Working in the community:** Pictures of charity events and training sessions with users

>> **Community members' photos:** Encourage users to send in photos depicting their use of the product

>> **Our pets at work:** Adorable pet photos that humanize your staff and make connections with other pet lovers who can upload their photos

>> **Contests:** Photos of contest entries by users and winner photos

>> **Featured staff members:** Video of staff members giving a video greeting (fifteen seconds long at most)

>> **Request for product improvements:** Photos of current products with questions from the company about how to improve them. Customers are asked to reply to these questions and offer some ideas of their own

>> **Inspiring photos just because:** A beautiful image from nature or daily life to make others feel good. While this story category might be the one least tied to your business, it will probably be the most popular.

Engaging users by using consistent story themes is the best approach. When users see a new image, they can relate it to all the other images that have made up that storyline for your brand. This creates a series feeling that keeps visitors coming back for more. Think of it like a TV show with particular stories that are continually updated.

Here are two other items that your team should pay attention to:

>> **Hashtags:** As discussed earlier, hashtags are how people find your content. Make sure to use ones that are already in use that relate to your brand. Using them is a habit people already have. In addition, create specific hashtags for your brand.

>> **Captions:** Any photo should have a caption. We are trained to look for them and read them. Therefore, captions are an important part of the marketing process on Instagram. Don't assume that they are optional. Users have been shown to favor long ones, so give careful thought to what you write.

Curating and sharing

Key to everything you do on Instagram is the idea that sharing will create buzz and new followers. If you are creating and displaying only your own pictures and not finding and sharing other people's content, you are talking to yourself. As we said, you are presenting stories. But you also need to spread other people's stories to demonstrate that you are interested in more than just your own company's activities.

Some brands known for their success on Instagram include Ben and Jerry's, Disney, GE, and Warby Parker. So what, for example, is Warby Parker (`http://instagram.com/warbyparker`) doing right?

Warby Parker is an eyeglass manufacturer and seller of high-end glasses that start at the $95 price point. In addition, whenever a customer buys a pair of glasses, Warby Parker donates money and glasses to train a person in a designated overseas community to sell them very affordably. So right away, the company has two story lines on which to focus their images:

>> Well-designed eyeglasses that are reasonably priced (see Figure 12-4).

>> A program called Buy a Pair, Give a Pair, shown in Figure 12-5, that trains others to give eye exams so that those in need can get eyeglasses.

FIGURE 12-4:
Warby Parker on
Instagram.

FIGURE 12-5:
Warby Parker's
Buy a Pair, Give a
Pair program
shows how
children are
receiving help.

As you go through the photos on the site, you see examples of the types of stories we suggest. Included are interesting street-life photos, product images, company events, people being served, users wearing the product, and others. Think about what images you might collect that tell your story in photos and demonstrate that you are thinking about the community at large.

TIP

Share your own images and others by linking your account to Facebook, Twitter, Flickr, and Tumblr directly from Instagram. It will help your message spread.

Using tools to manage your account from your computer

Because Instagram is a mobile platform, seeing your account on a larger computer screen is sometimes useful. For this purpose, several tools have been developed that allow you (and everyone else) to get the big-picture view on Instagram. These tools include:

» **Iconosquare** (`http://Iconosquare.com`)**:** Free; formerly Statigr.am. Iconosquare is used by 40 percent of the Fortune 1000 and has very robust features and a nice display of your own account. You can see your statistics and help promote your images to others.

» **Combin** (`https://www.combin.com`)**:** This is an Instagram growth tool that's aimed at organic audience attraction. With its powerful search, you can find accounts and posts from your target audience by hashtag, location, hashtag+location among followers and commenters of your competitors.

» **Boomerang from Instagram:** This app, which is available in the Apple and Android App stores, lets you create gifs of your photographs or videos that go forward and back in time. These videos don't have audio but allow you to capture perfect behind-the-scenes type moments in a very Instagram friendly fashion.

» **Foursixty** (`https://foursixty.com`)**:** With Foursixty you can sell your products on Instagram by linking them to your product pages. Your customers can add items to their shopping carts directly, instead of having to browse your website.

Chapter **13**

Discovering Snapchat

Snapchat (www.snapchat.com) is a multimedia messaging app that was originally created by Evan Spiegel, Bobby Murphy, and Reggie Brown as students at Stanford University. Launched first in July 2011, what makes Snapchat so special is that pictures and messages published on the social media platform are ephemeral, lasting only a very short period of time. Unlike Facebook or some of the other social media platforms, Snapchat is built from the ground up to be mobile driven and for snapping and sharing photographs. In fact, unlike other social networks it doesn't have an accompanyning website. It's built to be mobile driven and with a portrait orientation just the way you use your phone.

Snapchat is one of the newer social media platforms. It's also one of the fastest growing with over 210 million daily active users who use the app over 20 times a day and spend an average of 30 minutes on the app creating 30 billion snaps daily. With its new Discover platform for premium content, Snapchat has launched 100 Discover channels and reaches a monthly audience of over 10 million viewers. And with over a $1 billion in annual revenue through advertising, Snapchat is already a popular advertising medium for marketers.

TIP

Over the years, Snapchat has been most successful in engaging a younger audience than Facebook, Instagram, Pinterest, or Twitter. In fact, that's the most important fact to know about it — if you're a business that's trying to engage people younger than 25, then Snapchat should probably be your starting point for your social media marketing plans.

Exploring Snapchat

Similar to many other social media platforms, Snapchat lets you communicate with friends via a mobile app and use different features. Snapchat allows you to connect and follow friends, share messages, upload photographs, and shoot videos. The application also offers news, games, quizzes, and other forms of entertainment. With photography and video editing tools, the application also lets you enhance what you create before sharing it. See Figure 13-1 to see what the Snapchat interface looks like.

FIGURE 13-1:
The Snapchat
interface.

Looking at Snapchat's unique features

Snapchat is designed at its core to be a more casual, lighthearted, and idiosyncratic social media platform with features and functionality that at times appear intentionally difficult for older users to understand and appreciate. From the scores of whimsical photo filters and effects to the disappearing messages features, Snapchat can appear designed to be the polar opposite of a LinkedIn or even a Facebook.

Features that may benefit you as a marketer are:

- **Snap Map:** Friends can see each other's location on a map.

- **Snapstreaks:** Kids can exchange messages for as long as they can.

- **Snapscore:** Users are assigned Snapscores that are visible to their friends. The more they use the Snapchat features (such as Snapstreaks) the higher the scores.

- **Stories:** These are collections of posts or videos over a 24-hour period that represent a specific interest, moment, or activity by a user. A user posts it to their stories section in their account, and it is made available to that user's friends. You can tap anybody's name to view their stories in the order that they have been posted. And you can view them any number of times within a 24-hour period after which they're automatically deleted. To view the stories, you open the app and swipe left from the Camera tab.

- **Lenses:** Lenses have also made Snapchat incredibly popular over the years. Face lenses allow you to add cartoon cat ears or whiskers to your face (among many other whimsical elements). Similarly, world lenses let you overlay augmented reality elements such as rainbows that appear as if they're a part of the photograph you've uploaded.

- **Geofilters:** Another whimsical feature — they're location specific elements only available by visiting a specific location.

- **Snapcash:** Lets users pay for things.

REMEMBER

What makes Snapchat so truly unique is that everything you do on the platform feels very casual. For example, as you post stories, you can also respond to someone's story with a photograph. Plan to be more informal in your marketing on this platform.

Getting to know the Snapchat user

So who exactly is the typical Snapchat user? As with any other social media platform, you want to understand the demographics and psychographics of this user base before you begin marketing to them. A good source for understanding Snapchat users is the Omnicore fall 2019 analysis (https://www.omnicoreagency.com/snapchat-statistics/):

- Snapchat has 310 million monthly active users.

- 24 percent of U.S. social media users use Snapchat.

- 3 billion snaps are created everyday.

- » 90 percent of users are 13–24 years of age.

- » 73 percent of users are 18–24 years of age.

- » There are 14 billion Snapchat daily video views.

The stat that stands out the most is how young Snapchat users are. Snapchat allows 13-year-olds or older to use the platform, and as those users get older, they start migrating to other platforms such as Facebook, Twitter, and Instagram. That single fact differentiates Snapchat from other platforms.

Advertising on Snapchat

Advertising on Snapchat is in some ways very similar to and in others very different from the other social media platforms. You can choose a demographic that you want to target, create the advertising you want to share, and then assign a budget for the advertising. Similar to the other social media platforms, Snapchat allows you to run an advertising campaign on your own in a self-service fashion. (You're typically required to spend at least $3,000 a month on a campaign.)

However, with Snapchat being much smaller and much younger than the other social media platforms, you're limited in how you can target your customers and what advertising formats you can use. In addition, Snapchat has its own visual language and its own features with corresponding advertising opportunities.

You can't create ads once and assume you can use the same creative across Facebook, Twitter, Instagram, and Snapchat. In fact, it's quite the opposite. For example, what you create for Facebook and Instagram most certainly won't work on Snapchat. This is critical to consider as you choose which social media platform to focus on. You may quickly discover that you don't have the resources or the budget to spread yourself across many social media platforms. You'll need to choose where to focus quickly unless, of course, you're a very large brand with the ability to support active social media accounts on many platforms.

Choosing an objective and format

When you use the self-service functionality on Snapchat (https://forbusiness. snapchat.com/), you must first choose between different business objectives. The objectives you can choose from include:

>> **Awareness**: Branding

>> **Consideration**: App Installs, App Traffic, Website Traffic, Engagement, Video Views, Lead Generation

>> **Conversions:** App Conversions, Website conversions, and Catalog Sales

Then you need to choose the advertising format that you'd like to run:

>> **Snap ads:** These are the most common and basic advertising format and they function similar to display advertising. They appear as an ad between your stories and can drive users to your website, app, video, AR lens, or app store page.

>> These ads are ideal for brand building but can also be used at the consideration or conversion phase.

>> **Collection ads:** These are perfect for showcasing a series of products that you want people to purchase immediately. As Snapchat says, these are tappable, frictionless ways to shop and buy. These ads also appear integrated into stories in a more traditional fashion but allow a user to choose from different products within the ad itself and go deeper into that product. You need to include links, calls to actions, and swipe up URLs for them to work well.

>> These ads are useful if you're trying to drive conversions and want to showcase many products from your product catalog.

>> **Story ads:** These function similar to Stories in that they draw the user into a series of Snaps. The Snaps together form a story that should engage the user the way any other content would. The story ad appears as a sponsored Discover tile that lives alongside popular content tailored to their preferences. Each Story Ad can have anywhere between 3 and 20 placements and requires a headline, a brand name, attachments (if you're optimizing for swiping up), and the individual files for each ad in the story.

>> Think of Story ads as a branded content experience.

>> **Augmented Reality (AR) lenses:** These lenses are probably the most fun ad units on Snapchat. These ad units allow you to create and promote AR lenses that get superimposed on top of a user's face as he or she looks into their phone camera. Whether you're advertising a movie such as Westworld and want to superimpose a character's image onto a user, or you want to give users a pair of cool sunglasses, the AR lens allows you to do this. The AR lenses include two types — face lenses or world lenses. Regardless of the one you choose to use for your marketing campaign, you must include your brand logo in the ad and preferably in the top right-or the top left-hand corner.

>> **Filters:** Along with AR lenses, these are another really popular ad unit on Snapchat. These allow you to promote custom creative overlays that users can add to photo and video messages. In a similar fashion to AR lenses, these

allow brands to participate in native Snapchat conversations in more fun ways. As you design your own filter, consider ways to make it fun and ask yourself when and why would they be used. The filter shouldn't take more than 25 perecent of the screen; it's best kept simple and light.

>> **Commercials:** These are six-second, non- skippable, video-based ads within their high premium content units.

TIP

>> Commercials are the most traditional kind of marketing but have their place for building awareness and consideration for your brand or product.

Reaching your customers on Snapchat

It's one thing to have fancy ad units, but it's another if you have the ways to target them most effectively. After all, that's the power of all forms of digital marketing — you can reach exactly the people that you want to when you advertise online. Snapchat makes it easy by allowing you to target customers based on their interests (what they say they like) and their behaviors both on Snapchat and beyond the platform. You can also focus your advertising efforts by demographics including age, gender, household income, parental status, and the like. Targeting by country and within a category such as universities or by radius in an area is also possible. In other words, the way you're able to target on the other social media platforms when you advertise, you can do so on Snapchat as well.

The other side to reaching your customers is using the more advanced targeting tools provided by Snapchat. These include Custom Audiences that allow you to retarget Snapchat users who have already seen your ads or engaged with your business elsewhere and Lookalikes that allows you to find Snapchat users who are similar in demographics and psychographics to your current customers. You create a lookalike audience by uploading a file from your own CRM database or by sharing anonymous data about your website visitors.

Measuring Results on Snapchat

You should never advertise on any social media marketing platform unless you can measure the effectiveness of it. Fortunately, Snapchat makes it easy to measure the results of the various campaigns that you may run on the platform. On Snapchat, you can track the following metrics in your Ad manager dashboard.

>> **Campaign Performance:** This tells you how your campaign performed and includes your total spends by campaign, the paid impressions, the swipe ups, and the effective cost per swipe up.

- **Web Conversions:** This lets you track conversions across devices, develop retargeting audiences, and optimize bids for conversions using the Snap pixel.

- **App Conversions:** Similarly, this lets you use attribution and analytics tools to see how your Snapchat ads drove app installs and downstream actions within your mobile app.

Keep in mind that as you measure the effectiveness of your social media marketing campaigns on Snapchat, you can segment the results by campaign, custom audiences, and demographics.

TIP

As with most other social media marketing platforms, advertising on Snapchat can be confusing if you don't know the terms used. Here is a glossary of the most important terms to be familiar with:

- **Average screen time:** The number of seconds spent watching your ad across all impressions

- **Completions:** The number of snaps watched to 97 percent duration

- **Discover page:** A page available to all users that is full of content from premium publishers

- **eCPSU:** The average cost per each swipe up.

- **eCPV:** The average cost per qualified video view

- **Geofilters:** A filter applied to a user's photo or video when in a designated location

- **Snaps:** Photos and videos created by Snapchat users

- **Snapchatters:** The users of Snapchat

- **Sponsored lenses:** Ads that use facial recognition to activate hidden features of the lenses

- **Swipes:** The number of times Snapchatters view a filter when swiping left or right in an app

- **Swipe up rate:** The average number of swipes per impression, shown as a percentage

- **Top snap:** Your most popular snap

- **Use rate:** The rate at which a geofilter is used when made available in the filter carousel

- **Web view:** An attachment of snap ads that take viewers to a preloaded website after swiping up

Chapter **14**

Marketing with Pinterest

I magine that someone came to the virtual lobby of your business (or your real lobby) and offered to create a fabulous wall of your brand images and products. It would be colorful and contain clear labeling. The most exciting thing about this wall is that if you point at one of the images, you're taken to a screen that tells you more about the product and helps you buy it. That's an offer you wouldn't turn down. Well, that's what Pinterest offers your business — and it's free!

In March of 2010, Pinterest launched its beta. It was met with polite applause from friends and colleagues of the startup. But not many people were sure how to use it. A scant year later it was listed in Time Magazine's 50 Best Websites of 2011. As of 2019, according to Omnicore Agency (`https://www.omnicoreagency.com/pinterest-statistics/`), Pinterest had 300 million unique visits in the month of March. The site had 4 billion + boards with 200 billion + pins.

What caused this explosion of interest? The answer is visuals! It provided a fool-proof way for people to share pictures of things they liked and perhaps wanted to buy. It was just a quick hop from pinning pictures to a digital board to buying them online. In April of 2019, Pinterest had an Initial Public Offering (IPO) that was very successful and as of this writing, its stock continues to climb.

To optimize your use of Pinterest as a business tool, you need to understand how members use it. If you are already a user, you're ahead of the game. If you have never used it, help yourself by exploring it first as a user would.

In this chapter, you look at how to get started with Pinterest, find interesting pins, collaborate with colleagues, distribute marketing materials, and sell products. You'll also have some fun along the way!

Recognizing Pinterest Users

As you know, visuals instantly attract your eye. Your brain understands them more quickly than the written word and is more likely to respond to them. Posts with images have a greater response on all the social networks.

To understand the attraction of Pinterest, you need look no further than the home page. It contains hundreds of images of things you personally like and respond to. How does it do this? Take a look at getting started with Pinterest and you'll see how social media marketing with Pinterest attracts new customers.

As a baseline, it's important to note that Pinterest users (`https://www.fool.com/investing/2019/03/25/pinterest-ipo-4-key-points-from-the-companys-finan.aspx`) are approximately 66 percent female (majority of users between the ages of 18 and 64). If women aren't your target audience, however, don't turn away just yet. You have several important reasons to consider Pinterest as a social media marketing tool:

TIP

>> **Large number of users:** As we said, Pinterest continues to grow every day. You have an active group of women (50 percent have children) who are happy to re-pin and recommend items as well as buy for family members.

Men are starting to catch up and use Pinterest for organizing information like travel info and hobbies. Fifty percent of new signups are men (`https://blog.hootsuite.com/pinterest-statistics-for-business/`).

>> **Good distribution tool:** Sharing is the order of the day. You never know who will share something on your website and have it be found.

>> **Easy sales tools:** Selling from the gift section is very easy; you just have to put a link to your store to sell on your website.

>> **Excellent showcase:** Because of the way the system is constructed, almost every pin looks good. Why not take advantage of that?

>> **A lot of time spent pinning:** Users typically spend more than 34 minutes looking around (`https://adespresso.com/blog/pinterest-marketing-statistics/`). That's a long time to hold consumer eyeballs.

In this chapter, we focus on Pinterest for business. If you want to familiarize yourself before signing up as a business, you can sign up with a personal account. It's easy to convert to a business account by clicking a button.

Exploring the interests of users

To see topics of interest to you, Pinterest suggests that you choose three boards to start. Users have lots of ways to find interesting pins. One easy way is to just type keywords into the search box and see what comes up. When you start typing, a window pops up, displaying related categories and pins.

To see all the Pinterest categories available you can go to `https://www.pinterest.com/categories/`, as shown in Figure 14-1.

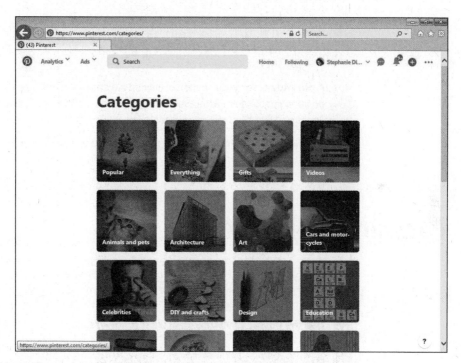

FIGURE 14-1:
Categories on
Pinterest.

To see what's trending on Pinterest make sure to scroll down in your search results list to see trending ideas. This shows you what people are currently pinning and may give you some ideas. You can also go to `https://www.pinterest.com/pinpicks/pinterest-100-for-2019/` to see what Pinterest labels as the top pins of 2019. They create this board on an annual basis.

Pinning as a social activity

Pinterest makes finding and sharing pins a truly social activity. Previously it would have been a marketer's dream to have potential customers trading pictures of her products and commenting on them. Now, customers can go right to the source of the pin and buy the product. According to AdEspresso (https://adespresso.com/blog/pinterest-marketing-statistics/) 80 percent of pins are re-pins.

Re-pinning, liking, and commenting create targeted groups with common interests. No more searching for marketing leads. They come to you and they also recommend your product to friends.

Make it easy for users to pin from wherever they are. Here are several to consider:

>> **A save pin widget**: This widget allows users to save pins directly from their browsers (https://help.pinterest.com/en/article/save-pins-with-the-pinterest-browser-button).

>> **A pin widget for your website:** Having a website pin lets users pin anything on your site to their Pinterest account (https://business.pinterest.com/en/save-button-for-websites).

>> **A build a widget:** For other widgets you can go to https://developers.pinterest.com/tools/widget-builder/ and build a widget of your choice.

Focusing on Strategy

Now that you've seen Pinterest through the eyes of a user, this section tells you about four key ways to use Pinterest to achieve your business goals:

>> **Use the power of visuals to attract followers.**

First and foremost, you need to think of Pinterest as a gigantic billboard for your company that can be seen by millions. Users can find images in all sorts of ways because they are pinned and re-pinned. You never know how many people you can reach until you start pinning and getting feedback. You can see what's popular and determine how to create more content of that type.

>> **Develop cross promotion.**

Cross promotion to and from Pinterest will power up your other marketing efforts and is key to optimizing your use of Pinterest. Every one of your social media channels should provide the capability for users to pin items to Pinterest and then send them to other channels. For example, a user can pin from your website to Pinterest, and on Pinterest you can provide a link to your blog. Or, say that you're planning a new marketing campaign that includes all sorts of exciting graphics and new pages. Make sure that all those items get pinned to a board that supports the campaign with the same discounts and promotions. With this strategy, you leverage what you've already created.

>> **Pay attention to mobile.**

According to Pinterest, approximately 85% of searches are done on mobile devices. Make sure that everything you promote can be viewed via mobile. The app makes it incredibly easy to find ideas for anything you need while you're on the go.

>> **Leverage your existing business strategy.**

Although leveraging your current business strategy might seem obvious, it's often overlooked. Because Pinterest is so different from other social networks, businesses hold it apart from their other business strategies. Actually, it's the perfect complement to any marketing plan. The key is to determine how it serves your current interests. As you develop a strategy for using Pinterest, remember to create hashtags that support your goals. Users can also use the hashtags they want, but don't leave it to chance if you have some strategic goals. For example, if you're planning a major conference and have developed hashtags, be sure to use them on your pins.

Becoming a Business Pinner

To get started with Pinterest for Business, go to `http://business.pinterest.com/en`, click the Sign-Up button in the upper-right corner, and enter your email address or your Facebook login. Getting started is easy — and free! After you're signed up and have chosen your name, you can start creating boards of topics that interest you, as shown in Figure 14-2, and pin items to them.

FIGURE 14-2: Creating a board on Pinterest.

TIP

Don't forget that if you want to pin to any of your boards from your mobile device, you need to download the iPhone app in the iTunes store `https://itunes.apple.com/us/app/pinterest/id429047995?mt=8` or the Android app from Google Play `https://play.google.com/store/apps/details?id=com.pinterest&hl=en_US`.

Setting up your profile

In this section, you can explore how you might set yourself up as a business user. As a business user, you want to make your brand clear and understandable. If you have a business, there is no real reason not to set your profile as a business user.

This section looks at how two lifestyle companies list themselves on Pinterest. One uses a person as a brand, Martha Stewart, Inc.; the other, L.L.Bean, uses the company brand. Both do a great job of conveying what their brand has to offer, but they do it in different ways. By looking at each type, you can see what might work for you.

REMEMBER

You don't have to be a giant conglomerate to succeed. Millions of people are enjoying and buying from small and midsized businesses, too.

When you sign up as a business, in the profile section for Pinterest boards are Name, Picture, Username, About You, Location, and Website. Here's what Martha Stewart and L.L. Bean do to communicate with customers.

Example profile: Martha Stewart Living

Martha Stewart (MS), who is known for her beautiful presentations of food, crafts, and home design, uses Pinterest to full visual advantage. Her main page, at `http://pinterest.com/marthastewart` is shown in Figure 14-3.

>> **Picture:** The name you chose previously would dictate the picture. If your name and face are part of the brand, you use your own picture. If you're not, you use your logo. Even though some companies have a logo, they use their CEO's picture because that person has "celebrity" status. For Martha Stewart, you see her picture, for L.L. Bean you do not.

>> **Name:** Obviously, Martha Stewart uses her name on her profile rather than Martha Stewart Inc. She names her boards in a way that helps her bridge the gap between personal and business. Give some careful thought to the name you want to use to identify your company. If you are a "solopreneur" or small business owner, you can use your name and, in the description, list the name of your business. It depends on how closely you're identified with your brand.

>> **Location:** The headquarters of your company. For MS, it's New York.

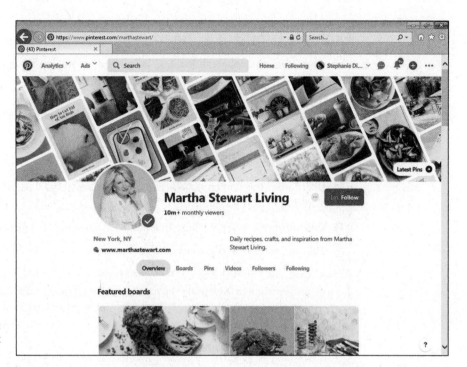

FIGURE 14-3:
Martha Stewart
on Pinterest.

>> **Username:** This is the URL by which your site will be identified. For example, on Pinterest MS has `https://www.pinterest.com/marthastewart/`.

>> **Description:** This descriptive content shows up to the right on your username.

Below the description you see several links in a row. For Martha Stewart, the links take you to instructional information that has value for the reader. The site has no hard sell and the text comes across in an authentic manner. The company focus is to be the authority on how to create a beautiful life. She mixes crafts with recipes, gardening, and everything in between.

- *Overview:* You see the boards featured by MS.

- *Boards:* You see boards by category.

- *Pins:* Here you see all the pins across MS's categories.

- *Videos:* These are the videos uploaded to the site.

- *Followers:* This is a list of people who follow MS on Pinterest.

- *Following:* This is a list of people MS follows.

>> **Website:** MS links to her website. (You must have your site verified by Pinterest.) You can also link to Twitter and Facebook. Also notice that she has additional pinners (staff people who post pins), MS Living, and Plaid Craft.

Example profile: L.L. Bean

The main site on Pinterest for L.L. Bean shown in Figure 14-4, displays the following:

>> **Name:** The company name, L.L.Bean. It also shows monthly views.

>> **Picture:** The company logo, which is well-known to users.

>> **Location:** Freeport, Maine.

>> **Username:** This is `http://www.pinterest.com/llbean/`. Here you also find a link to the L.L. Bean website.

>> **Description:** You see the description and L.L. Bean hashtag #BeanOutsider.

The links across the page are:

- *Overview:* This is the official Pinterest site for L.L. Bean. This area also invites users to "Celebrate the joy of spending time outdoors. Discover something fun with [them]." The boards focus totally on the outdoor user experience with L.L. Bean products.

- *Boards:* You see the boards by category.

- *Pins:* Here you are shown all the pins across L.L.Bean's categories.

- *Activity:* Pins people saved from `www.llbean.com`.

- *Followers:* This is a list of people who follow L.L.Bean.

- *Following:* This is a list of people that L.L. Bean follows.

One interesting comparison is between LLB's Weddings board and MS's Weddings board. The brands clearly delineate themselves visually. LLB focuses on the outerwear and outdoor activities that wedding goers are experiencing. MS focuses on elegant fashion, flowers, and food. Think carefully about the visual statements you want to make, and never stray from that focus.

Starting a group board

A group board is a board that several people can share. The owner of the account simply has to invite people to add pins to the board by clicking the pen icon (Edit) at the bottom of the board showing collaborators and typing a user email as shown in Figure 14-5. Once a user accepts, she can pin anything she wants.

This system works really well if you have several people on your team who need to supply marketing pins. It also allows you to add colleagues and vendors from outside your team. It's an efficient way to collaborate with everyone who needs to have access to the boards.

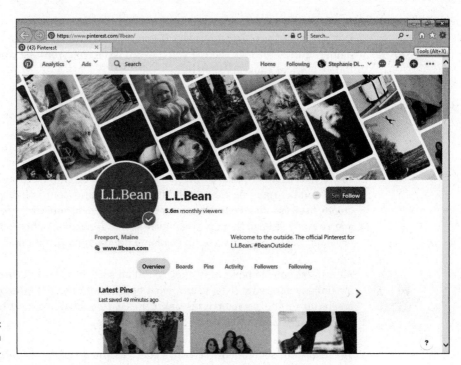

FIGURE 14-4:
L.L.Bean on
Pinterest.

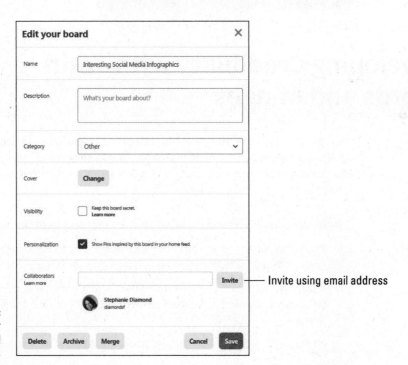

Invite using email address

FIGURE 14-5:
Editing your
board to add
pinners.

Don't be reluctant to add pinners if you need to. Anyone on the team can delete pinners and even block them if you have an issue. You won't be stuck with pinners if they leave or cause a problem.

Creating secret boards

Does the title grab your interest? Secret boards sound so mysterious. They are really a great tool for personal or business use. Secret boards are just what they sound like. They are boards that only you and your chosen friends can see; they aren't public. Imagine the possibilities for you and your collaborators! You can create projects and keep them under wraps. Then you can unveil them when you're ready or keep them permanently secret. How about a board for new product development or perhaps one for personal dream trips you'll take?

After users got the hang of it, they found all sorts of ways to utilize secret boards for holiday shopping lists, secret wish boards, and more. Pinterest now lets you create up to 500 secret boards any time. We doubt that you'll have that many secrets, but it's worth a try!

To create your secret board, create a board as you do normally and check the Keep This Board Secret box.

Developing Credibility with Your Boards and Images

This section explores the types of images that you should consider for your business. Obviously, you want to choose images that are colorful and convey the essence of your brand. Pinterest has several kinds of pins that you can create, as follows:

>> **Image pins:** JPGs or videos, which make up the majority of pins you see.

>> **Promoted pins:** Pins you pay for. We provide more details in the section "Experimenting with promoted pins," later in this chapter.

>> **Rich pins:** These pins allow you to add extra information that makes it easier for customers to find your pins. Use them liberally. The four types of rich pins are:

- *Product:* These show pricing and where you can buy the product.

- *Recipe:* These show ingredients, serving sizes, and cooking times.

- *Article:* These are articles you have pinned to save or read later. You see the author name, headline, and a brief description.

- *App:* If you have an iOS app the user can install it without leaving Pinterest.

TIP

Go to `https://business.pinterest.com/en/rich-pins` to learn about the different types of pins.

TIP

You can create as many boards as you need to communicate your message. Don't skimp, and don't worry about whether each one is perfect.

The key aspects of a board are its title and cover picture (see Figure 14-6). These aspects are what the user sees first. If the name and picture are enticing, users are likely to at least click to see the board. You have no guarantee that users will stay and perhaps even click other pins, but you want to get their attention by making a good first impression. Liken your board to a book cover and title. If your board's title and cover picture aren't immediately intriguing, users won't click.

FIGURE 14-6:
Cover picture and title of a board.

Encourage your audience to do the following:

>> **Re-pin your pins:** Get them circulated!

>> **Comment:** As you know, the opinions of friends and colleagues are most valuable.

>> **Share and use your hashtags:** Let your customer be your best salesperson; make sure to have your content pinnable from your website using widgets.

>> **Buy:** Ah, yes, your favorite customer activity. Make it easy to click the Buy button. Evaluate each pin for its usability.

Sony Electronics is using Pinterest to communicate with its audience effectively. Sony has to appeal to both genders and make a strong visual statement. Sony has interesting shots on its site and encourages people to provide lively, interesting shots, too, using bold graphics and colors.

Sony's account on Pinterest, shown in Figure 14-7, displays 37 boards. The boards present an interesting mix of topics. You can scroll down to find titles including Minimilist Lifestyle, Fitness, and For the Moms.

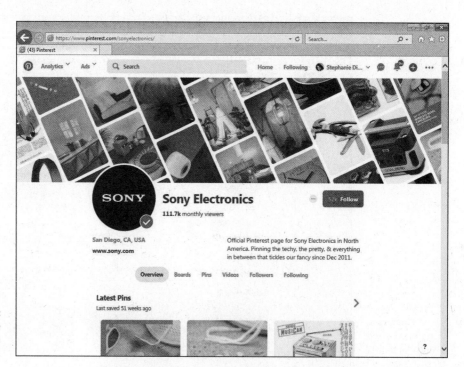

FIGURE 14-7:
The Sony home page on Pinterest.

Some images and videos to consider are

>> Employees in action

>> Charity events

>> Infographics

>> Something related to food

>> Pictures with pets

>> Celebrity tie-ins (the use of celebrities to extol the virtues of the products)

>> Pictures of customers using products

>> Colorful graphics taken from brochures, product pages, and other marketing material

>> Glamour shots of products

>> Videos that communicate your company's history

TIP

Have someone go into your company's archives or digital folders and seek images that may be forgotten. Just because it wasn't already used on your website doesn't mean that it might not be right for Pinterest.

Drilling down with Guided Search

Pinterest wants to make it as easy as possible for you and your customers to find exactly what they're looking for. To that end, it offers Pinterest Guided Search for iOS and Android. Guided Search is useful because it lets you drill down within a category.

For example, say that your customer is looking for plants for her shaded patio. First she types in **shade** and gets items including shade garden, shade plants, and shade flowers. She chooses *shade plants*. Then she is shown additional categories to pick from. These include perennial, outdoor, and container. She chooses *container* and is presented with hundreds of pins that meet this criteria.

As a marketer, it's important that you conduct these searches for products on mobile devices. You want to know exactly what users will find and how you can make it easy to find your products first.

Experimenting with promoted pins

To help marketers advertise their pins, Pinterest developed Promoted Pins. Brands pay for these pins to show up in searches and category feeds. (They don't show up in a company's Home feed.) A Promoted Pin, shown in Figure 14-8, displays the notation "promotional pin" at the bottom.

FIGURE 14-8:
A Promoted Pin.

Promoted Pin

Just as with any other form of advertising, you need to decide whether advertising specific pins will work for you. Think about how your users are currently sharing your pins and commenting. Most people on Pinterest are used to the idea that they can buy something, so determine whether you will get a reasonable bump from a Promoted Pin.

Tracking your results

It's easy to assume that your Pinterest traffic is converting customers. But perhaps it's not. You need to analyze what you're doing. Several tools are available to help you see what your customers are doing on Pinterest. These tools include:

» **Pinterest's free built-in analytics dashboard.**
You can access this dashboard by clicking the Analytics link in the upper-left corner of your page. You can choose to look at an overview of your analytics or Audience Insights. You can track such items as how many pins are coming from your website in a certain timeframe, what users share most often, and what pins get clicked most.

» **Tailwind** (`https://www.tailwindapp.com/`)**:** Tailwind is an app that you can use with Pinterest. It allows you to schedule pins, monitor their performance, and optimize your content.

Chapter **15**

Interacting with Tumblr

Which social media platform has approximately 471.6 million blogs as of August of 2019 and 1.1 billion posts published monthly? If you guessed Tumblr, then you're in the know. What started out in 2007 as a way for David Karp, Tumblr's founder, to easily post media turned into a visual power-house now owned by Verizon with millions of users.

What makes a Tumblr blog so appealing? It's easy to use, and your image types look great. Tumblr blogs differ from other social media blogs because you aren't encouraged to include long, involved text posts. They are meant to serve the images that they display, and humor is encouraged. In this chapter, you look at what you need to do to get started with Tumblr and how to show off your content to its greatest advantage.

Setting Up Shop on Tumblr

Tumblr is free to join and is hosted for you on Tumblr's site. You don't have to worry about getting your own hosting site or paying for a suitable WordPress or other blogging templates. This is not insignificant. You probably don't need to hire a developer at the beginning to help you set up your site. However, if you want to customize the template and develop special features, you'll want to consider some assistance.

So who uses Tumblr? According to Statista (`https://www.statista.com/topics/2463/tumblr/`), 43 percent of Tumblr users are between the ages of 18 and 24. Is that your demographic? If so, Tumblr is a must for you. Also, as with Pinterest, users spend a lot of time looking at and posting images, so you'll have the opportunity to grab their attention.

To sign up on Tumblr, you need to fill out a quick form, which is shown in Figure 15-1. You just need to put in an email address, username, and password.

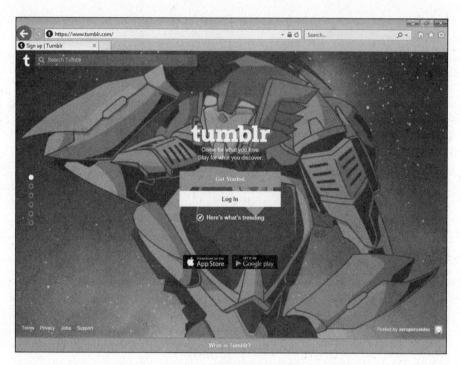

FIGURE 15-1:
Signing up for
Tumblr.

To set up your Tumblog, you need to pick a name that will have Tumblr in the title, as in, *blogname*.tumblr.com (replacing *blogname* with your chosen name). Then you can pick a design for your site by choosing the gear icon at the top right and choosing Edit Appearance, as shown in Figure 15-2.

You have hundreds of themes to choose from. Just look through the designs available to you. Some are free; some have a fee. If you're matching your own branding, you can customize the theme with help from your webmaster. Your blog's appearance is important, so take the time to look through the options.

FIGURE 15-2:
Choosing to edit
appearance.

Two kinds of Tumblr blog types are available to you, as follows:

>> **Primary:** The first site you create is designated as your primary blog.
A primary blog has all the available features but can't be made private.
You can gather likes, followers, and so on.

>> **Secondary:** A secondary blog can be public or private. If you make it private,
it won't have the social media functions such as follow and like.

For marketing purposes, you most likely want to start with a primary blog and get
it all set up and working before you branch out to other blogs. If your company is
small, one blog will probably suffice. Consider a secondary, private blog for your
team collaboration or working with other vendors or colleagues.

Finding and Sharing the Good Stuff

You already know that the first two things you need to consider when adding a new platform to your social media strategy are the following:

>> **How it will serve your customers.**

Are your customers currently on Tumblr? Make sure to confirm this and understand how your customers are using it. If you serve a young demographic, make sure to incorporate the playful spirit of other Tumblr blogs. If your audience fits the demographic but is a bit older, don't be afraid to use your blog to show off your media. IBM does a great job of using Tumblr to communicate its message (check it out at `http://ibmblr.tumblr.com/`), by displaying a variety of categories, as shown in Figure 15-3.

>> **How it will integrate with your channel strategy.**

Your strategy must be the centerpiece of everything you do, and you need to conduct your Tumblr in a way that integrates this strategy. If a majority of your users are not yet on Tumblr in any great numbers, you might consider using it to enhance your current distribution — for example, include links on your other channels to media on Tumblr.

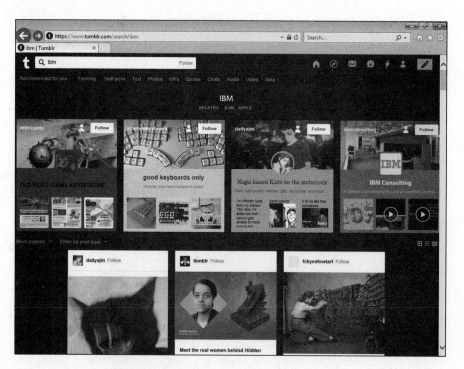

FIGURE 15-3:
IBM categories on Tumblr.

REMEMBER

It's most important to note that your Tumblr blog should not be a carbon copy of the content you have on Facebook or Twitter. Tumblr allows you to integrate multimedia in a more effective way. One of the most useful aspects of having a Tumblr blog is that it forces you to think about more than just text. This is a good thing because most business blogs are pretty dull, and companies don't even realize it. You're challenged to break out the media you own or create something new.

With a Tumblr blog, you have no excuse for posting a few paragraphs and calling it a day. The world of visuals and multimedia is open to you. As a social media marketer, you can make this cornucopia of media choices work to your advantage. You can put up multimedia on Tumblr that's not on your other platforms and then link it. Just don't make your other platforms a twin of Tumblr. It just won't work.

REMEMBER

To make it easy to select items to curate from your browser, you can add a browser extension. To do this, go to `https://www.tumblr.com/apps`, as shown in Figure 15-4.

TIP

The variety of media is one of the reasons that the average age of the Tumblr user skews so young. These users are comfortable sharing every type of media that comes their way, and they want to see what's new.

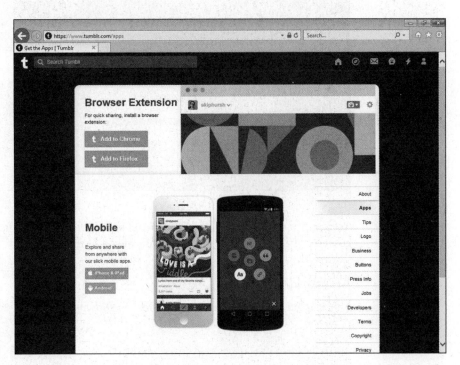

FIGURE 15-4:
Adding an extension to your browser.

Using your dashboard

So now that you have completed the basics, what will your visitors see in your feed? They will see your favorite blogs, your own posts, and anything that has value to you. You need to be active and provide a variety of different types of content. To understand how this works, let's look at what tools are available to you and how you can manage them.

Tumblr provides a dashboard, which you use to navigate the structure. This structure is shown in Figure 15-5.

FIGURE 15-5:
The Tumblr blog dashboard.

To simplify, we have broken down the dashboard into four sections: menu options; content types; posts and feeds; and followers and finds.

Menu options

This section displays your menu options, as shown in Figure 15-6.

Menu options

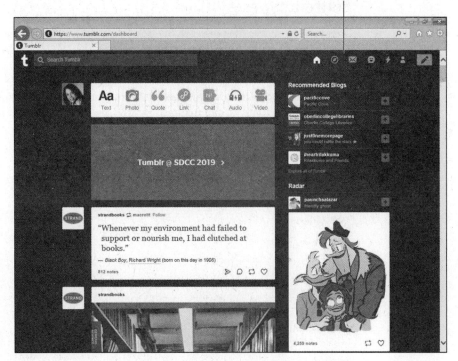

FIGURE 15-6:
Menu options.

The menu holds the following options:

>> **Home:** This links to the Main page where you see your dashboard.

>> **Explore:** This link shows you what's on Tumblr that might interest you.

>> **Inbox:** This is where you get messages from others, including "fan mail," questions, and submissions. This area also has a button that allows you to send fan mail to other blogs.

>> **Messaging:** This link shows you messages from tumblogs you follow.

>> **Activity:** This link shows you the activity (likes, reblogs, and so on) that result from a new post you have to create.

>> **Account:** Here you see analytics on posts and followers. You also see links for settings and help.

>> **Make a Post:** When you click this link you are shown the media types you can choose to create a blog post.

Content types

This section shows the icons for the type of media you want to post, as shown in Figure 15-7. For example, if you want to post a video, you click the video icon, and a window pops up that makes setting up the video easy.

The primary focus of Tumblr is media sharing, and Tumblr's dashboard has seven types of media that you can instantly share (see Figure 15-7), as follows:

- » Text
- » Photo
- » Quote
- » Link
- » Chat
- » Audio
- » Video

FIGURE 15-7: Your media options.

You can see from the choices that you have a wide range of options. Sharing the same kind of content on a WordPress blog isn't as easy as it is on Tumblr. For example, when you think about sharing audio in a WordPress or other blog post, you probably realize that you'll need to know the best way to do it, and you have to find the icon in the post window, among other tasks. But to post an audio in Tumblr, all you need to do is click the audio icon, and a window pops up, as shown in Figure 15-8.

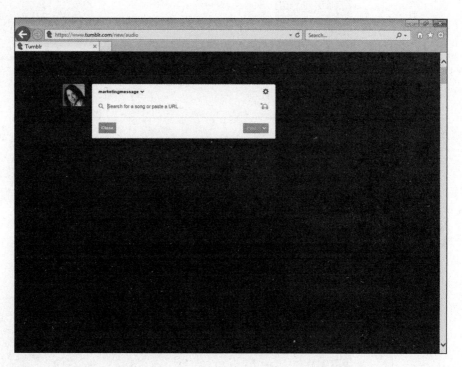

FIGURE 15-8:
Posting an audio on Tumblr.

Posts and Feed

In this area of your Tumblr blog, your current post and post stream are displayed, as shown in Figure 15-9.

One of the other nice features about posting is that you can schedule a post, as shown in Figure 15-10. Scheduling a post (as opposed to posting immediately after you write it) is useful for the times when you plan to be away and don't want to have the flow of steady posts interrupted, or when you have several things you want to post right away but don't want them to go all at the same time.

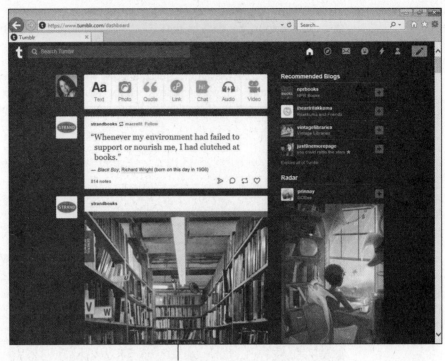

FIGURE 15-9:
The post stream
of a Tumblr blog.

Post and feed

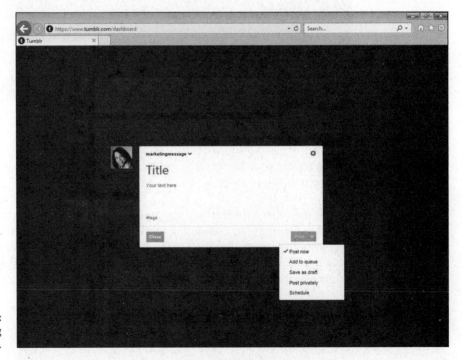

FIGURE 15-10:
Scheduling
a post.

The options to post are the following:

>> **Post Now:** Post immediately.

>> **Add to queue:** Put it at the end of the list of postings that have been scheduled.

>> **Save a draft:** Continue to edit the post at a later date.

>> **Post privately:** Send a post to a select person.

>> **Schedule:** Choose a specific date.

These options allow you to coordinate your posts with specific campaigns, people, or dates. Also, at the bottom of each post are icons for sharing the post (to email, Facebook, Twitter, and a permalink, which is the link where the post will be found even if it moves from its current spot in your post list), replying to the writer of the post, reblogging it, and liking it. These icons help others engage with you. You can also use them on other people's posts to engage with them and make your ideas known.

Note the tag icon at the bottom left of your post stream. Click this icon to create a tag (or multiple tags) for your post — and you want to be sure to tag your posts. Tagging your posts is how people find that content in addition to using categories and hashtags (#). For example, if you're citing a specific product in your post, you can add the product name as a tag so that people searching for it via tags will be sure to find it.

REMEMBER

One great feature of a Tumblog is that no one can post without your consent. When you authorize apps on some of the other social platforms, you may be giving consent for them to post in your name. Tumblr does not permit this. There is a setting called Submissions that asks whether others can submit posts into your submission queue for approval.

Followers and Finds

This section shows who is following you in addition to showing you all your posts. As shown in Figure 15-11, you can see the blogs of those who follow you, who you follow, and your likes. In this section, you also see recommendations for new blogs to follow.

This is where you discover new, interesting people and other blogs to interact with. In the final heading, called Radar (see Figure 15-11), you see sponsored posts.

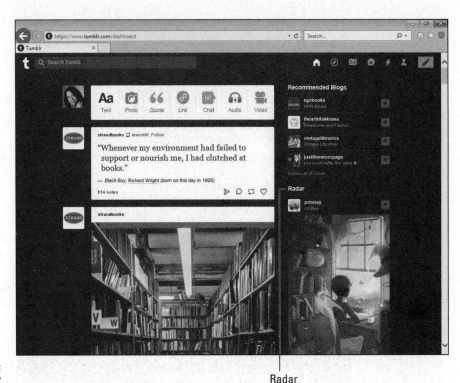

FIGURE 15-11:
Who follows you?

Radar

TIP

Although a Tumblr blogger can see his or her own follower numbers from the dashboard, bloggers can't see follower numbers of other people's blogs. Knowing this fact should help you get over that feeling of being new and unestablished yourself. By contrast, on platforms like Twitter, it's hard to miss follower numbers.

Observing other blog successes

As with other platforms, you always want to see who is successful and why. Tumblr is no exception. So what are some of the top business Tumblr blogs? Brands that typically generate buzz on Tumblr include Disney, Facebook, Apple, Nike, and Nintendo.

When you think about the visual nature of Tumblogs, it's no surprise that design-conscious brands like Disney and Apple are succeeding. If you look at Disney's Tumblr blog (http://disney.tumblr.com/), you see that it posts animations, videos, and photos of its properties. It's a natural winner.

So where else should you look to see successful blogs? Check out https://www.tumblr.com/search, as shown in Figure 15-12. When you click the link, you're shown recommended blogs. Blogs are listed that are suggested by the topics you have already searched. Look around and see what intrigues you.

Recommended blogs

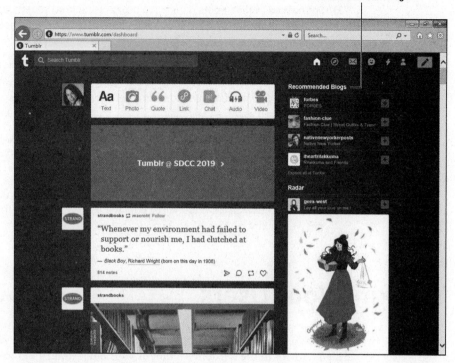

FIGURE 15-12:
Recommended
blogs.

Looking at Paid Media

The idea of advertisements showing up in their feed is usually met with a negative response by users. Mindful of this distaste, Tumblr has been very cautious about introducing advertising into the mix.

One thing Tumblr prides itself on is the fact that it uses native advertising. This means that the posts in a user's feed look pretty much like a regular post. Depending on your point of view, this can be good or bad.

TIP

There can be quite a bit of exposure for your posts. According to Tumblr, 60 percent of engagement with Sponsored Posts comes from non-followers who see the post in someone else's feed.

Several types of posts are paid for, including the following:

>> **Sponsored Web posts:** These posts are just what you'd expect them to be. They are found in your feed when you access your feed from a desktop or laptop.

>> **Sponsored Mobile posts:** When you access Tumblr on your mobile device, you see Sponsored posts in your feed. These posts have been approved by Tumblr and tested before they are posted.

>> **Sponsored Trending blogs:** These posts are seen in your mobile feed when you click the search icon at the bottom of your screen. This display is created by Tumblr for you. You need to submit three representative posts, and they are displayed as a Trending blog.

>> **Sponsored Radar:** There is a section labeled Radar on the right side of your dashboard. (Refer to Figure 15-11.) This is where sponsored Radar posts show up. The post is very visible in the dashboard and gets some good exposure.

>> **Sponsored Spotlight:** This type of post is chosen to be displayed by Tumblr based on the value it has to the community. To have your post chosen, you need to submit it no less than 24 hours before you plan to run it.

Tracking Your Users

The quickest way to see follower activity is to click the dashboard item called Activity in the Account section of your blog. Here, you can see the number of followers you have. You can segment them based on when they began following you.

Knowing when people started following you doesn't tell you anything about how engaged they are, but it does let you know that there are people actively reading and appreciating your blog. Of course, other indications are your fan mail, comments, and likes.

If you want more detailed information, you could add a Google Analytics tracking code.

Chapter **16**

Engaging Customers Using Other Platforms

Y ou know that not all social media platforms and tools are created equal. If you use sites such as Facebook, YouTube, and Twitter you find an incredibly large audience that is direct messaging, tweeting, sharing, and other social activities. But these platforms aren't the only choices you have for engaging with your fans and prospects. New platforms are being developed all the time. Some, such as Pinterest, started out with little fan fair and gained traction in a short amount of time. If you consider adding some other choices to your marketing roster it may help you attract a broader audience.

In this chapter, we look at three social platforms that are not as big as Facebook or Twitter but may help you find followers and spread your message. They are Medium (a blogging platform), Reddit (a content discussion site), and (TikTok), a social media video-sharing app.

Blogging on Medium for Your Business

We begin by looking at Medium, a blogging platform started by Twitter founder Evan Williams in 2012. Williams says he created Medium to provide a place for Twitter users to share ideas and tell stories using more than 140 characters (now 280 characters). As of 2017, there were sixty million monthly readers. The audience is mainly interested in such topics as lifelong learning, business, technology, entrepreneurship, and marketing.

Anyone can join Medium. To publish, you have three options. You can:

>> Create and edit your own publication (if accepted by the Editors) to which others can submit content.

>> Be designated as an author and publish to your own feed.

>> Submit content to an already established Medium publication.

TIP

If you want to look at a list of the top one hundred publications on Medium, you can go to `https://toppubs.smedian.com/`, as shown in Figure 16-1, to see which ones are most popular. It's also helpful to browse there to orient yourself to the type of content that's successful.

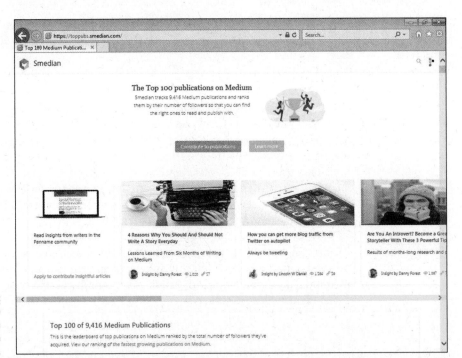

FIGURE 16-1:
Searching top publications on Medium with Smedian.

REMEMBER

Readers can subscribe to Medium for a small monthly fee and become a member (as of this writing it is five dollars per month). For their subscription fee, they receive hand-curated content and other features not available to non-subscribers, such as podcasts. When subscribers clap (see the "Reviewing a profile" section for more on claps), the author is allotted some of their subscriber money. There is no advertising on the site.

There is a debate going on among some marketers as to whether a business should consider setting up their first blog on Medium instead of one of the major blog platforms such as WordPress over which they have full control. In the next section, you look at some of the pros and cons of setting up a blog on Medium.

Looking at the pros and cons

The good news about Medium is you don't have to choose it or another blogging site. You can, in fact, do both. You can set up a blog on Wordpress.org (with your own domain) or other blogging tool and still have a blog on Medium at the same time. This is because you can repurpose content. You can take the content you have published elsewhere on the web and re-purpose it on Medium.

Those who are inclined to use Medium as their first or only blog include the following arguments:

>> **Distribution:** You have a built-in audience on Medium. You can take your Twitter and Facebook followers onto Medium (Medium links followers from both and adds them) and gain new followers who find you there when they look for your topic.

Just because Medium has a larger audience than your blog (presumably) doesn't ensure that you'll find additional readers. But it does put you in a position to be found by new audiences. The potential exposure to new groups is significant.

>> **Structure:** Medium has an almost effortless blog setup. You fill in the blanks, take your content from anywhere on the web, and publish it. They allow you to use visuals, so the content looks appealing. Also, because they handle the blog structure, you don't have to pay for hosting or other fees associated with running a blog.

>> **High quality:** If you're a member, you receive hand-curated content by Medium editors who present the best stuff first. This also cuts down on clickbait headlines and poor-quality content. Subscribers are serious about reading good content.

>> **Expertise:** You can create collections of content that can establish you as an expert in that topic.

Those who are less inclined to use Medium as their first or only blog include the following arguments:

- **No control:** You don't own it or have control over your blog on Medium. Just like Facebook or Twitter, the platform administrators have control over what happens. Rules can change.

- **No Google credit:** Medium gets credit for organic search ratings because Google recognizes the content coming from Medium, not your site. This doesn't add anything to your domain's authority.

- **Friction:** Users are asked to subscribe, which puts some friction between you and the reader. This can hamper the building of your own list although you can use external links back to your website blog.

Making a choice

Some of the key determinants as to whether it's a good idea to set up your blog on Medium relate to whether content marketing is a big part of your marketing strategy and whether you have time to devote to two blogs. Getting your content seen and read is usually a vital business factor. But only you can decide the number of resources you want to deploy on blogging and that the conditions are right for you. Here are some choices to consider:

- **Setting up your first blog on your website:** Are you just launching your business or blog online? Do you have the resources needed to create and launch a website? If so, you may want to first test blog content by creating your own website. If you aren't clear about what content resonates with your audience, you'll want to learn that first.

- **Setting up your first blog on Medium:** Do you already know the type of content your audience likes, and you're looking for a way to get wider distribution? Or, do you have minimal resources and can't or don't want to set up a complete blogging platform from scratch? Medium provides the structure for users to quickly get up and running.

- **Setting up a second blog on Medium:** There is no prohibition against repurposing content from your own blog site on Medium so you can use the knowledge you gain on your own site content to populate your Medium site. This means that you believe that the time and resources you devote to a second blog with a built-in audience will benefit your business and help it grow.

Utilizing analytics

Before we look at examples of business content on Medium, we look at some of the data analytics you can gather when you post on the site:

>> **Views:** People who looked at the post

>> **Reads:** People who read the post

>> **Read ratio:** The difference between reads and views

>> **Average time reading:** The amount of time (estimated) that people spend with the story

>> **Fans:** People who clapped for a story

>> **Referrers:** What sites your traffic came from

>> **Reader's interests:** You see the topics that your readers follow. You need to reach a threshold number of readers (determined by Medium) for the story before you can view this content.

As you can see, this is useful data that helps you learn more about your audience. Take a close look at these stats and use them to optimize your content.

Delving into Medium content

In this section, we look at how content is presented for a profile on Medium for both a thought leader, Larry Kim, and a software company called Buffer.

Reviewing a profile

Larry Kim founded WordStream and is currently the CEO of MobileMonkey (http://mobilemonkey.com), a Facebook Messenger solutions company. He participates on Medium as an author and thought leader. He edits the publication Marketing and Entrepreneurship, and he is a top author who submits articles for the publications, Entrepreneurship, Education, Inspiration, Life, Productivity, and Life Lessons. Figure 16-2 shows his Medium profile.

>> **Profile:** Medium pulls information from your Twitter profile if you have one, or you can set up a one-hundred-and-sixty-character description, with a photo and link to the business location you want readers to know about. Here you see the number of followers that Larry Kim has, which as of this writing is one hundred and ninety-seven thousand.

>> **Claps:** At the claps link you find content that was approved of by Larry Kim with "claps." If your content receives claps, you know it is resonating with your audience, so this is an important number to watch.

Followers

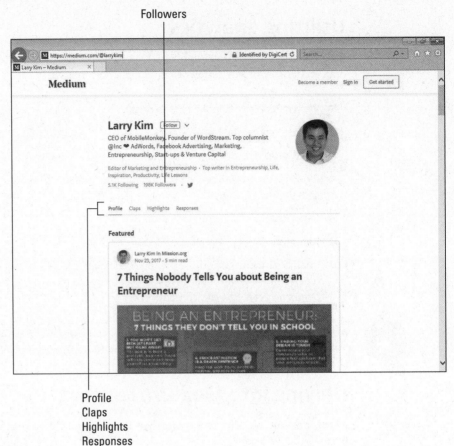

FIGURE 16-2:
Larry Kim's profile
on Medium.

Profile
Claps
Highlights
Responses

>> **Highlights:** This is where you find the list of content that has been highlighted on Medium by Larry Kim. When your content is highlighted, you know the topics that get your reader's attention.

>> **Responses:** Here, you see comments written about content by Larry Kim. Naturally comments written about your content can lead to insights and perhaps create a networking opportunity with the commenter.

Viewing a company's blog

Buffer (http://buffer.com) is a software company that has several different publications and authors on Medium. Their staff may write a blog post on their own or add it to one of their publications. One of their profiles is shown in Figure 16-3.

Followers

FIGURE 16-3:
One of Buffer's
profiles on
Medium.

Profiles
Series
Claps
Highlights
Responses

As you can see, this profile includes the same links as Larry Kim's profile: Profile, Claps, Highlights, and Responses. It also has one additional link called Series. Series are stories that you read on your mobile phone that are displayed "card by card" and can be added to over time. To explain this type of post they say, "there is no ending, just to be continued." In this way, readers can continue to check in and read about a topic as writers add to them. The Series tab is present when you download the Medium app.

TIP

After experimenting, Buffer found that Medium helped them reach a variety of new audiences and have continued to update their content. They also started a blog on Customer Support https://medium.com/customer-support to explain their commitment to customer service.

Discussing Ideas On Reddit.com

Reddit (http://reddit.com) is a community discussion and rating platform where participants vote content up and down. It was founded by Alexis Ohanian and Steve Huffman in 2005. It calls itself the "front page of the internet" and lives up to that billing; Alexa ranks it as the sixth most visited site in the U.S. You can submit blog posts, images, audio, and original content. In fact, there is a separate link for original content on the front page.

TIP

According to Statista in 2017, the Reddit audience skews male (sixty-nine percent), and the majority were in the 18–29 age range (fifty-eight percent). If this is your audience, you need to look into what's being shared here.

Marketing on Reddit

Should your company consider joining Reddit to become one of its "Redditors"? That depends on how much you want to spend time digging deeper and connecting with your niche audience. It's likely that there's an audience online that is discussing your topic. According to Statista, Reddit has:

>> Five hundred and forty-two million monthly visitors; two hundred thirty-four million unique users) as of March 2019

>> Over one hundred and thirty-eight thousand active communities

>> Almost 1.6 billion visits to their online forum (from February 2018 to April 2019)

Reddit has gotten the interest of brands because it has a mass audience and marketers are eager to grab their attention. But, not surprisingly, marketing behavior is virtually shunned on Reddit. Therefore, figuring out the best way to participate as a company takes time and effort.

TIP

Determine whether you have the time to spend learning the rules and determine the best way to join the conversation. You don't want to associate your company with inappropriate content and be banned.

To avoid being banned, think about the following:

>> **You first goal is to understand the lay of the land.** You want to find subreddits (threads) that have content related to your business topic and determine how you want to participate in discussions.

>> **Think about adding value by doing things like answering questions.** If you act like a marketer who only talks about their products, you won't be welcome. You want to develop a community and serve them well.

>> **See how content is presented.** Make sure not to use cheesy headlines or clickbait. The administrators can ban you.

Setting up

To join Reddit, you have to register and verify your account. Here are a few important things to note:

>> **Username:** You can't change your username after you pick one, so give careful thought to your choice ahead of time.

>> **Rules:** After your account is verified, you receive a welcome letter from Reddit that outlines acceptable behavior (reddiquette).

>> **Subscriptions:** Reddit automatically subscribes you to fifty of the most popular subreddits when you join. Communities on Reddit are called subreddits. You can keep or delete them as you choose. All subreddits names start this way: reddit.com/r/ name.

>> **Premium:** You can subscribe to a premium version of Reddit for $5.99 a month. This gives you an ad-free version, access to the r/lounge community, and seven hundred coins to spend each month. Coins are virtual tokens that can be used to show the writer of the content that their contribution is exemplary.

>> **Account:** To view your account as others see it, go to https://reddit.com/user/youraccountname.

>> **Search:** To search subreddits type a term related to your business as shown in Figure 16-4 (https://www.reddit.com/search/?q=content%20marketing).

TIP

To keep up on the latest communities, you can find new subreddits as they are created by searching at https://www.reddit.com/r/newreddits/.

Knowing the lingo

When you join any community, it's helpful to know the special terms used by its members. As a marketer, here are two you should know:

>> **Karma points:** Karma points are earned by upvotes to your posts or comments. This is your currency. Other users can judge you by this, so pay attention to this metric.

Digital marketing

FIGURE 16-4:
Searching for
subreddits about
digital marketing.

>> **Shadow ban:** If you violate the rules you may be shadow banned by the administrators. This means that no one else can see your account although you think your account looks fine.

Analyzing content

One of the reasons for participating on Reddit is to see the kinds of things others in your communities are writing about and how they're using it. Here are two free/paid tools you can use to analyze subreddits users and determine how well your content is performing:

>> Snoopsnoo (https://snoopsnoo.com/), as shown in Figure 16-5, is a free tool that lets you look at other member profiles to see how they're using Reddit. You can see such things as how long they have been on the site, how long it's been between postings, and their karma scores.

>> TrackReddit (https://www.trackreddit.com/), as shown in Figure 16-6, is a tracking tool that lets you set up alerts for topics (two are free). For example, you can monitor what's being said on Reddit about a brand name or person.

Reddit username

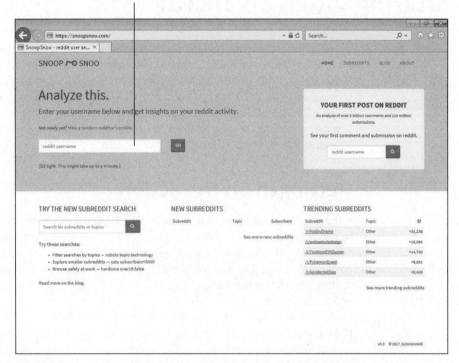

FIGURE 16-5:
Snoopsnoo.

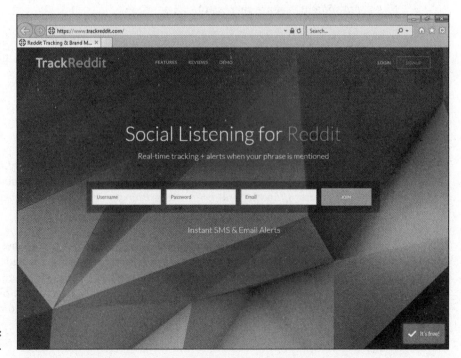

FIGURE 16-6:
TrackReddit.

Sharing Video on TikTok

Looking for something new in social media? Are you a brand hoping to attract attention from a teen audience? If so, you may want to check out TikTok. In 2017 ByteDance, a Chinese Internet company, introduced a new social media video-sharing app called TikTok. In 2018 ByteDance bought Musical.ly that had a substantial U.S. based audience and merged it with TikTok and is gaining a presence among Americans. Forty-one percent of TikTok's audience is between the ages of 16 and 24 (Global Web Index, 2018).

Getting in on the action

Although the platform may be new to you, TikTok was the most downloaded app in the Apple App Store in the first half of 2018 — one billion downloads (CNBC Sensor/Tower) worldwide, which surpasses downloads of platforms such as Instagram, YouTube, and Facebook. Currently, it has more than five hundred million monthly active users.

TIP

Interested in exploring the app? You can download it free from the App Store (https://apps.apple.com/ro/app/tiktok-make-your-day/id835599320) and at Google Play (https://play.google.com/store/apps/details?id=com.zhiliaoapp.musically&hl=en_US). You'll want to look around and see the types of content that are successful.

So, what is TikTok? It's a video sharing app on which users create fifteen-second videos that play on a loop with music tracks. The videos are largely made up of lip-synching, stunts, pets doing tricks, and other humorous music-backed content. The app supplies tools to create something unique and fun.

Experimenting with TikTok

If you think that major companies aren't interested in an app such as TikTok, you forget that five hundred million monthly users are a lot of eyeballs. Companies like Guess, Chipotle, and even the *Washington Post* are experimenting with this new social media app.

Of particular interest to brands is the Challenges tab. Companies are trying out challenges that relate to their products. A challenge asks the reader to participate in a themed action. For example, in 2018, Guess (https://shop.guess.com/en/) a fashion brand, partnered with TikTok to create TikTok's first branded content challenge using the hashtag #InMyDenim, as shown in Figure 16-7.

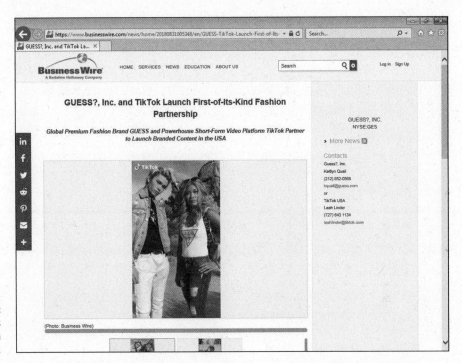

FIGURE 16-7:
Guesse's #InMyDenim challenge.

Guess asked popular fashion influencers on the channel to create content and asked users to take photos of how they looked in their new denim line (https://www.businesswire.com/news/home/20180831005348/en/GUESS-TikTok-Launch-First-of-Its-Kind-Fashion-Partnership). So how did it go? Guess considers the campaign a great success with thirty-four million views and lots of attention to their product.

REMEMBER

If you want to reach this Gen Z audience, research carefully and see what others are doing. This is an audience that will let you know if you're missing the mark!

4

Getting Your Message to Connectors

Chapter **17**

Marketing to Millennials

Regardless of what you've heard or observed about the difficulty of marketing to Millennials, you *can* create successful social media marketing campaigns aimed at them. You just need to understand that they are very different from previous generations and have grown up with a social media lifestyle that's "always on." They haven't known a time when the web wasn't their constant companion. It would be helpful to remember that many were coming of age during and post the recession of the late 2000s. This event had a definite effect on their outlook for the future and their fear of further potential downturns.

In this chapter, you look at the characteristics that make up the Millennial cohort (also know as Gen Y); what they want from brands and how you can successfully connect with them. We also look at some brands that Millennials favor.

Learning About Millennials

Millennials are the largest generation in the workforce today. They are the last generation born in the twentieth century and the first to grow up with technology as their constant companion. They are entirely comfortable finding online information and keeping their mobile devices close.

Take a look at how they compare to other generations in size and age (https://www.kasasa.com/articles/generations/gen-x-gen-y-gen-z):

>> **Baby Boomers:** 76 million people born between 1944 and 1964

>> **Gen Xers:** 82 million born between 1965 and 1980

>> **Millennials (also known as Gen Y):** 73 million born between 1980 and 1994

>> **Gen Z:** 74 million born 1995–2015 or after

TIP

Millennials' buying power is substantial. It's believed that in 2020, Millennials will account for 30 percent of retail sales in the U.S. (approximately $1.4 trillion). You can't afford to ignore their economic might just because they are somewhat more difficult to reach.

In the following sections you look at several key characteristics of Millennials that you need to know if you are going to engage them.

Technically savvy

It's no mystery why Millennials are tech-savvy. They've grown up with technology. According to Pew Research in 2018, more than nine in ten Millennials (92 percent) own smartphones, and 28 percent are smartphone-only users. If you're courting a Millennial audience, you need to make mobile a centerpiece of your marketing campaign efforts.

Seek a balanced life

Unlike Baby Boomers who champion a "work all the time" ethos, Millennials want to have a more balanced life. At the time of this writing, Millennials are between the ages of 25–39. The older ones have families and want to enjoy spending time with them. The younger cohort prefers social experiences and travel.

TIP

Millennials are interested in participating in the *gig economy* (short term, freelance work) because it allows them to have more flexible hours. Consider whether freelancers would enhance your team. Also, if you're able, consider flexible work hours for full-time employees.

Follow influencers

Millennials hate ads, but 58 percent of them are influenced by online celebrities and are even willing to sit through a short advertisement that includes their favorite influencer. They want to be entertained, and a message from someone they follow is acceptable. (See https://www.forbes.com/sites/andrewarnold/2018/01/21/millennials-hate-ads-but-58-of-them-wouldnt-mind-if-its-from-their-favorite-digital-stars/#28063ff459ca) for more information.

REMEMBER

If you market to this group, you may want to invest in advertising with influencers that hold considerable sway with this population. They will sit through an introduction by a celebrity but ignore a short ad.

Look for recognition and feedback

Parents of Millennials made sure that their children received encouragement for their efforts. They gave them recognition for small wins and provided input on how they could do better. For this reason, Millennials expect their managers at work to act similarly. They look for encouragement and solicit feedback. If they don't receive it, they're likely to look for work elsewhere. They want to feel that each job they take contributes to their career advancement.

Prefer to share or barter

Millennials are careful with their money. One of the myths about Millennials is that they are cheap. However, this isn't accurate. There are several reasons why they're careful spenders, not the least of which is the amount of college debt that many have accumulated. They are also unsure about the economy, having experienced the 2008 recession. They don't want to bet on smooth sailing in the future.

This is one reason the sharing economy has become so popular among Millennials. They would rather not buy a car when they can share or barter for one. For example, Zipcar (http://zipcar.com), as shown in Figure 17-1, is popular with Millennials. They can rent a car for a set amount of time for a fee. The time can be a short as a few minutes to a few days. Millennials often prefer to use a service like this instead of investing in a car.

TIP

It's worth your time to figure out if there is a sharing option for your product that you can present to your Millennial audience. In this way, you can develop a new revenue stream and perhaps increase your reach.

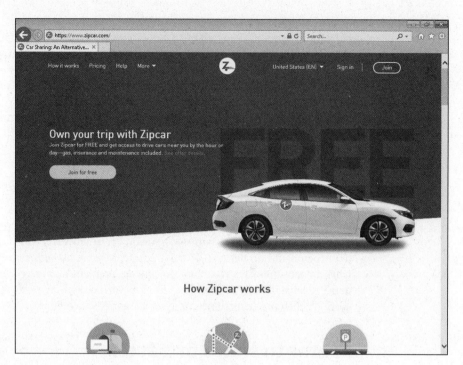

FIGURE 17-1:
The Zipcar
home page.

Understanding What Millennials Want from Brands

Understanding the mindset of Millennials makes it easier to understand what they expect from your company. There are specific things that Millennials look for when connecting with a brand. They would rather respond to useful information that speaks to their needs rather than their checkbook. They want an honest connection that is meaningful to them.

In the next sections, we look at what Millennials want to see from your company.

Trustworthiness and authenticity

Millennials are particularly interested in buying from brands that are trustworthy and authentic. They have grown up with traditional advertising, and many ignore it completely. They want something (or someone) they can trust. They know that images can be faked and changed in Photoshop and are likely to disregard them when deciding what to buy. For example, they care about the ingredients in their packaged goods and the chemicals in their cleaning products. Brands need to step up and demonstrate their commitment to "clean and real' rather than just displaying nice images of trees and farms. They want to see a commitment to the farmer.

Cause-minded attitude

As we discussed, Millennials are careful about how they spend their money. They are also concerned about how your company spends its money. They want to see that you are worried about the needs of the broader community. According to research by Millennial Marketing (http://www.millennialmarketing.com/who-are-millennials/), as shown in Figure 17-2, fifty percent of Millennials would be more likely to buy from a company when their purchase supports a cause, and would even be willing to pay a bit more!

FIGURE 17-2: Millennial Marketing's research on Millennials.

Respectful of privacy concerns

With all the concerns about data theft and misuse, Millennials are much less willing to trade their email addresses for information like Baby Boomers and Gen Xers did. They also eschew "sneaky" ways of showing them ads. According to its study "Marketing to Millennials in 2019," listwithclever.com (https://listwithclever.com/real-estate-blog/marketing-to-millennials-in-2019/) found that Millennials are "creeped out by ads that follow them." These ads are facilitated by a technique called *remarketing*, which lets advertisers show an advertisement for a product in your browser after you have shown an interest in it on its website. If you're targeting Millennials, it's a good idea to use less intrusive ads that don't make them feel that their privacy is being violated.

Open to collaboration with customers

Millennials are used to being asked about their opinions and enjoy giving feedback to companies about their products. Many of them have created online content and consider themselves creators. You can gain their loyalty by soliciting their thoughts about how they use your products and how to improve them.

REMEMBER

Trust matters. Don't ask them for their input if you don't intend to use their suggestions. They consider their time way too valuable to spend with companies who don't care about them. After you have shown that you are uninterested in their ideas, they won't come back.

Recognizing Millennials Shopping Habits

It's essential to understand the way Millennials like to shop. According to an article in *Forbes*, "What Millennials Want When They Shop Online (https://www.forbes.com/sites/forbesinsights/2019/07/09/what-millennials-want-when-they-shop-online/#7fe49db94ed9), Millennials leverage technology to enhance their shopping capabilities. They found that Millennials are more likely than other generations to:

>> **Prize convenience:** They care more about convenience than free shipping or low prices. They want to be able to buy online and pick up or return to a store.

>> **Want same day delivery:** 45 percent of Millennials value same day delivery over other factors.

>> **Begin searching for a product online:** Even if they intend to buy in a store, they want to thoroughly research it online.

So, what exactly are Millennials spending their money on? An infographic by the University of Southern California (USC) Online Master of Science in Applied Psychology (`https://appliedpsychologydegree.usc.edu/blog/psychology-of-successfully-marketing-to-millennials/`) found that they spend their money on:

- » **Socializing:** This includes "food away from home" and transportation.
- » **Education:** Their substantial debt is well-known.
- » **Apparel:** They care about their appearance.
- » **Services:** They want to make their life easier and more convenient.
- » **Food:** They buy groceries for "at home eating."

These preferences paint the picture of a shopper that is interested in spending time socializing with friends, dressing well, eating out, and generally focusing on convenience. If you're marketing to Millennials, be aware that they value experiences over goods.

Smaller budgets and the ability to find the lowest price online has turned Millennial shoppers into seekers of experience over the collections of things. Previous generations were excited to find coupons and would be likely to buy when they had one. On the other hand, Millennials are adept at finding discounts and are looking for an experience or event that they can enjoy and remember.

BUT ARE THEY REALLY SHOPPING?

According to HubSpot, Millennials enjoy *Fauxsumerism* (`https://blog.hubspot.com/marketing/marketing-to-millennials?__hstc=185882614.ddd60d13feb6f888fb3f9ef4935689ef.1559601376373.1559674260383.1562183250867.3&__hssc=185882614.2.1562183250867&__hsfp=953835470`). That is, searching for items to buy more than actually buying them. This may be a clue as to why platforms like Pinterest are so attractive to them. Because of their limited budgets, they like to make lists on Pinterest of all the things they'd like to buy. In fact, according to Pinterest Business 2017 (`https://business.pinterest.com/sub/business/business-infographic-download/2017-11-07-millennial-report-final.pdf`) fifty percent of Millennials use Pinterest every month. They find sourcing pictures of products to be a fun pastime. The buying part not so much.

Succeeding with Millennials

One way to determine the best marketing tactics to use with Millennials is to look at the retailers that are currently succeeding in their efforts. According to Business Insider, (https://www.businessinsider.com/top-100-brands-according-to-millennials-from-netflix-to-walmart-2019-8#1-amazon-105), the top five retailers chosen by Millennials are Amazon, Apple, Nike, Walmart, and Target.

Hitting the target

Target (one of the top five brands mentioned in the previous section) is going all in on a bet that the "Millennial family" is its audience. It's partnering with the underwear brand Jockey on a new line of intimates called the Jockey Generation that will be carried exclusively in Target stores. Target will sell such items as t-shirts, socks, and loungewear, as shown in Figure 17-3. They are using innovative fabrics like those made from plastic bottles and will be giving a portion of each sale to the Jockey Family Foundation that educates and supports adoptive families. By all accounts, they have put all the right pieces in place to attract their Millennial audience https://fashionunited.com/news/fashion/target-and-jockey-team-up-on-underwear-for-the-young-millennial-family/2019070828835.

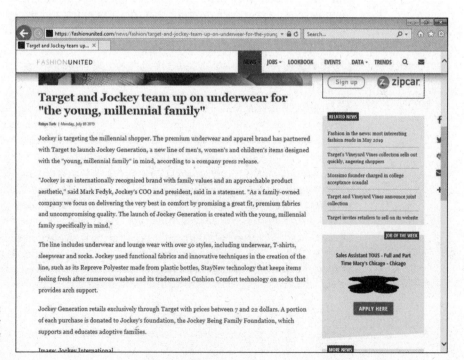

FIGURE 17-3: Target and Jockey launch the Jockey Generation line.

Interestingly enough, a Millennial's reason for choosing a brand may be different from what you expect. Millennials choose brands that enhance their *own* brands on social media. They focus on their followers and are aware of which brands will enhance their reputation. Among Millennials, brands are seen as an extension of their own socially conscious attitudes. They want to associate themselves with companies that demonstrate an interest in the community issues they care about.

More than any other generation, Millennials see themselves as brands. They often develop their own content, images, and video. So, for example, when they choose Nike as a brand, they choose it because it says something about them. They want to be perceived as caring about such things as health, innovation, and trustworthiness. Look at your Millennial audience to determine what they think your brand says about them. If your audience is not responding, develop content and images that speak more clearly to what your brand represents.

Appreciating the convenience of subscription services

Are you looking for a business model that attracts Millennials? One to consider is the subscription model. It's a curated selection of items that arrives at your house each month for a set fee.

One reason Millennials favor subscription services (more than other generations) is that it allows them to return items without having to go to the store. They value the convenience.

A new study by First Insight, "The State of Consumer Spending: Millennials Flexing Their Retail Market Influence in U.S. and U.K.," found that 25 percent of U.S. Millennials subscribe to subscription box services and when asked about their plans, 32 percent of those who hadn't subscribed yet, intended to in the next six months.

One such offering is Birchbox (https://get.birchbox.com/index-v7-pc.html), a monthly beauty subscription service, as shown in Figure 17-4. (They also have a Birchbox app that is available in the Apple App store and Google Play.)

Birchbox is attractive to Millennials because they allow you to customize their offerings and create a sense of adventure — two essential keys to engaging Millennials (https://artplusmarketing.com/how-to-market-to-millennials-5-brands-who-are-doing-it-right-9273d35b43cf).

Many products and services lend themselves to a monthly subscription model. Think about how you might customize a subscription offering for your target audience.

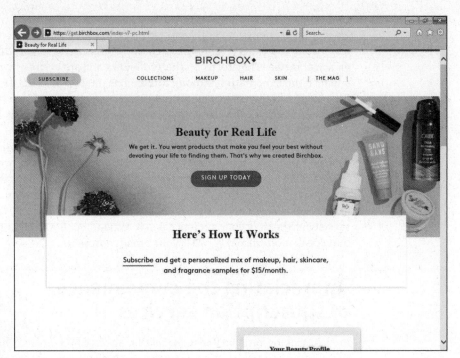

FIGURE 17-4:
Birchbox
subscription
service
home page.

Chapter **18**

Accounting for the Influencers

I n Chapter 1, we briefly introduce the social influencers and how they affect pur-chasing decisions. In this chapter, we discuss social influencers in greater detail and explain why they matter, how you can reach them, and what best practices to deploy in the process of doing so. We focus on the social influencers who reside within your customer's networks and how you can account for them in all your marketing efforts.

How influencers are defined is a controversial subject among marketers. Some marketers focus on what they consider to be key influencers, whereas others place more emphasis on everyday influencers. Back in Chapter 1, we introduce the three types of social influencers, which we believe accounts for all the types of influence taking place around a customer. Here's a quick recap:

- » **Expert influencers** are considered authorities in the specific domain or are people whom others depend upon for information advice. They do a lot to build awareness and affect purchasing decisions at the consideration stage. One example of an expert influencer is a subject-matter expert.

- » **Referent influencers** are in a friend's social network, but they may not be tightly connected with the user. One example of referent influencers are your work colleagues.

>> **Positional influencers** are that inner circle around the user; often they have to live with the choices of the purchasing decision. One example of positional influencers are your family members.

The next sections delve into the social influencer categories, starting with the expert influencers.

Knowing the Expert Influencers

The *Word of Mouth Marketing Influencer Guidebook* explained that you need to account for five types of influencers. When you think of expert influencers, be sure to cover these five types:

>> **Professional/occupational influencers:** People in formal positions of authority

>> **Citizens:** Everyday individuals who are recognized as having influence based on their social network

>> **Ambassadors:** Individuals who may be paid by the brand or are in a mutually beneficial relationship with the brand

>> **Celebrity Influencers:** Celebrities, artists, musicians, and so on

>> **Advocates:** Socially connected individuals (neighborhood leaders, members of community groups, online networks, and business networkers)

You can find out more about the Word of Mouth Marketing Association, (acquired by the Association of National Advertisers) at `https://www.ana.net/content/show/id/womma`.

As you scan the preceding list, you may be asking yourself the following questions:

>> **Are your PR people nurturing online relationships with expert influencers via all the social platforms on which they have set up presences.**

In many companies today, the PR department is part of the social media group because their functions now overlap. Your public relations people are probably concerned with these expert influencers and have already developed relationships with them. It's not enough to know what the expert influencers are doing and saying in the physical world — you need to track their activity, commentary, and points of view online. And most important, you need to build relationships with these influencers online.

>> **Is it possible to develop a relationship with expert influencers online? Will they care what you think?**

You may wonder whether you *do* even need to track their online activities. If you're a marketer in a small business or maybe chief executive officer of a small business that doesn't have a formal marketing department, you may wonder whether they will respond to your tweets, personal Facebook friend requests, and prodding emails. Those are all valid questions. Social media is now the great leveler. Social media responses are courted from anyone who may potentially influence another's purchase.

>> **Are you pursuing the wrong list of influencers?**

The final thing you may ask yourself is whether you have the right list of expert influencers. Thanks to the excesses of several mammoth corporations, we now live in an age in which trust in formal authority is at an all-time low. Consumers are increasingly distrusting big business and are turning to each other for advice. The experts that your consumers depended upon when making purchasing decisions are probably not the same experts that they are looking toward today.

What does all this mean? Quite simply, it means that you must begin by analyzing who are the expert influencers affecting brand affinity and purchasing decisions for your target markets.

In the final analysis, you need to know the following:

>> Who these expert influencers are

>> Where they are active online

RECOGNIZING THE IMPORTANCE OF INFLUENCE

Can influence really be that important? Most studies say yes. Research studying the influence of people who regularly review products was done by University of Rhode Island business professor Kathleen Ferris-Costa (Marketing Professor at Bridgewater State University). She found that these reviewers were 50 percent more likely to influence purchases.

How about social networks? Are people on these networks really influenced? Google did a study in 2018 that found influencer marketing was considered effective by 92 percent of the participants. That's evidence of real influence.

>> Whether it is feasible to develop a relationship with them on the social platforms in which they are participating

>> How much influence they actually have

REMEMBER

In larger organizations, other departments within your company may already have relationships with the expert influencers that they have nurtured over a long period of time. That's a good thing. Find out whether existing relationships are in place before knocking on the doors of the expert influencers. They certainly don't want to be harassed by multiple people from one company.

Reaching the Expert Influencers

Different strategies exist for reaching and activating the expert influencers. How you reach them varies based on who they are, what you want them to accomplish, and where you think you have the best chance of establishing a relationship with them.

You may want to consider the following tactics:

>> **Introduce yourself to them at conferences.**

Most people at business conferences respond to a face-to-face introduction. Make use of that but beware of seeming too intrusive.

>> **Reply to their tweets.**

Responses to a tweet are expected. Just don't assume too much, too soon.

>> **Comment on their blog posts.**

A thoughtful reply to a post may get you more positive attention than you expect.

>> **Friend them on LinkedIn.**

You may not get a response if you have a personal profile page, but you may at least get on their radar screen.

The good news is that influencers like to influence, and as long as you have a promising value proposition, they will at the very least listen to you.

Keep in mind that nurturing expert influencers is an investment in the long term, and you may not always get the response you want from them immediately. Also remember that influencers draw their strength and importance from being unbiased, independent, and credible. Don't ask them to compromise that position.

TIP

Expert influencers like to be in the know. Provide them with exclusive sneak peeks, and they'll be grateful for the opportunity to see and talk about your product before anyone else does. You can use that access to information to deepen your relationship with them.

Reaching the expert influencers may be easy depending upon your industry, the size of your business, and the product you are selling. But for other marketers, that may not be the case. For example, if you're a marketer for a small business, reaching expert influencers is going to be harder because these people may not be high profile or visible. You'll have to really seek them out. Here are some tips for reaching expert influencers:

» **Ask your customers who they seek out for advice.**

Very little in marketing beats firsthand customer research, and the same applies to social influence marketing. You can identify and reach the expert influencers by asking your consumers who they are and where they spend their time.

» **Pay attention to the media.**

Keep an eye out for the experts who are quoted frequently by the media when your product or category is discussed. Also keep an eye out for who appears on television. Make a list of these experts and use that list as a basis to research their influence.

» **Look at your competitive environment.**

Your competitors, suppliers, and business partners probably seek out the experts just as you do. In many cases, these experts sit on the advisory boards of other companies that operate in your space. Understand who these people are. A lot of that information is freely available online.

» **Attend conferences and exhibitions.**

The expert influencers are often called upon to give keynote addresses to industry conferences, lead seminars, and pass judgment on new products and services at exhibitions. Pay attention to these people at those events.

» **Seek out the industry analysts.**

The analysts often have an outsized influence on customers in your product category. Their influence increases dramatically in the business-to-business space, where customers depend upon them for advice when making large-scale purchasing decisions. Pay attention to them and to what they have to say.

» **Evaluate their online footprint.**

Use professional tools for rankings, such as Buzzsumo as shown in Figure 18-1 (http://app.buzzsumo.com/influencers), which lets you find influencers by keywords and hashtags. Two other good tools to find influencers is TweetDeck (`http://www.tweetdeck.com`), which helps you discover influencers by topic, and Followerwonk (`https://followerwonk.com/`), which lets you search influencers by number of followers.

>> **Become an influencer yourself.**

Sometimes there's no better way to influence than to become an influencer yourself. Seek out leadership positions in your community and in your industry by joining trade groups and industry associations. Make it a goal to speak at conferences in your field. Using these tactics, you'll become an influencer and will get access to other influencers.

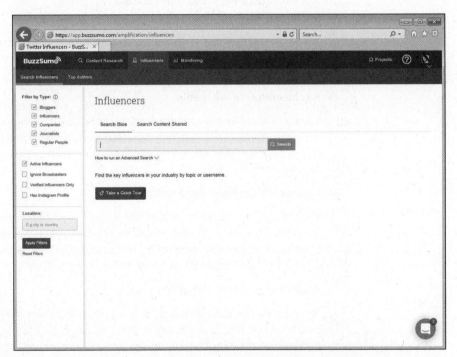

FIGURE 18-1:
Buzzsumo influencer search page.

Tapping into the Referent Influencers

Consumers connect with their friends and make their social networks available through social media platforms. These people are referent influencers — people in your friendship circle, such as your high school friends or people you've become friendly with at work. You may be close to only a few of them, but you probably observe the activities of them all on your favorite social platforms.

The holy grail of social influence marketing is the ability to identify which referent influencers are most powerful and have the highest impact on brand affinity and purchasing decisions. After you've identified them, the next question is, how does a marketer reach these referent influencers who surround their customers? They matter because it has been statistically proven that networked neighbors (or those consumers linked to prior customers) adopt the service or product at rates three to five times greater than baseline groups. The research shows that these network neighbors impact purchasing decisions very directly, too.

The referent influencers themselves break down into two categories, which we cover next, and differentiating between the two is important.

Anonymous referent influencers

These are everyday people who are extremely active on the social platforms and blog, upload, comment, rate, and share much more than other consumers who share their same demographics. By virtue of the volume of their activity on the various social platforms, the anonymous referent influencers carry weight. Your customers probably don't think of them as experts, but they do notice what these people are doing online.

Known referent influencers

These are the everyday people who reside specifically within the social networks of your customers and are known to your customer. The best way to think about this group is to consider your high school class. Of the approximately 300 kids who may have been in the class, there were probably 10 or 15 who everyone else looked up to and followed. These are the cool kids whom everyone wanted to be like. These are the referent influencers.

Reaching the Referent Influencers

Marketing to the referent influencers is all about knowing who they are, the weight they carry, whether they reside within your customer's social graph, and how to reach and activate them to influence your customer. In the next sections, we discuss how companies help you reach the referent influencers.

TIP

Not all tactics for reaching referent influencers need to be paid for. Your company's Facebook page can be a place to build a community and encourage referent influencers to influence your customers by incentivizing them with competitions, coupons, and special offers. Your customers who like your Facebook page will probably bring their referent influencers to the page, too, if you give them incentives to do so.

You may want to consider using Facebook's Custom Audience tool that allows you to upload your own company's email list. When you create your next ad, Facebook matches the emails on that list and makes sure that audience sees the ad.

Cookie data

Many technology companies analyze cookie data to infer the relationships between people and target similar advertising to them both. If one set of users responds well to the advertisements, companies then present the same advertisements to other similar people or to the friends of the original group in similar social networks, conversations, or websites. This strategy allows a company's advertising to reach anonymous referent influencers.

Keep in mind that this strategy applies to you only if you have an advertising budget and are advertising online. Otherwise, you won't be able to take advantage of the cookie data. Two companies that focus on this method are 33Across (www.33across.com) and dstillery (https://dstillery.com/).

Website behavior

You can do a lot on your website to allow for the referent influencers to converge and positively influence each other. From the most basic of solutions, such as implementing customer reviews, to creating discussion forums in which customers can talk about issues of concern, your website can be a destination where people congregate and talk to each other.

After you've identified these referent influencers, be sure to give them the best possible service if they're customers. Not only will you increase the sales from them, but you'll also increase sales among the people that they influence directly. As a *Huffington Post* article pointed out (https://www.huffpost.com/entry/6-examples-of-influencer-marketing-done-right_b_59eef009e4b06bbede69b380), American Express gives its influencers (whom American Express identifies by how much they spend) a distinct credit card with special benefits that include a concierge service and first-class upgrades.

Use your referent influencers to improve your products and services, too. They're typically people who have strong opinions, care about the products, and want to impact product design. Ask their opinions — or at the very least, share new products with them — before you do so with anyone else. Similarly, also consider giving them special discounts and coupons and cultivate their loyalty by marketing to them with additional care.

Tapping into the Positional Influencers

The final category of influencers to cover in this chapter are the positional influencers. These are the people who are closest to your customers and influence them the most at the point of purchase. Because they are the people who have to live with the purchasing decision, they are the most vested in it. But they're not celebrities, so they're not always noticeable and can be the hardest to find. They're important, but marketing to them can be similarly difficult.

What makes tapping into the positional influencers harder still is the fact that how big a role they play in a purchasing decision varies dramatically by the purchase. For example, if you were to buy a desk for your home, your spouse or significant other (arguably the most important positional influencer in your life) would have a huge impact on the purchasing decision. That person's opinion would heavily influence where you shop and what you choose. On the other hand, if you were purchasing a laptop for professional use, that person would play a much smaller role in the purchasing decision. This is because the choice doesn't impact that person significantly and the product isn't of interest to him or her even though it's a high-consideration purchase.

Without a doubt, positional influencers are important. Identifying them can be challenging, as can developing an understanding of the weight they may carry.

Separating the referent influencers from the positional influencers can be hard sometimes, especially when you're marketing on a social platform. In those cases, separating these two types of influencers doesn't matter as much. What matters is to give your customers incentives to bring their influencers to you so that you can market to them as well. Focus on getting your customers' influencers, and the right influencers will be influenced, and then they'll do the influencing for you!

The following sections cover tips to allow for positional influencers to play the role they normally do best.

Understanding the circles of influence around your customers

It is important to understand who will be most impacted by the purchasing decisions of your customers. That alone will tell you who the positional influencers are and how important their influence is. For example, with first-time car purchases, family members are very important positional influencers because they'll be riding in the car and, in some cases, driving it.

Letting consumers shape and share the experience

Reaching positional influencers may be hard, but your customers will reach them for you. Make sure that your e-commerce website or even your campaign-centric microsite allows for the sharing of content and posting to Facebook and other social platforms. Let the consumers shape and share the experiences in any format that they want. Make it easy for customers to pluck information from your website, such as product sheets and e-books, and carry that information elsewhere and to their positional influencers.

Articulating your product benefits for multiple audiences

You probably always assume that you're selling a product to your target customer, ignoring the fact that social influencers play a big role in the purchasing decision. If you know who the influencers are, articulate your product benefits so that they resonate with the influencers.

TIP

Regarding the example of purchasing a car: If you're selling a car to a college student demographic, tout the safety benefits, because the students' parents will most probably be involved in the purchasing decision. Don't ignore them.

Fishing where the fish are

Marketing to your customers where they spend their time online is a cliché in social media marketing, but the point holds strongest in the context of positional influencers. Because these influencers are the hardest to find yourself, you need to make sure that you're marketing and selling your products where these positional influencers probably influence your customers. So it goes without saying that you need to have a deep presence on all the social platforms where your customers and their influencers are congregating.

But locating your positional influencers also means that you need to design your website or your presence on the social platforms to encourage your customers to reach out to those influencers. You need to include the built-in share functionality that most blog platforms have — that is, functionality that lets users take product information from your blog and socialize it with their influencers. You can allow users to share your blog info as shown in Figure 18-2.

Share link

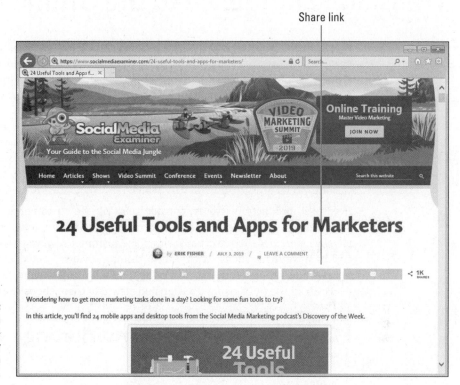

FIGURE 18-2: Social media share functionality in use on a blog.

Offering friends and family incentives

When talking about social influencers and the role they play in brand affinity and purchasing decisions, you can easily forget that many marketers have been practicing these concepts in the physical world for decades. One of the most popular examples of reaching out to social influencers is in the form of "friends and family" incentives. For example, AT&T has a special family plan for its mobile phone service. If your whole family uses the service, you get discounts on the monthly plan.

TIP

The best way to engage the positional influencers around your customers is to have your customers engage them for you. You get them to engage the positional influencers by giving them incentives to do so or by converting the purchasing decision into a group decision.

Translating Influence to the Offline World

For all the discussions about social influencers, we would be remiss if we didn't discuss how the concept of influencers ties into having influence in the offline space. The online world is not separate from how influence works in the real world. The following sections include recommendations for how you can tap into social influencers to affect physical-world purchasing decisions.

Putting your customer reviews in your stores

If you sell products in stores, consider putting the customer reviews that have been created by customers on your website next to the actual products in the physical stores. If there isn't space to place customer reviews, at least include the customer ratings. Along with the customer reviews, consider adding expert reviews and ratings. Reviews and ratings do a lot to give your customers confidence about the purchasing decision and also help them choose between products.

Marrying social media marketing with events and PR

TIP

Here's a tip about social media marketing that's worth paying a lot of attention to: Marketers who tie together social media marketing initiatives with traditional events and surround them with PR tactics invariably have immense success. When you're trying to tap into social influencers, consider organizing an event that your customers can bring their social influencers to. Promote the event heavily on the social platforms, and use your presence on those platforms as a way to manage invitation lists and reminders and to post event communications.

For example, send invitations through Facebook, and encourage your potential customers to RSVP through Facebook itself. You can also create a special hash tag (#) for your event so that when you're tweeting about your event, others will see it. It helps generate buzz for your company and encourages people to attend future events. In addition, you can use Facebook Live (`https://www.facebook.com/facebookmedia/solutions/facebook-live`; see Figure 18-3), which is a live video on Facebook, before the event to create excitement and momentum. Another possibility is to hold a live Twitter Chat or Instagram pics.

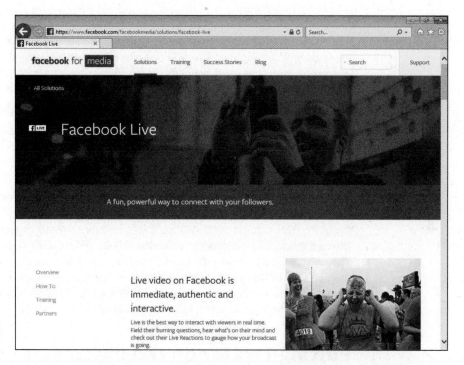

FIGURE 18-3:
The Facebook
Live home page.

Measuring online buzz and offline influence

There's a very direct relationship between online buzz and offline influence. What is talked about on the social platforms often gets translated to real-world conversations when people interact with each other at work, in the shopping malls, and at home. Consider tracking how your social media marketing activities translate into offline influence. How? By using surveys to track conversations about your brand before, during, and after a social media marketing campaign. If you're a large brand, you may want to use a market research firm to help you understand the ongoing buzz about your brand in the physical world.

If you're a smaller brand, you can check out Chapter 30 for tools you can use.

Connecting influencers at meet-ups

We've talked about marrying events with social media marketing so that your potential customers expose their influencers to your brand, too. You may want to run specific programs just for the influencers who play a significant role in impacting brand and purchasing decisions in your category. Whether they be expert, referent, or positional influencers, you may want to consider organizing programs that address them directly.

Some of these can be real-world events, too. Insurance companies put a lot of effort into developing relationships with parents of new drivers because they know they heavily impact the first car purchase. And because parents are always concerned about the well-being of their children, they're more likely to push for better auto insurance. One service that you can use to create those events is Meetup (`www.meetup.com`), which enables companies to connect with local communities around their products or categories.

Treating your stores as cafés

Bookstores such as Barnes & Noble have blurred the lines between their physical stores and their online storefront. You can buy books online and return them in the store. You can get notifications about in-store events in your neighborhood through email, and customers can look up books online while they're in the stores. They also organize readings and book clubs and encourage customers to bring their friends to them and promote the events online, too. Online or offline, these bookstores don't care: They encourage deeper interaction and encourage customers to bring their social influencers with them at every stage.

Putting Twitter on the big screen

Twitter is the twelfth online social media site in 2019 ranked by number of users (`https://www.statista.com/statistics/272014/global-social-networks-ranked-by-number-of-users/`).

The follow-follower dynamic and the 280-character limit lend themselves to frequent, short bursts of communication. Consider promoting your Twitter account in your physical stores. Or better still, have you considered having a live Twitter stream on a screen in each of your stores to show customers how you're answering the queries of others, responding to problems, promoting specific products, and deepening relationships with your community? Call it the Twitter influence, but the way in which you're interacting with your other customers on the social platforms can strongly influence a customer to purchase from you as well. Don't miss that opportunity.

TIP

One great tool that you can use to accomplish an impressive display of posts is Tint by Filestack (`http://www.tintup.com`). You choose what to display — for example brand posts or a specific hashtag, and let it run. This tool is great for events to encourage attendees to spread the word.

» Creating content to capture attention

» Preparing your content for voice search

Chapter **19**

Disrupting with Voice Search

D o you remember a time when using your mobile device to type search terms seemed like a novelty? That's where we are now with voice search. Currently, you probably think about voice search being mostly confined to voice commands for Siri (iPhone) or other smartphones, or Alexa (Amazon) Echo or another voice assistant (also called smart speaker). However, voice search is coming to your online business and you need to be ready.

In this chapter, we look at what you should know about the coming transition to voice searching and what you need to do to be prepared.

TIP

This chapter covers voice applications using speech. To learn more about messaging applications and chatbots where users type their queries, see Chapter 20.

Understanding Voice Search

If you're wondering why voice search is gaining in popularity so rapidly, the answer is simple. People are finding smart speakers such as Google Home in their Christmas stockings and are getting used to telling these devices to carry out daily commands. In fact, in 2018, Adobe reported that people who owned smart speakers were planning to purchase another one for themselves during the holiday season.

Also, Siri, your Apple iPhone voice assistant is ready for your commands right out of the box. You can book flights, order flowers, or make hands-free calls from the car, without a learning curve.

Benefitting from voice searches

When you undertake the effort to optimize for voice search, you and your management need to be confident that implementing it will have a positive effect on your business. Here are some benefits that you can expect. Voice search:

>> **Makes your company more competitive:** It's still early, so getting a jump on it will help you stand out.

>> **Improves the customer relationship and reduces churn:** Making it convenient for the customers to get answers will create more loyal customers.

>> **Gets traffic to company sites:** If you include links to your sites in your voice searches, you make it very easy for traffic to come to you.

TIP

Emarketer estimates that currently, 111.8 million people in the United States use a voice assistant monthly, which is up 9.5 percent from 2018. Don't wait to plan your voice search strategy. Your competitors are already looking into it.

Reviewing smart speakers

Take a look at the current line of devices that you can choose from. According to voicebot.ai (https://voicebot.ai/2018/03/08/amazon-echo-maintains-large-market-share-lead-u-s-smart-speaker-user-base/), the market share of the most popular home devices are:

>> Amazon Alexa: 71.9 percent

>> Google: 18.4 percent

>> Other: 9.7 percent

So, who owns a smart speaker? According to voicebot.ai, in 2019 here is the age distribution of smart speaker owners:

- » 34.1 percent are under 30.

- » 29 percent are ages 30–44.

- » 26.2 percent are ages 45–60.

- » 20.1 percent are over 60 years old.

Interestingly, the research found that once someone owns a smart speaker, there is no difference in usage patterns. Everyone seems to use them at about the same rate. They become part of your daily routine.

Interacting with Voice Assistants

As a marketer, you want to know how people are currently using voice assistants so that you can provide the right content. According to information collected in an infographic from Visual Capitalist (`https://www.visualcapitalist.com/smart-speaker-market-share-fight/` called "the Fight for Smart Speaker Market Share":

- » 84 percent are asking questions

- » 83 percent are streaming music

- » 80 percent are checking weather

- » 62 percent are setting alarms/timers

- » 55 percent are listening to the radio

PRIVACY FEARS ABOUT VOICE ASSISTANTS

According to a study by Microsoft, 41 percent of current smart speaker users have concerns about trust and privacy. In 2019 Bloomberg reported that Amazon staffers listened to Echo audio clips to help improve the response to commands. Several users were alarmed at the notion that others were listening to their conversations. It was also revealed that Apple listens to Siri clips, and Google does the same. Amazon and the other companies responded by saying that employees don't have information that can identify the person. It's up to you as to whether this concerns you enough to eliminate the device from your home.

TIP

As you can see, asking questions plays a big part in the current use of smart speakers. Knowing this gives you the opportunity to create content for voice search that answers questions you know your customers ask.

Discovering What Customers Want

When you're preparing your online content for voice search, you need to be aware of the kinds of things that people will ask. According to a 2017 Google study, "Voice Activated Speakers: People's Lives are Changing," here's the content that people want to be able to get from companies via voice search:

>> 52 percent want deals, sales, and promos.

>> 48 percent want personalized tips and information to make life easier.

>> 42 percent want information about upcoming events or activities.

>> 39 percent want business information such as store hours.

>> 38 percent want access to customer service or support.

These tasks give you a solid understanding about the kinds of questions users will ask their smart speakers as voice search expands. You'll note that this is the same kind of content you expect them to want when text searching for information about your company. The key is to structure it for voice searching.

TIP

To accommodate voice search, you need to prepare your content. To learn how to prepare your content, see the section, "Getting Your Content Ready."

Providing Answers

Most marketers are always looking for ways to provide their prospects and customers the information that makes it easy to buy and use their products. There are currently things you can do to capture the attention of voice searchers. We look at two: flash briefings and actions.

TIP

Although these voice assistants don't allow marketers to advertise, they do allow companies to create content that can provide their audience with helpful information or a way to place orders.

Creating flash briefings and Actions

It's still early days, but brands are starting to catch on to the idea of creating marketing apps for smart speakers as a way to easily connect with their audience. These apps come in the form of *flash briefings* for Alexa and the equivalent *Actions* for Google Assistant. These apps take the form of short audio commands such as "Alexa ask Grubhub to order food" or messages that users can hear by asking their device to connect them to a company. For example, a local business can set up a way for people to hear about their spa treatments.

These promotions can be placed in your emails, on home pages, or even in YouTube videos. For example, when presenting a new product in an email you could have a line of copy that says, "Hey Google, talk to <brand name>." or "Alexa, tell me about <brand name>." When they do that, they hear more about the product and can ask additional questions in a conversational way. There is less competition for voice searches right now, so if you have an excellent idea for an app, you might want to explore this option further.

Looking at brand examples

Some brands have created flash briefings or Actions to promote their brand without explicitly advertising. These are apps that when invoked, provide information, tips, and other messages.

For example, Unilever has created a recipe app called Best Recipes for Hellman's Mayonnaise (`https://www.amazon.com/Unilever-Best-Recipes/dp/B01MRISWRV/ref=sr_1_5?keywords=recipes&qid=1569528182&s=digital-skills&sr=1-5`), as shown in Figure 19-1.

REMEMBER MY NAME?

Companies are starting to experiment with ways to get their products in front of voice searchers when they don't specifically ask for a brand name. *The Wall Street Journal* (`https://www.wsj.com/articles/big-consumer-brands-dont-have-an-answer-for-alexa-1519727401`) reports on this problem that affects smaller or less well-known companies. If users ask Alexa to put tissues on their shopping list, they are given one or two choices. That's great for Kleenex, who is likely at the top of the list, but bad for a smaller brand. If users searched Amazon directly on screen, they would see a multitude of brands and price choices.

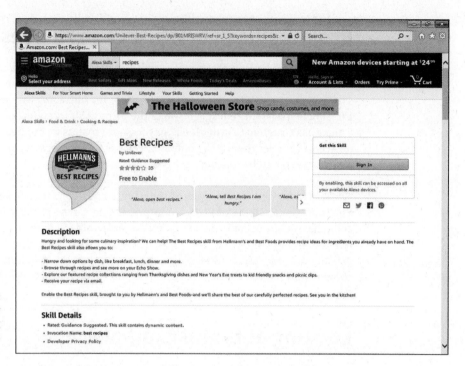

FIGURE 19-1:
The Unilever
flash briefing
for Hellman's
Mayonnaise.

To invoke it, you say, "Alexa open best recipes." When you do, you get recipes that don't all feature mayonnaise, so it's useful to a variety of customers. The key is it still keeps the name Hellman's Mayonnaise in the forefront.

Cosmetics company Estee Lauder has also created an app on Google Home that provides information on beauty, makeup, and other topics, as shown in Figure 19-2.

To invoke it you say, "Hey Google Ask Liv at Estee Lauder about <topic>." These messages include skincare, nutrition, and sleep tips. (https://assistant.google.com/services/a/uid/00000072e8771a94?hl=en-US).

Developing your apps

If you want to create these apps for voice assistants, you can check out:

>> Flash Briefings on Alexa: (https://developer.amazon.com/en-US/alexa/alexa-skills-kit/learn?sc_category=paid&sc_channel=SEM&sc_campaign=SEM-GO^Brand^All^LD^Professional_Developer^Evergreen^US^Eng1) as shown in Figure 19-3.

>> Google Home, check out Actions on Google Assistant: (https://developers.google.com/actions/), as shown in Figure 19-4.

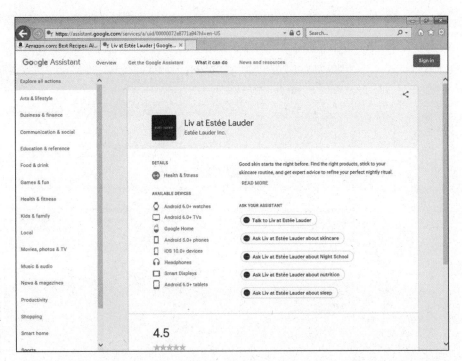

FIGURE 19-2:
The Estee Lauder
Google Action
for Ask Liv.

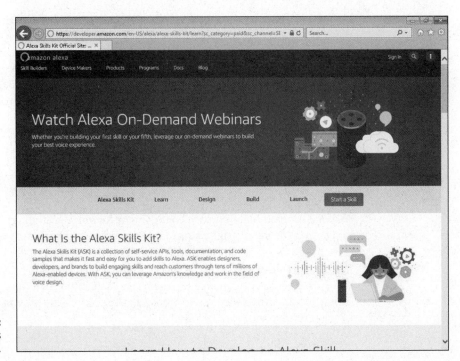

FIGURE 19-3:
Flash Briefings
instructions.

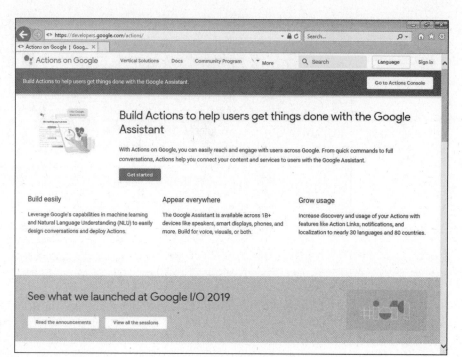

FIGURE 19-4:
Google Action
instructions.

TIP

If you're interested in seeing what other marketers are doing with flash briefings, check out Marketing School with Neil Patel and Eric Siu (https://www.amazon.com/Single-Grain-Marketing-School/dp/B0713YTNYG/ref=sr_1_1?keywords=marketing&qid=1569527852&s=digital-skills&sr=1-1) or the Unofficial Gary Vee Flash Briefing (https://www.amazon.com/Unofficial-Gary-Vee-Flash-Briefing/dp/B01MZFKEW3/ref=sr_1_4?keywords=gary+vee&qid=1569528036&s=digital-skills&sr=1-4).

Getting Your Content Ready

So, what can you do to prepare your content for voice searching? There are a few things that you can do right now to make a difference going forward:

>> **Prepare answers:** Learn the specific questions asked by your customers and provide answers to them. Keep them short and to the point. Then make sure to test and refine them, so your answers are succinct and provide the specific information they are looking for.

REMEMBER

Voice searches are typically longer than text searches. People use conversational language that includes lots of filler words. Make sure to account for the fact that they will use more than just keywords and phrases.

>> **Improve site performance:** Customers won't wait around for your page to load. Whether they are on a mobile device or voice assistant, make sure that your content loads in 4.6 seconds or faster.

>> **Accommodate user intent:** Make sure you prepare content for phrases that have buying words in them such as "how much" or "what is the cost?" These indicate the user intent to consider buying, and you want to help them do that.

>> **Be aware of the buyer's journey for mobile as well as smart speakers:** Just like with regular SEO content, make sure to have voice searches mobile-ready for each stage of the buyer's journey. Your users are already doing this. Helping them get all the information they need to buy from any channel on any device is still the name of the game.

Chapter **20**

Utilizing Messaging Apps

As a communications technology, online messaging is overtaking social media as the preferred way of connecting with brands. One reason for this is that messaging is a private targeted communication between a customer and the brand with no interference — and it's immediate. People also embrace messaging as a better way to communicate with friends and family. In fact, over 87 percent of the worldwide Internet population uses a chat or messaging app (Global Web Index Messaging App Report 2018).

In this chapter, we look at two major messaging platforms: Facebook Messenger (Messenger) and WhatsApp from Facebook. We also see how your business can use chatbots to increase your reach, provide better customer service, and engage customers.

Looking at Messenger

In this frenetic Internet environment where developing customer relationships is crucial, direct messaging is a welcome addition. It's like email only better because it's faster and as of this writing, it's still somewhat of a novelty. Users find it intriguing. According to Hootsuite in 2018, 98 percent of mobile messages are read, and 90 percent get opened within three seconds of being delivered.

Reviewing benefits for brands

So, why are messaging apps good for brands? There are several reasons that brands benefit from using messaging apps:

» Companies can develop a closer relationship with customers when they can chat with them directly.

» Companies can supply the correct information right at the point when their customers want it.

» Customers can buy directly from the app (if they choose) so there's no 'friction' or impediment to buying.

» Companies can gather customer feedback in a secure format.

» Companies gain another channel from which to communicate and can reach customers who don't open their emails.

Don't be reluctant to try messaging. Customers are more willing to authentically communicate because they rightly believe that their messaging content is more secure (better encryption).

Learning what users want when messaging brands

To create an effective marketing messaging strategy, let's look at what users of messaging apps want from companies. According to the Global Web Index Messaging App Report 2018, some of the reasons consumers want to message with brands include what we call the five Cs:

» **Community:** They want brands to connect them with others in the community.

To consider: With community in mind, don't overlook the opportunity to develop a community forum or to establish a group on Facebook to let fans interact with one another. Users want to communicate with you privately, but they also like the idea of meeting and sharing with like-minded people. You will also get the benefit of social proof — other people vouching for your product or service.

» **Contribution:** They want to contribute ideas for products and features to the brand.

To consider: Customers (especially Millennials) have given thought and attention to how your products fulfill their needs. They're eager to let you know what they have concluded and how they can improve your product. Create a way to collect their ideas so that they feel heard. Also, make sure that they can see that you value these ideas, or they will feel disconnected from you. Don't let them feel like they have wasted their time.

» **Customization:** They want to customize/personalize products.

To consider: You know that personalization and customization are potent forces. You can develop a better relationship with your customers if you make them feel part of the product by helping them customize it. This will go a long way toward developing brand advocates.

» **Content:** They want brands to provide them with entertaining and informative content.

To consider: This is an obvious one. Entertain them, and they will come back for more. Check analytics data frequently to see what content is resonating with your audience. Also, consider the type of questions they may have and be ready to supply the answers.

» **Coolness:** They want to feel "cool/trendy" by conducting one-to-one conversations with the brand.

To consider: Don't discount the "coolness" factor. People are more likely to share information about the products with their friends when they can show they have a "special" relationship with the brand. They are able to articulate the benefits of your product in a way tha's compelling and authentic.

REMEMBER

Customers want the personalized attention that messaging apps offer so that they can become part of your cohesive community of fans. However, it's critical that you're authentically interested in them. If you're feigning interest as a marketing ploy forget it, you will do more harm than good.

AN ALTERNATIVE TO WhatsApp AND MESSENGER

If your primary customers are located in Indonesia, Thailand, Taiwan, and Japan, you may want to consider using Line. It's a freeware app for messaging on mobile devices and desktops and has similar features to WhatsApp and Facebook Messenger. You can send texts, images, video, and audio, and hold free VoIP calls and video conferences.

Line was launched in Japan in 2011 and is owned by the subsidiary of a company in South Korea called Naver Corporation. In 2019, it had 600 million registered users and 165 million are monthly active users. It's currently Japan's largest social network. You can find the downloads for Line at https://line.me/en-US/download.

Setting Up Messenger

Enabling Messenger on your Facebook page so that you can receive communications from others is quick and easy, as shown in Figure 20-1.

General to Messages   Settings

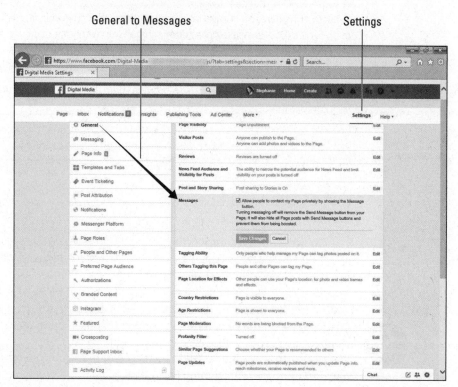

FIGURE 20-1:
Enabling
Messenger.

Do the following:

1. **From your Facebook Page, click Settings at the top right.**

2. **Choose General from the list of links on the left.**

3. **Click the Edit link next to the word Messages.**

4. **Select the Allow People to Contact My Page Privately by Showing the Message button box.**

5. **Click Save Changes.**

Now you've enabled Messenger, and you're ready to start receiving communications from your customers on Facebook. Be sure to review the Messenger marketing guidelines, so you don't violate the rules.

If you're new to messaging on Facebook, you need to know that as a company, you cannot send a direct one-to-one message to a customer if they haven't first started a conversation with you. They need to reach out to you. Once they have communicated with you, you're free to respond.

Also, even if they have communicated with you, you can't download their email address or send them messages if their Facebook page is set to private. This ensures that, as a brand, you don't violate their privacy or spam them.

Did you know that according to Facebook data, people exchanged over one billion messages with businesses every month using FB Messenger? Perhaps it's time to join the action if you haven't already done so.

Understanding Chatbots

One of the best technologies to come out of the use of messaging apps is the development of chatbots. Chatbots are pieces of code that automatically respond to queries in a natural way. They vary in complexity from extremely simple to using artificial intelligence (AI).

Chatbots are gaining in popularity because they can be used in several different ways. Consider using them to provide tech support, make product recommendations, schedule meetings, and generate leads, among other things.

In its most advanced form, when a customer asks the chatbot a question, it replies in a conversational way as though a human was at the other end of the chat. Chatbots are becoming relatively easy to create, but key to its success is determining the best type for the job you need to do. We look at three types in the next section.

Classifying chatbots

As you can imagine, new technologies like chatbots spur different conversations about classification. The industry designates chatbot types in various ways ranging from identifying them as either tied to a platform like Facebook Messenger, standalone like Slack, or scripted versus transactional. I (Stephanie) like the designation used by *Chatbots Magazine* that classifies them as the following three types (https://chatbotsmagazine.com/the-3-types-of-chatbots-how-to-determine-the-right-one-for-your-needs-a4df8c69ec4c):

>> **Menu or button chatbots:** These are the simplest form and are like the phone decision trees we use (for example, "Press one if you want support.").

These are the least complex group because their content is limited. However, if you have simple information to depart, this works well.

>> **Keyword chatbots:** These bots "pick out" the keywords that are presented to them by the user and supply answers related to those keywords. These bots can handle more complex queries but are limited by their knowledge of the keywords used. If your content is straightforward and doesn't have very technical terms that can be used in several ways, this type can work for you.

>> **Contextual chatbots:** These chatbots are the ones users find most satisfying when they need complex answers. They use artificial intelligence (AI) and machine learning (ML) to "learn" about the content and get more informed as they mature.

Within these categories, you can find chatbots that provide a multitude of different services. In the next section, you look at companies that are using chatbots successfully. Perhaps they'll give you ideas about how you can maximize your use of them for your customers.

Dipping into chatbots

Chatbots are very versatile, and depending on what you need to do, you can either find an already created one that will do the job or create one yourself. To see how other companies are using chatbots, here are three different ways that companies use them.

>> **To get information:** Staples (http://www.staples.com), an office supply store, deploys a Messenger chatbot that answers questions about its products as shown in Figure 20-2.

>> **To book an appointment:** Sephora, a cosmetics store, uses a Messenger chatbot (https://www.facebook.com/sephora/?epa=SEARCH_BOX) to set up appointments for makeovers at its stores as shown in Figure 20-3.

>> **To chat with insomniacs:** Casper, a mattress company, uses a standalone chatbot (http://insomnobot3000.com/) as shown in Figure 20-4. The implication they probably want you to draw from using this chatbot is that if you are still awake, you don't own a Casper mattress.

You can see that each branded chatbot is designed to engage the customer and encourage them to buy from the brand. The key is that when customers have the right information at the right time, they're motivated to buy.

FIGURE 20-2:
Staples chatbot.

Ask questions

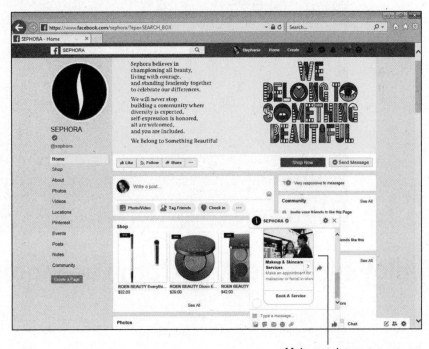

FIGURE 20-3:
Sephora
appointment
bot.

Make appointment

Chatting with Insomnobot 3000

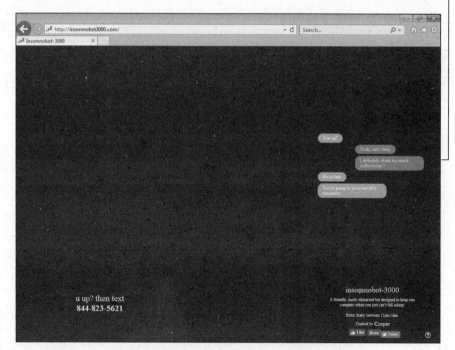

FIGURE 20-4:
Casper's
Insomnobot3000.

Deploying WhatsApp from Facebook

As of 2019, WhatsApp has over 1.5 billion users worldwide, so it's worth a look. Here are several things you should know:

REMEMBER

>> **Mobile:** WhatsApp was created for mobile. To get started with WhatsApp you need to install it on your mobile phone (iPhone and Android) so that it's connected to a single phone number and country. After you've done that, you can also use it as a web app and on Macs and PCs.

Because WhatsApp is tied to a single phone number, it's hard to hide behind a fake identity.

>> **Limited:** You can only message those in your phone contacts who have downloaded WhatsApp. (In Messenger you can message anyone who downloads the app.)

>> **Free:** It's a mobile app that provides Voice over Internet Protocol (VOIP) calling. When you use VOIP, it means you don't incur short message service (SMS) text charges.

>> **Content:** The app handles all types of content. You can send free text messages, voice messages, voice calls, video calls, photos, videos, images, docs, emojis, and PDFs. (There is a ten-photo limit for WhatsApp but not on Messenger.)

>> **Global:** The main reason that WhatsApp adoption was so quick was that it's free and works well across countries and devices. For this reason, it's very popular with international audiences. If you target global markets, you'll want to consider using it.

Communicating with users

As you decide what marketing content you will send, there are three communication types you can deploy:

>> **Personal one-to-one chat:** You can message (or video call) directly with a customer. (You can also delete sent messages if you've made a mistake in the message.)

>> **Broadcast to many:** You can send the equivalent of an email that reaches several users at once. They can only message back to you and not to each other like in a group message.

>> **Groups:** You can create a group(s) of up to 256 users, and they can communicate with each other as well as with you.

Creating mobile messages with WhatsApp

As with chatbots, the objective of using messaging is to help the user ask questions and develop a relationship with the brand. Mobile messages are no different. You have to decide what you're trying to accomplish and how sending a marketing message via a mobile device makes it more appealing to the customer.

Using the WhatsApp Business App

Because of the demand, Facebook created a free business app called WhatsApp Business so that you can keep your business and personal accounts separate. They say it was specifically built for the small business owner to automate, sort, and answer customer messages. There are built-in statistics that allow you to see how many messages were sent, who read, who answered, and so on.

TIP

You can download it to your iPhone or Android from `https://www.whatsapp.com/business/`.

Here's what you need to know to get started after you download and confirm your phone number and country:

>> **Business Profile:** You're asked to create a business profile that includes:

- Your business name
- Business category
- Description of your business
- Business hours
- Email
- Web address

>> **Set up these options:**

- *Automated messages:* This includes a personal greeting and who receives your messages.
- *Quick replies:* Set up these messages to deal with frequently asked questions.
- *Short link:* If you have a link that you want to send your visitors to, you can include that here.
- *Labels:* You can organize your different chat categories by giving them a label (for example, new customer).

If you're a small business owner and Facebook Messenger is too big a commitment for you to manage, you may want to consider WhatsApp.

REMEMBER

If you're already using WhatsApp for personal or business communications, you need a separate phone number to use with WhatsApp for Business.

5

Old Marketing Is New Again with SMM

Get recommendations on how to retool your corporate website to develop effective social media marketing efforts.

Find out what it means to be an authentic and engaged advertiser — in other words, how to take your existing advertising efforts social and get more mileage out of them.

Learn how to tap into the mobile phone market to spread your SMM campaign.

Discover how to encourage employees to be brand advocates.

Find out how to adapt measurements to fit your campaigns.

Learn how social media can work seamlessly with other areas of your company.

Learn how to strategize in real time to reach your customers.

Know what data is at your fingertips and how to safeguard it.

Chapter **21**

Practicing SMM on Your Website

Corporate websites have gone through many changes since their introduction. When Stephanie began working at AOL in 1994, the companies she worked with to create their AOL websites were initially concerned that having a website might be too big a step, but as they watched some of their adventurous competitors do it, they started to become a bit more comfortable. Remember, there was nary a social media platform in sight at that time. Myspace didn't come into being until the early 2000s.

Companies needed websites to be all things to all people. They had multiple audiences, they sometimes needed to sell the product directly, and they had to create a timeless, stable impression. The corporate site didn't cater just to prospective customers but to existing customers, shareholders, members of the press, business partners, and suppliers as well. The site also needed to carry information and include functionality that met all their needs. What's more, the corporate website needed to reflect the company's brand; the company couldn't change its look and feel based on the whims of a specific campaign.

For this reason, the concept of microsites came to be. Companies built these mini-websites to support display ad campaigns, and the microsites were time-bound and oriented toward specific events or audiences. These events could be Christmas shopping, Father's Day, or back-to-school promotions for teenagers. Creative uses for the display ads directly reflected on the microsite, which would typically contain information about the specific offers. After all, with companies spending so much money on the display ads, they needed to drive visitors who clicked the ads to a site that extended the experience of the ad. This strategy of separating the corporate website from the microsite and treating the microsite as an extension of the display ads worked for a long time. But then the social media revolution came, and it all began to change. Now social media sites co-exist along with microsites.

Currently, savvy website owners realize that "owning" their website is a good way to protect themselves from the whims of social media platforms that could change policies on a dime. Websites have again become the hub of corporate activity. From this hub, you can do things like hold contests, acquaint customers with your local store, and provide them with the review information they need to make purchasing decisions. To make sure you understand why websites are still important in 2019, consider that websites give you control over your:

>> **Message and stories:** On your website, you can take all the time and space you need to tell your story your way. You can sprinkle your message throughout the site and emphasize your changing priorities as they develop.

>> **Website data:** You have access to all your data and you can analyze it in any way it makes sense. Of course, you want to analyze data from all the social media sites you are on. But you don't need to worry if a social platform changes its policy about access to their analytics.

>> **SEO:** By optimizing your website content for search engine optimization (SEO) you can help your customers find you.

>> **Product sales:** Selling directly from your website gives you total control over how the product is presented and received.

>> **Customer information:** Your mailing list and subsequent customer information are protected by your website controls.

In this chapter, we give you recommendations on how to retool your corporate website to allow for the most effective use of social media marketing, along with tips for integrating your corporate website to the social web in a meaningful way.

Focusing on the SMM-Integrated Website

Today's consumers are not as easily impressed as they once were. They want more than an ad campaign; they want a committed, longer-term relationship with your company to which they give their time and money. And given that you spend money advertising to your customers, it only makes sense to generate more than an impression or a single sale from your campaign. Yes, consumers will always want those short-term deals and the back-to-school offers, but they want more.

When consumers click links today, either from advertisements or social networks, they expect to be taken to a website that tells them everything about your product or brand that they're interested in. They want to be able to view your offer and make a purchase, but also navigate the rest of your website. These consumers want to be able to view what else you have for sale, learn more about your company, and share that information with their friends. Everything needs to be integrated.

Today's consumers visiting your website don't want to just depend on your brand or company to tell them what to buy and whether the offer you're pushing at them is special. They want to draw that conclusion themselves with the assistance of their social influencers. So, as you think about social media marketing on your website, first and foremost consider that your consumers want more than an ad click to a home page.

Making the Campaign and the Website Work Together

The best way to make the advertising campaign and your website work harmoniously in a social world is to make sure you link the two in every way possible. In the sections that follow, we tell you how you can optimize those links.

Treating your website as a hub, not a destination

The first step in practicing SMM on your website is recognizing that it's a hub that fits into a larger digital ecosystem supporting your brand. This digital ecosystem includes the following: your website; your ads across the Internet; your presence on various social platforms; and the conversations about your brand on blogs, the social platforms, in online communities, and on discussion forums. Your purpose shouldn't only be to bring people to your website and entice them to stay on it as long as possible. That might contradict every traditional marketing principle, but it's true.

REMEMBER

If someone wants to know everything about your company — good, bad, or ugly — he should feel that your website is the best *starting point* for him.

If you design your website as a hub versus a destination, your website will immediately become more valuable to your customers. Even though this may mean that you'll be pointing your consumers to external sites, they may treat yours as a starting point in the future.

The Mars corporate brand designed its current website (`https://www.mars.com/`) so that you can learn everything about its corporate philosophy, various brands, and work in local communities all in one place (see Figure 21-1).

FIGURE 21-1:
The Mars
website.

Linking prominently to your presence on social platforms

As long as customers interact with your brand, it matters little where they're interacting with it. For consumers, the Internet is the social platform on which they share information, connect with their friends, develop business relationships, and get entertained. They're also interacting with brands on these social platforms. You must highlight your presence on these social platforms right on your website, too. If your customers want to interact with you on social platforms, help them to do so by showing them how they can. For example, The Content Marketing Institute (`https://contentmarketinginstitute.com/`) has links to all its major social platforms on the right side of each page on its website, as shown in Figure 21-2.

Social media links

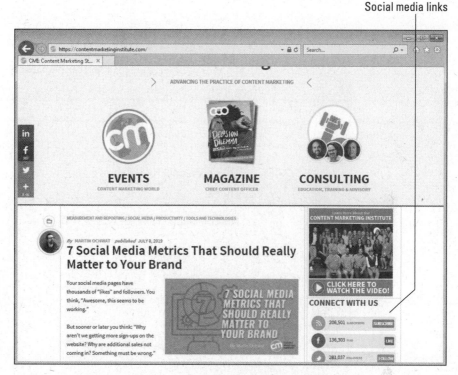

Depending on your business model and the strength of your brand, how prominently you link to the social platforms may differ. For example, if you're a luxury handbag brand that likes to entice customers by creating a feeling of mystique and exclusiveness, linking extensively to the social platforms may do more harm than good. However, if you're Coca-Cola and are keen to deeply immerse yourself in the pop culture, linking to social platforms where conversations are happening (potentially about events that Coke may sponsor) becomes important.

Promoting campaigns on your website home page

As we mentioned earlier in the chapter, your corporate website serves many audiences and has many purposes. But that shouldn't stop you from using the featured zone on your home page to promote something (for example, a conference, an ad, or a product). That's the first step in linking campaigns with your website. This may be obvious to you, but many companies don't do this. Anthropologie displays its products that are on sale from a link on their home page, as shown in Figure 21-3.

Sales

FIGURE 21-3:
Products for sale
link on the
Anthropologie
website.

WARNING

If you're using featured zones on your home page to promote campaigns, be sure to update them frequently with new promotions. No one likes to see the same promotions again and again. It implies that the company is neglecting its website.

Encouraging deeper interaction through your website

Consumers who respond to your campaign want to learn more about the products or services you're selling them, and you can do more than just provide them with that information. Instead of just bringing them the information, you can connect them with other prospective or current customers by pointing them to a discussion area on your website (if you have one) or third-party review sites that discuss your product. You can also introduce a live-chat feature, whereby they can talk to you in real time.

Asking customers to give you feedback on your content

Customers feel they own a bit of your company when they're loyal to your products. These fans are typically called *ambassadors* because they will likely tell their friends and family about how much they enjoy your product. They become like an external sales team. They want to have the inside scoop on your company, products, and advertising campaigns, too. The behind-the-scenes assets fuel their interest in the company. Make sure that your TV, print, and digital advertisements are available for your fans to view on your website. Allow them to critique the campaign assets and provide feedback. It serves to build trust, enthusiasm, and ownership among them. Be prepared to accept both positive and negative comments. While you can't control the conversation, you can and should help shape it.

Rethinking Your Website

Practicing SMM philosophies on your website isn't only about approaching campaigns differently and tying them into your website more strategically. You should rethink your whole website experience to enable more direct social influence to take place. Redesigning your website with social influence elements can increase sales and deepen relationships with your core customers. In the following sections, we give you some recommendations on how to enhance engagement on your website.

User experience

User experience (UX) has become a competitive advantage. Consumers can shop around to find the lowest price for most goods. Therefore, differentiation has to be derived from something other than price. Marketers realize that a great experience brings people to their site and keeps them there.

Simple design

When companies created their first websites, the tools were not very advanced. It took a long time and a dedicated team to make things happen. Now, you can easily plan a website and execute quickly. The focus should be on navigation and the right content. Everything has to be easy and the design needs to be simple. No one will wait for websites to load. They also won't be willing to search around looking for something. The competition is such that the same answer can probably be found on your competitor's website.

Conversational user interface (CUI)

Technology has now made it possible for customers to hold conversations with company sites and social media platforms instead of having to click an icon or type a command. You want to have a two-way conversation with your customers and chatbots make that possible. Make sure that you use these messaging tools on your website.

TIP

See Chapter 20 for details about using chatbots and messaging apps.

Content marketing

According to the CXL Institute (`https://conversionxl.com/blog/first-impressions-matter-the-importance-of-great-visual-design/`), it takes .05 seconds for a user to determine whether they will continue to stay on your website or leave. This means that you need to do everything you can to make your site engaging at first glance.

Content marketing is now an integral part of any website marketing strategy. You need to audit your website to analyze the content you currently have and determine what's working. You also need to see what you're missing and how you can reach more of your target audience.

Here are three things you need to review to make your website more powerful:

>> **Search engine optimization (SEO):** In order to be found, you still need to write content that accommodates search engines. There are lots of shiny objects to try, but this is not optional.

   What you should do: Identify the keywords your customers use when they search for your topic. There are several good tools that you can use for SEO. For example, you could try Ahrefs (`https://ahrefs.com/`) or KWFinder (`https://kwfinder.com/`).

>> **Video:** Video has become essential. According to Hubspot, 54 percent of users want more video content from brands. You can repurpose any video content you create to use on social media sites.

   What you should do: Jump into video creation if you're holding back. Your users probably want to see you on sites such as Instagram where InstaStories gets a great deal of traffic.

>> **Podcasts:** Podcasts are increasingly popular. According to the Edison Research and Triton Digital study, "The Infinite Dial 2019" (`https://www.edisonresearch.com/infinite-dial-2019/`), in the U.S. 50 percent of people over the age of 12 have listened to a podcast. This makes podcasts mainstream. It's likely that some of your audience members fall into this group.

What you should do: Think about how you could use podcasting to increase your reach. You don't need to create an elaborate thirty-minute podcast. You could create a quick tip podcast that is five minutes long. The idea is to provide content in the most popular formats.

Customer reviews

The most critical change you can make to product pages on your website is to include customer reviews. Nothing sells a product better than actual customer reviews and ratings of the products. The customer reviews provide the shopper with the perspective of other customers. They give your customers the inside scoop on your products — the ins and outs of them and why they're good or bad.

You can be sure that customers will go online to look for your product reviews. In fact, a 2017 study by the Speigel Research Center called, *How Online Reviews Influence Sales* (https://spiegel.medill.northwestern.edu/online-reviews/), found that a product with five reviews is 270 percent more likely to be purchased than a product with no reviews. Reviews are critical to the success of a product. Amazon is the most well-known example of a company that provides customer reviews, as shown in Figure 21-4.

You'll find that customer reviewers serve a couple of purposes. They:

>> **Help sell products, no matter the review.**

Even though you may be worried that customer reviews may damn your products, they invariably convince customers to purchase, and they lead to more sales. Unflattering customer reviews may drive your customers away from certain products, but they also drive customers to peruse other products on your site, which could result in a purchase. Very few products receive perfect scores, so some negative reviews demonstrate that the system isn't being gamed.

>> **Get feedback from customers about what does and doesn't work.**

The customer reviews also serve as a valuable feedback mechanism, telling you what products are liked and why certain products are purchased more than others. Many a marketer has learned valuable insights about missing features of their products by reading the customer reviews on their websites.

A case study done by Bazaarvoice.com in conjunction with Petco.com found that by adding Bazaarvoice ratings and reviews to its site, the conversion rate for dog food products with one review was 20 percent higher than those with no reviews (https://www.bazaarvoice.com/success-stories/petco/). That's quite a difference!

Customer reviews

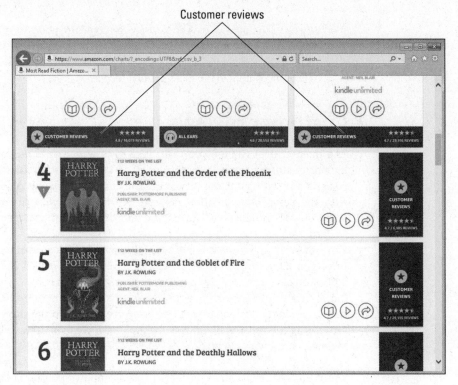

FIGURE 21-4:
Amazon
customer
reviews.

In addition to adding customer reviews on your website, you can incorporate them in other ways:

>> **In your search engine advertisements:** Some retailers have found customer reviews and ratings to be so successful that they now include customer ratings in their search engine advertisements. Including the ratings in those advertisements has also increased the *click-through rate,* which is the number of clicks in an advertisement that drives users to the website.

>> **On your physical shelves:** Other companies, such as Staples, include customer ratings sourced from its website on the display shelves of its physical stores. Even when customers see the ratings in a physical store, they're influenced.

REMEMBER

The customer reviews and ratings are where your customers truly influence each other. Allow for that social influence, and you'll probably see it building trust, increasing sales, and improving customer service.

About Us and Contact Us pages

The About Us pages of a website have traditionally included management team profiles, investor information, company history, contact and address information, company values, and fact sheets. Those sections are extremely important, and you can make them all the more so by injecting social features. For example, include links to the blogs and Twitter profiles of the management team along with the traditional profiles.

The chief executive officer of your company may want to include a YouTube clip of herself sharing her vision for the company and how the company can serve customers. The company history page can link to external websites that explain more about the company's history, and the fact sheet can include quotes and factoids from third-party providers and individual experts. On these pages, you can feature expert influencers who endorse the company. See Chapter 18 for more information on the expert influencers.

The Contact Us page requires special attention. It must not be a page that lists only telephone numbers, email addresses, and locations. In today's world, customers assume that *Contact Us* means that they can talk to an employee right away about a problem. Include live chat technology on the Contact Us page (if your company sells a consumer product) and link to your company's Twitter feed.

TIP

The Twitter feed matters because the customer may want to engage in a conversation with someone in your company directly, then and there. What better place than Twitter, where you can invariably make a statement that you're authentic and transparent?

Another potential solution for a Contact Us page is to enable customers to provide product and business ideas to your company. Call it crowdsourcing, but customers often don't mind giving free advice to companies. The Salesforce Trailblazer Community (https://success.salesforce.com/), as shown in Figure 21-5, solicits feedback from customers and encourages customers to interact with one another. In recent years, it has received thousands of ideas from customers about every part of its business.

On the site, customers can comment on the ideas submitted and rate them, pushing the best ones to the top. The most successful ideas are implemented in some form or the other. It is a win-win situation already. The customers feel empowered to provide constructive feedback, their voices are heard, and the company benefits from the fabulous ideas.

Another great way to get feedback is to use a tool like GetFeedback (https://www.getfeedback.com/), shown in Figure 21-6, which surveys customers to get their opinions. The feedback is easily obtained by sending a thank-you email with a link in it.

FIGURE 21-5:
Salesforce
Trailblazer
Community.

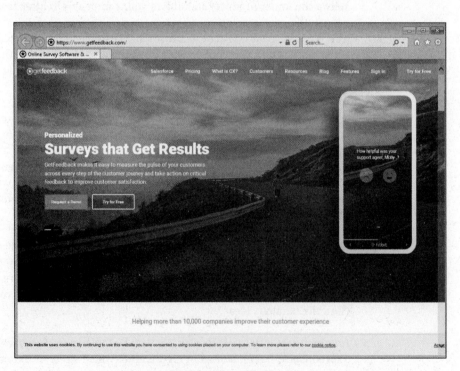

FIGURE 21-6:
GetFeedback.

Tips and Tricks for Website SMM

Follow these steps to enhance your website's social media potential. Many of these tips and tricks may seem small, but time and again, we've seen them directly impact how a potential customer views a brand on a website. They are easy to remember as the four As — Aggregate, Amplify, Align, and Apply.

Aggregate information for your customer's journey

Social media has empowered consumers to form stronger opinions and express them more broadly. More people are blogging, commenting, and rating than ever before. According to a 2018 article by Orbit Media (`https://www.orbitmedia.com/blog/blogging-statistics/`), the average blog post is 1,151 words (an increase of 42 percent over the last five years).

These contributors provide a rich base of knowledge for other consumers to use while making a purchasing decision. Consumers who tap into these blogs know more about your brand than you probably do. Rather than try to control the message, serve as the hub and the aggregator of all information regarding the brand. Let your website become the amphitheater for the conversation. Even if the conversation is negative, you win over the long term, as Chevy did with its Tahoe campaign. The user-generated advertisement contest resulted in 629,000 visits to the website, and Tahoe sales took off.

Amplify business stories

So, you can't control the message anymore. Your consumers would rather listen to each other than to you. But you still have messages that you want to disseminate. You can do that by shaping, influencing, and amplifying business stories that play to your brand's strengths.

REMEMBER

Just because your consumers are more interested in talking to each other doesn't mean that you have no voice at all. Publish your favorite business stories as widely as possible and direct consumers to the individuals or groups already predisposed to your products.

Align your organization into multiple, authentic voices

Social influence marketing is about providing space for consumers to influence each other during the purchase process. As a brand, you want consumers to positively impact each other. Provide the space for consumers to influence one another by aligning your entire organization into a network of multiple, authentic voices. Don't leave customer interactions to the sales and marketing teams. Empower other internal constituents across the organization to serve as brand ambassadors, maybe via blogs. They'll talk about your brand in their own voices to their own communities. They may not be totally on message, but they'll be authentic — and they'll have a strong, positive influence. Trust them. See Chapter 5 for more information on SMM voices.

Apply share buttons

It's incredibly easy to make sure that you provide sharing tools for content on your website. There's no excuse for not using them. Use tools such as Click to Tweet (https://clicktotweet.com) or a WordPress plugin for your site (https://wordpress.org/plugins/better-click-to-tweet/).

Chapter **22**

Becoming an Authentic and Engaged Advertiser

I n earlier chapters, we briefly touch on social advertising and how it can play an essential role in your marketing efforts. We also allude to paid and earned media in the context of the different marketing opportunities on social platforms, as well as discuss native advertising.

In this chapter, we go into each of these topics in more detail. Knowing how they can help you achieve your SMM objectives is critical as you become a more authentic and engaged social media advertiser. But that's not all; it's also important to leverage SMM efforts with offline marketing efforts, whether through television or any other form of media. We discuss your offline efforts, too, in this chapter.

Social Advertising: An Online Advertising Game Changer

Display advertising has stopped growing the way it used to, with fewer people noticing, clicking, and interacting with those advertisements everywhere. This is primarily because other forms of online advertising — including social media advertising — have come to the forefront. For the most part, the industry has responded by making the display advertisements more immersive, with *rollover* states (which means that something happens to the display when you mouse over it), forms, pull-down menus, expandable units, and streaming audio and video clips all built within them. The advertising industry has also developed technology to make targeting consumers more precise using demographics, psychographics, past purchasing behavior, website usage behavior, look-alike data (putting ads in front of people who are similar to those who have already purchased a product) and other programmatic means.

Those incremental innovations help grab users' attention and provide a stronger return on investment (ROI) for the advertisers. But social advertisements, which infuse social content and a user's *social graph* (mapping of the person's friends) directly into the ad unit or adjust who the advertising reaches based on a person's social graph, makes display advertisements far more interactive, engaging, and better performing than other forms of display advertisements that have come before.

DISPLAYING ADVERTISEMENTS ON SOCIAL NETWORKS

Every year, Internet pundits predict the demise of online display advertising. They prophesize that consumers will stop looking at display ads, and as a result, the multibillion-dollar industry will die a sudden death. And each year, the statistics prove them wrong. In fact, display advertising has largely remained flat, with minor declines. Marketers continue to invest in display advertising and with good reason. Year after year, display advertisements produce results, especially for direct-response campaigns, where the dollar investments in display advertisements are traced directly to customer acquisition. The amount they spend on display advertising may decrease as some dollars shift to social media marketing, but it's still a core component in their media mix simply because those advertisements prove to be worth their investments.

But one type of online display advertising has never really worked well and continues to provide dismal click-through rates: display advertising on social networks. The reason is simple: People click display advertisements less when they're in a social environment engaging with their friends. You've probably seen display ads on social platforms such as Facebook over the years. They do exist, but they don't perform well. As a result, Facebook has moved away from display advertising, and social networks such as Twitter, Tumblr, and Pinterest now focus much more on native advertising solutions that place the ads more directly in the user's content stream.

The Interactive Advertising Bureau (`https://www.iab.com/`) defines a social ad as "an online ad that incorporates user interactions that the consumer has agreed to display and be shared. The resulting ad displays these interactions along with the user's persona (picture and/or name) within the ad content." This definition serves as a good starting point but should be expanded to also include user-generated content.

To explain this in laypeople's terms, imagine seeing a display advertisement on a website such as CNN.com or NYTimes.com and uploading a photograph to it. Or you could see tweets (Twitter messages) by other people appear within it, and you could respond with comments or tweets of your own. Or imagine that you're browsing Facebook and you see a display ad that includes a photograph of a friend with a movie recommendation. Those are all social advertisements because they're either infused with social graph data or with user-generated content. In the second example, only people who know your friend will see that advertisement.

Rather than depending on just creative images to influence your customers to make a purchasing decision, you allow customers to influence each other in the display ads. And rather than consumers seeing just static quotes from other consumers (after all, customer quotes aren't new in advertising), the consumers can respond to those messages with questions, comments, or endorsements of their own within your advertisement.

From being a medium through which to push a message, the online ad is a location for conversations in which consumers can influence each other. The display ad becomes a tool in your social media marketing toolkit. That's powerful. This matters more than ever because as Josh Bernoff, well-known strategist and CEO of Wellness Campaign (`https://wellnesscampaign.org/`), said, "People don't want to talk about products; they want to talk about their passions or their problems and solutions." Let them use those ads to carry on those conversations and influence each other in meaningful ways.

Native Advertising and How It Can Work for You

An innovation in the online advertising space is native advertising, which bridges the worlds of advertising and content. (The phrase *native advertising* is based on the premise that the advertising is more native to the way the content is displayed and positioned on the website or application.) These native advertisements are intentionally made to look and feel like regular website content and often are even produced for the advertiser by the editorial team of the website. Native advertisements provide direct entertainment or educational, social interactivity, or utilitarian value to consumers while also communicating a specific brand message. In some cases, they take the form of advertisements, and in other cases are more like editorial content. But in both instances, they are more "native" to the core experience that the user is already in.

When these native advertisements provide value, consumers are typically comfortable with the sponsored branding that becomes part and parcel with them. The native ads are successful when they have the following attributes: emotional, engaging, social, relevant to the user, contextually appropriate, and simple. We discuss some of these attributes in the sections that follow.

As you consider building and launching native advertisements on a social platform such as Facebook and Buzzfeed, or a media outlet such as the *New York Times* or beyond, consider these numbers: The majority of both Facebook and Twitter's advertising efforts are native advertising — they're in the content stream where user contributions appear and look and feel like regular content.

One example of native advertising that has been successful is Fidelity's ad, "Should You Accept Your Employer's Pension Buyout Offer?" seen in *Forbes* magazine, as reported by Buzzfeed (https://www.wordstream.com/blog/ws/2014/07/07/native-advertising-examples). It provides substantial information about the topic and doesn't hide the fact that it's recommending their services as a solution. Because the intention is clear and provides useful information, this ad has been well received.

TIP

Should you continue to invest in native advertising? The answer appears to be yes. According to eMarketer, (https://www.emarketer.com/content/us-native-advertising-2019), native advertising is maturing but shows no indication that spending is abating. MediaRadar says that native campaigns renewed at an average renewal rate of 40 percent in 2019, up from 33 percent in 2017.

The following sections describe the attributes that make native advertisements successful.

Emotional

Native advertisements are typically emotional and engaging. They solicit a response from consumers and encourage deeper participation. For example, Chase Bank created a Million Dollar Sweepstakes for their Freedom card. Participants had to buy all their purchases with the Freedom card. This advertisement resided within Facebook, and at the end of the sweepstakes, a million-dollar winner was crowned. The value of this app to Chase was that people were spurred on to use their card for every purchase. Figure 22-1 shows the sweepstakes winner.

FIGURE 22-1:
Chase Freedom
Million Dollar
Sweepstakes.

Engaging

For native advertising to succeed, it must continuously engage users. It should be designed to encourage repeat use and sharing of the native advertisement. On Buzzfeed, the article "14 Ultra-Pimped-Out 'Sims' houses you wish you could actually own" does a perfect job of making an advertisement for Sim4 suddenly appear immensely engaging.

Simple

Probably the most critical attribute of successful native advertisements is that they're typically very simple. You shouldn't try to build Microsoft Office into your native advertisement. Users are more likely to adopt apps that are simple, straightforward, and focused on doing more with less, or using less to tell a story in a way that's still deeply engaging.

Making Paid and Earned Media Work Together

Earned media — editorial, radio, or television coverage of an event or product that you don't have to pay for — has its roots in the public relations world. Earned media is usually free publicity through promotional and marketing efforts outside advertising. Public relations professionals have mastered the art of getting their clients earned media at a cost significantly lower than buying the media attention through paid advertisements or promotions of one form or another.

With the continued growth of social media, earned media has taken on a new dimension. Your brand no longer has to depend on the mainstream media to earn attention among its consumers. Your brand can also earn that attention directly by interacting and engaging with its consumers and their influencers across the social web. All of a sudden, earned media means engaging with consumers on social platforms from Instagram, Twitter, and Facebook to YouTube. If you can attract your consumer's attention directly, why bother with the mainstream press? And for that matter, why bother with paid media, either? In fact, journalists, too, use social media for story ideas. Keep in mind, though, that earned media in the social space isn't necessarily predictable, and although it can be a critical element to communicate your brand messages, it can't be depended upon.

Working harder to gain attention

In the early days of the social media phenomenon, brands that engaged in direct conversations with their customers, and their influencers automatically gained prominence. After all, what they were doing was revolutionary. The first time a user got a response from a customer service agent via Twitter must have been quite a seismic moment. Similarly, the first time a chief executive officer of a Fortune 1000 company started blogging, it drew a lot of media coverage and won him praise among his customers. Zappos developed a reputation for phenomenal customer service through Twitter; Figure 22-2 shows the Zappos Twitter feed. Zappos was among the first to leverage Twitter strategically for customer service.

The days of participating in the social web to simply earn attention are over. Your brands absolutely must still receive attention, but doing so has gotten harder — and it requires more of your time. Every other brand is doing what you're doing online.

So the question is, how can your brand earn the trust and attention of consumers online in a meaningful sense? This is where paid and earned media needs to work together. We discuss this in the section that follows.

FIGURE 22-2:
The official
Zappos
Twitter feed.

REMEMBER

The most important myth about earned media is this: It isn't, as many people believe, free media. You still have to work for it. In fact, it takes a lot more effort to earn media than to buy media. The difference is that earning media requires time and effort and changing your company from within, whereas paid media is about buying online advertisements. Earned media requires you to devote time to monitoring conversations, building relationships, and engaging with influencers online.

Making paid media jump-start earned media initiatives

So how do earned and paid media work together in this socially driven digital world? In earlier chapters, including Chapter 7, we discuss paid media and earned media opportunities on various social platforms. We also discuss when to use which technique. Here, we explore how paid media can support earned media efforts.

At the most basic level, you can use paid media to jump-start your earned media endeavors. Grabbing your customers' attention and initiating dialogue with them can be hard. All your competitors are trying to do exactly what you're hoping to do, after all. Breaking through the noise can be difficult. The sections that follow highlight some specific ways in which paid media can support earned media.

It's essential to analyze the value of paid media in relation to the value of *incremental reach* (users passing it on) and the value of the endorsement effect (users promoting a brand via an image on their profiles and liking a specific piece of content and sharing it). The point is that when you use paid media to jump-start an earned media effort, you must analyze the value of all components to assess the total value of the campaign and how the components support each other.

Build awareness

Paid media is most valuable for building awareness among consumers about a product, service, or promotion. If you're beginning to engage with customers on a social platform or in a hosted online community, an effective way to build awareness for those experiences is to create awareness via paid media across the Internet. Most of your consumers may not know that you're interacting with others on a social platform and providing product sneak peeks, offering discounts, or answering customer-service queries. You can build that awareness by using paid media. This paid media can be in the form of advertisements on mainstream websites or social advertisements on social platforms.

Promote interaction

You may have already developed a thriving community and could be looking to increase engagement with a new audience segment. One way to do this is to use paid media to profile community members and highlight the value that the community provides.

For example, Intuit has a very successful QuickBooks Live Community (as shown in Figure 22-3), where customers help each other solve problems. Today, more than 70 percent of customer-service–related issues are resolved with other users answering questions. One accountant has posted more than 5,600 answers. Intuit now has the opportunity to promote the Live Community to prospective customers as a benefit of buying their software. That can be done through paid media.

Win friends and influence

If you want to engage with your customers in a more meaningful way but don't have the resources, skills, or permission to do so, use paid strategies. For example, American Express hosts the popular business site called OPEN Forum. The site pays experts like übermarketer Mike Michalowicz to blog on various topics, which cultivates discussion among the readers. The conversations triggered on the OPEN Forum percolate to other parts of the Internet, rapidly giving American Express additional exposure. American Express builds its reputation as a company providing valuable advice to its customers, the expert bloggers get a larger audience, the customers get the information, and each post builds brand awareness for the AmEx brand.

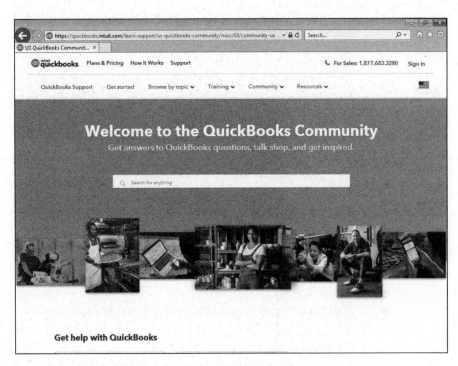

FIGURE 22-3:
The Intuit
Quickbooks
Community.

Tips and tricks for campaigns

When launching and running online campaigns, you can sometimes forget to make sure that your paid and earned media efforts work well together. Your earned media efforts can save you precious dollars and enhance the paid media campaign.

Here are some tips to consider when launching an online media campaign:

>> **Ask for earned media recommendations.**

If you're working with an ad agency, ask them to provide recommendations for a media campaign, ask them to also offer earned media recommendations at the same time. There is no reason they shouldn't.

>> **Request a social advertising component.**

Always ask your agency to include a social advertising component to the campaign and push them to explain how you can use social advertising to jump-start earned media efforts.

>> **Survey the landscape.**

Look at your presence on various social platforms when you're about to launch a campaign. Can you do anything to amplify the effects of the campaign?

>> **Design the campaign to be inherently social.**

Ask more of the participants in your campaign and offer more in return. For instance, direct them to your presence on a social platform — where you encourage them to friend, fan, or follow you — instead of directing them to a microsite.

>> **Promote your brand on social networks.**

Use your social influence on the platforms to highlight the campaign, and use places such as Twitter to answer queries, amplify the coverage, and share tidbits about it.

>> **Establish a fan page.**

Create a permanent home for the campaign to allow deeper social interaction. A permanent home strengthens relationships with your customers and helps you on the search engine optimization (SEO) front, too. Or use your social network presence as that home.

>> **Set influence goals and evaluate how well you meet them.**

Make an explicit secondary goal of the campaign to increase your followers on Twitter, your fans on Facebook, and your friends on YouTube. With that goal, your creative team will bring more synergistic ideas to the table.

>> **Don't forget the metrics.**

Measure all digital interactions with your customers, and especially find out how they reach your microsite or your website. Determine how many people were driven from paid versus earned media strategies and how many came from social platforms. We talk about how to measure a campaign in Chapter 25.

>> **Identify and reach out to the social influencers.**

Do it as soon as you launch the campaign; maybe they can help promote it for you. Show them all the campaign elements — basically everything that a consumer would see. Provide them something in return. See also Chapter 18 for more information about working with influencers.

>> **Offer some sort of reward to consumers who participate.**

Before you launch the campaign, think through whether you can provide something to consumers who engage with you more deeply on the social platforms. They'll reward your generosity by creating buzz that will nicely complement the paid media campaign.

Making SMM Work with TV

Second screen experiences (where a mobile device interacts with social media in addition to a TV set) that support the primary television experience of an ad have grown increasingly important. In fact, Nielsen has weekly social media ratings that track the number of social media interactions between TV shows and social media platforms (https://www.nielsensocial.com/socialcontentratings/weekly/). This explains why marketers are increasingly focusing on how they can make their television advertising support their social media marketing efforts, and vice versa.

Some traditional advertisers believe that nothing can replace television to build awareness for a brand. These advertisers scoff at the notion of digital advertising displacing television advertising. Asking marketers to choose between the two is a false choice. Each form of advertising has its place, and each one can complement the other effectively to meet the objectives of the marketing campaign. In the following sections, we outline two scenarios of how digital SMM campaigns can effectively complement a television campaign.

REMEMBER

Social media has created a perfect storm in the advertising world, which results in new advertising units, such as social ads and the rise of earned media, working in conjunction with paid media. And the technological innovations in live streaming is changing the nature of television online, leading to a whole new set of marketing implications for traditional TV advertisers.

Awareness through TV; engagement via the Internet

The reach of television is still insurmountable for any other marketing channel. Television advertising provides awareness for a brand, a product, or a new campaign better than other techniques. But television is most effectively used when it serves to build awareness and drive consumers to more deeply engage with a brand on other channels, such as the Internet.

Take Levi's 501 *Project Runway* Challenge, for example. Levi's 501 sponsored the reality television series *Project Runway*, in which up-and-coming fashion designers compete against each other in a string of design challenges for a big prize.

Levi's sponsored the TV show to build awareness for its jeans among young women, a target customer that had eluded the brand. Levi's also created a *Project Runway* design challenge of its own on a specially-built website. On this website, users were asked to submit their own clothing designs for a competition. Other users voted on the submissions, a panel of celebrity judges weighed in, and a winner was chosen. The online program was promoted extensively through paid media across the Internet and through the television advertisements that aired around the TV version of *Project Runway.*

Thousands of consumers submitted their designs for this online challenge, with many more visiting the website to critique the designs and vote for their favorites. The television advertisements built awareness for the online competition; paid media online promoted it across the Internet; and consumers engaged with the brand more deeply on the website by submitting designs, rating others, and discussing them. It was the perfect success story, with television advertisements working in conjunction with a social influencer marketing program to meet the brand's objectives. And yes, during the period of the campaign, sales to their target audience jumped.

Awareness, engagement, and conversion with television

Over the past dozen years or so, as digital advertising has gained in prominence, a slew of traditional marketers have bemoaned the attention that the digital space has been getting. Digital marketers have been too proudly explaining how important their form of marketing is because it's more measurable, more quantifiable, and more results-driven than other forms of marketing. This tension has created a false divide between television and digital.

Television is fundamentally going digital itself, in a way that none of us could have imagined a few years ago. The infrastructure that drives television — the content distribution models, the content formats, and the advertising opportunities — have all changed. And what's more, the lines between television and the Internet are blurring. Market research shows that consumers increasingly multitask. They don't just search the web while watching television; they talk to each other online while watching television. And online television sites in the form of platforms, such as YouTube and Twitter, have built-in functionality.

The face of television has gone digital, with major cable networks streaming live broadcasts. This means that as television continues to go digital, marketers have the opportunity to get the same advertising benefits from television that they've always obtained, but with some of the unique attributes of digital such as measurability, social capability, and interactivity.

Measuring the effectiveness of TV and the second screen

Today you can see episodes of all your favorite shows on your iOS or Android device in addition to your desktop computer or television. The same can be said for some broadcast channels that supply advertising along with their content.

With the feedback that can be obtained from the watching community on social media, advertisers are very excited about the depth of information they can obtain. Never before have executives been able to get such direct comments during a TV season. They have gone so far as to make changes to upcoming episodes based on comments about likes and dislikes.

Chapter **23**

Building an SMM Mobile Campaign

P eople use all kinds of social media to share experiences and create, refresh, develop, and maintain relationships. Consumers use full-fledged communities like Facebook, as well as blogs, comment forms, and the like to speak their minds and be heard.

As we explain in Chapter 1, social media marketing is about employing social media and social influencers to achieve the marketing and business needs of an organization. Using mobile devices like smartphones and other handheld devices in social influence marketing helps you leverage the devices' many capabilities to engage your prospects and customers with your brand. It also enables the users of these devices to communicate with each other and share their individual experiences with your brand, products, and services.

In this chapter, you find out how the mobile phone is the most pervasive communication, entertainment, and social media channel out there, with a future filled with possibilities. You get a feel for what consumers are doing with their mobile devices and the factors that affect their use.

We explain how you can use mobile search, branded apps, and mobile-enhanced traditional and new media to engage consumers within a marketing and social media context. Finally, we discuss how you can leverage the convergence of social media and the mobile channel to benefit your business today!

Looking at Consumer Trends in Mobile

The smartphone is a key fixture in the lives of nearly everyone in the United States and around the world. According to leading research firms, 96 percent of the U.S. population has a mobile phone. And Pew Research Center reports that worldwide there are approximately 5 billion people who own a smartphone as of 2019.

In 2018, Apple reported that the top five iPhone apps downloaded by users were the following:

>> YouTube

>> Instagram

>> Snapchat

>> WhatsApp Messenger

>> Facebook Messenger

A telephone and much more

The mobile phone is more than a simple tool for making and receiving phone calls. Sure, you can still make phone calls with it, but for most of us, the smartphone has become a portal to the world and a multipath channel for the world to reach us.

TIP

The Global Web Index 2019 (http://globalwebindex.com) reports that 16-24-year-olds spend 28 percent of their time on mobile — more than than any other age group. If this is your audience, you need to communicate with them via their mobile devices.

Today's mobile phones are newspapers, maps, books, magazines, cameras, radios, stores, game consoles, video and music players, calculators, calendars, address books, stereos, TVs, movie theaters, and concert halls. More specifically, people are using smartphones to

>> Access news and information

>> Check up on the latest celebrity gossip

>> Check the weather

>> Look up addresses and find directions

>> Access competitive business information

>> Buy products, images, ringtones — and pizza

>> Receive the latest coupons and promotional discounts from their favorite stores

>> Monitor their fitness, count calories, and record daily running scores

>> Play games

>> Listen to music and watch movies

>> Respond to their favorite brand's mobile messages

>> Participate with and support political candidates

>> Donate money to their favorite charities

>> Socialize with friends and marketers

>> Update friends and family on their locations and activities

This list is just the tip of the iceberg. Every day, consumers are doing more and more with their mobile phones, and you can create innovative campaigns that fit in with those uses.

REMEMBER

The key to successful consumer engagement, especially in the social media context, is to combine both information delivery and exchange with entertainment — in other words, focus on "infotainment" services.

The release and adoption of smarter phones

If you took the Wayback machine to 1983 (the Wayback was the time-travel machine in the old *The Rocky and Bullwinkle Show)*, you'd see innovative and/or fashion-conscious road warriors carrying around a mobile phone shaped like bricks and weighing a whopping 30 ounces or more. For all its heft, the grandfather of mobile devices could do only two things: make and receive calls. Today you find thousands of smartphones that come in all shapes and sizes. True, some phones are still dedicated to the single purpose of making phone calls, but these devices are smaller than their ancestors, have longer battery lives, and provide clearer calls.

Here are the categories of devices that currently exist:

>> **Regular phones:** These are lightweight, dedicated devices for making and receiving phone calls and text messages.

>> **Smartphones:** These are full-featured, multipurpose, high-bandwidth, networked, multimodal, interactive information, communication, entertainment, and commerce solutions. Some of the more popular smartphones include the Apple iPhone and phones running the Google Android operating system, such as the Samsung Galaxy.

>> **Wireless-enabled devices:** These devices aren't phones, but each has some form of wireless connectivity — either through Wi-Fi, Bluetooth, or an embedded wireless access card. The Apple iPad and iWatch are among the most popular wireless-enabled devices as this book goes to print. With Internet access, these devices naturally support interactive marketing.

Most people are adopting the requisite data plans to send text messages, acquire Internet connectivity, and enjoy related value-added services. This fact means that you must make your SMM campaigns mobile-device friendly. Also, keep in mind that the percent of the overall population using smartphones today is a much larger percentage of your target audience than it was only five years ago.

To learn more about the thousands of mobile devices that are out there (we're not kidding; there are that many), check out DeviceAtlas at www.deviceatlas.com/device-data/explorer (see Figure 23-1). Click the Device Data tab.

REMEMBER

Even though the iPhone captures the lion's share of the press today, according to statcounter (http://gs.statcounter.com/os-market-share/mobile/worldwide), in 2019 the iPhone accounts for 22.04 percent of the worldwide smartphone market; Android had 76.03 percent.

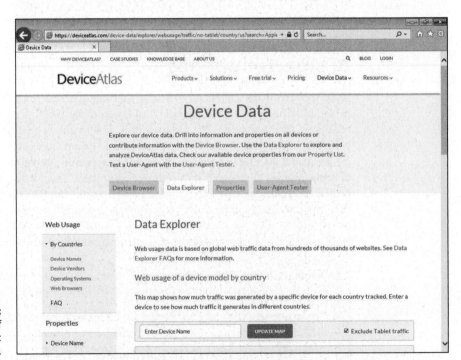

FIGURE 23-1:
The myriad of mobile devices: DeviceAtlas.

Understanding the Many Paths
within the Mobile Channel

As you know, a smartphone really isn't *just* a phone. Sure, you can make calls with it and engage in social practices, just as people did with the old landline phones. However, the telephone capability is just the tip of the iceberg. Today's mobile devices are capable of so much more. In fact, for many people, these devices are the primary method of personal communication, social interaction, and even commerce.

Figure 23-2 illustrates the many paths you can use to reach the mobile phone.

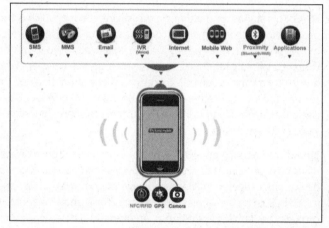

FIGURE 23-2:
The paths through the mobile channel.

The term used to interact with consumers through all these paths is *mobile channel*. The mobile channel refers to the collection of companies and systems, wireless networks, mobile phones, application providers, marketers, and so on that make it possible for you to interact with an individual audience member directly through a mobile phone or wireless-enabled device. Each of these paths — SMS, MMS, email, voice and IVR (integrated voice response), Internet, mobile web, proximity, and applications — is unique.

REMEMBER

Keep in mind what media scholar Marshall McLuhan taught us in 1964: "The medium is the message." Each of these paths changes how your message is received and accepted. In the social media context, this is important because if your message isn't accepted, it certainly won't be talked about and shared.

The paths are

>> **SMS:** This is short message service, also commonly known as *text messaging*. A text message is comprised of 160 or fewer letters, characters, and numbers delivered through the mobile channel. You can send longer messages (called Concatenated SMS) by linking the messages together. SMS is ideal for the sharing and exchange of contextually relevant, timely bits of information — including a brief message to a friend, celebrity gossip, details on your latest sale, impulse impressions, and thoughts on a product or service. In the social media context, SMS is popular with Twitter because people update their accounts (tweet) and/or receive alerts via SMS, even though SMS is just one very small part of the Twitter experience. Keep in mind, though, that SMS is permission based. If you're a marketer trying to reach customers via SMS, they need to have given you permission to market to them.

>> **MMS:** This stands for multimedia messaging service, which is a unique protocol for exchanging digital content, such as videos, pictures, and audio via mobile phones. The term *MMS* is often generically used for all forms of digital content, including ringtones, images, video, and so on, even if the delivery doesn't follow the proper MMS protocol; more often than not, this content is sent via the Internet rather than through MMS. MMS works well with an SMM campaign in which you're inviting customers to share their own pictures and videos with each other.

>> **Email:** Traditionally, email had been delivered to a mobile device, such as a BlackBerry or Palm Treo, through a special email service connected to the device. Now, regular email can be delivered through mobile applications (often built in by the wireless carriers or mobile phone manufacturers) or through the mobile web. iPhones, Androids, and devices such as tablets, deliver and render HTML emails, as opposed to the text-only versions of old.

>> **Voice:** This can take the form of talking with a live person working in a call center, who in turn may trigger mobile data services as a response to the call. Voice can also refer to an interactive voice response (IVR), or automated attendant, system in which your audience can interact with your service through various system prompts and menus, such as "Say or press 1 to tell us what you think of the service." The greatest opportunity here is with social media marketing campaigns that start online and invite users to have special customized voice messages sent to their friends on their mobile phones. For example, the mobile campaign for the movie *Snakes on a Plane* encouraged participants to create customized voice messages for their friends. When the receivers answered the calls, they heard a message about the movie in the voice of the actor Samuel L. Jackson. The message also said that their friends (you could include any name) wanted them to watch the movie together. It appeared as if Samuel L. Jackson was telling them this. This widely successful

campaign resulted in more than 4 million calls being placed between friends during the promotional period.

TIP

Check out Chapter 19 to see more about how voice search is taking over the search space.

>> **Internet:** Many mobile devices can connect to the Internet for a wide range of data-enabled services, including the mobile web, applications, location-based services that tell you about special discounts or recommend restaurants around you, content services like streaming video (for example, mobile TV or MLB games), as well as mobile-carrier-managed portals, such as Verizon.

>> **Mobile web:** Mobile web refers to the experience of browsing the Internet via the mobile phone — for example, such common practices as going to the Facebook website on your smartphone and posting a status update. You can do this using either the web browsers built into many of the smartphones to visit mobile versions of websites (or in the case of the iPhone, you can actually see the regular website) or by using specially-created applications that connect you to specific websites or web services. As mentioned previously, the YouTube application is the most popular mobile app.

>> **Proximity spectrum (Bluetooth/Wi-Fi):** This refers to the short-range Bluetooth radio channel and Wi-Fi network capability for connecting to the Internet. Think of *proximity spectrum* as technologies that let you connect your mobile device with others close to you. Typically, Bluetooth is used to connect phones with wireless headsets and related periphery devices, but you can also use it to deliver content to the mobile phone, as you can with Wi-Fi technology. Bluetooth plays a role in social media at live events where you can send content to the phone and encourage users to share it, whereas Wi-Fi plays a huge role in that it provides the data network connectivity for mobile Internet, Internet, and application services.

>> **Applications:** These are software utilities and services downloaded to mobile phones, and they take many forms. Some are unique to the particular platform they're deployed for, such as the Apple iPhone and Google Android. Applications are incredible ways to interact with social media programs because of their ease of use and integration into the features of the phone.

Keeping in Mind Mobile Phone Capabilities

There are many paths through mobile devices to engage and interact with members of your community, as we discuss in the preceding section. Phones today increasingly have a wide range of enabling technologies, including cameras, location detection, and motion and touch sensors to enhance the experience.

It's a snap: Using the camera

Most mobile phones today come with a high-end camera. A consumer can use the camera in her phone to opt into a mobile marketing campaign by taking a picture of an ad in a magazine, a bar code, a physical product (such as a DVD or soda can), or herself and then use it in the social media context to contribute content to the community.

Because their phones are always with them, most consumers find that they reach for their camera phones rather than try to remember to take a standalone camera. And social network applications make it easier to upload photos directly from a phone's camera than downloading images from a traditional digital camera to a computer and then uploading them to the community site. Most social platforms, such as Twitter, Facebook, and Instagram, allow you to take photographs on your mobile phone and easily upload them to the service. For example, customers take photographs of products with their phones, share them directly on Facebook, and ask their friends for feedback on whether they should buy the products.

Location, location, location

Location information is a very powerful tool, and it's one of the unique features of a smartphone. When mobile subscribers are out and about, they *usually* know where they are, but their phones *always* know (unless they turn off the GPS tracker).

Location information can make your programs more contextually relevant to a user's location, and you get those details, depending on the phone, from the user, the service network, global positioning and network triangulation technologies, Wi-Fi networks, and a wide range of other technical alchemy.

All you need to remember is that you can use location to make your programs more contextually relevant with the user and the community. For example, you could run a special SMM campaign targeted toward people who are in a three-mile radius of your flagship store, encouraging them to visit and get an additional discount if they bring a friend into the store with them.

WARNING

Location-based mobile campaigns can be controversial. If they're not permission-based or aren't explained clearly, they can come across as an invasion of privacy. If you're planning an SMM campaign with location-aware elements, we recommend targeting it toward audiences like Millennials who are already comfortable with location-aware services and advertising.

NEXT-GENERATION MOBILE SERVICES AND BEYOND

If you think that mobile networks and devices are going to stop innovating . . . well, don't hold your breath. The horizon holds many exciting developments. Some of the key drivers are increased network bandwidth, longer battery life (including batteries that charge from ambient radio waves), higher-resolution screens, faster processors, and more. Companies are even working on making their processes greener.

Just think of what you could do with faster data speeds on the phone. Today, 4G networks are the norm and 5G is starting to compete. (4G is the term commonly used for fourth-generation mobile networks. The first generation, or 1G, began in the early 1980s; the second generation, or 2G, emerged in the 1990s; and 3G was formed in the late 1990s.) With each successive generation, mobile network capabilities and data transfer and network speeds increased. 4G networks, with data-transfer speeds reaching 100 Mbps (megabits per second), allow you to do full-motion video conferencing and video exchange on phones and other mobile devices. This capability has a big impact on mobile devices' roles in social media.

Near-field communications and RFID

RFID and NFC technologies are going mainstream. Many phones and other devices are equipped with them. These systems — radio frequency identification (RFID) and near-field communication (NFC) — are similar in concept to Bluetooth in that they're both short-range communication systems, but they have unique identification and commerce capabilities.

In Germany, for example, NFC-enabled phones are used to purchase train tickets. A user simply hovers the phone near an NFC reader, and the reader charges his linked billing account (to a credit card, for instance) for the purchase of the ticket.

RFID chips can be used to identify you and can even personalize signs as you walk by. (Have you been in a store like Staples and walked by a sign that talks to you? That's what we're talking about.)

Phone interaction

It just takes a tap, a shake, a swipe, or a swing to interact with many of the phones. One of the most recognizable phones on the market leveraging this motion and gesture technology today is the iPhone, but other phones have it, too. The motion- and gesture-sensing capabilities of these phones improve their usability and convenience. For instance, on the iPhone and the Samsung Galaxy S10, you can make pinching motions on a picture or mobile website to zoom in and out on the screen. With some games, you can tap with one finger, two fingers, three, or more, and the number of fingers you use determines what happens. You can even give commands by shaking or tilting the device.

In a social media context, you can have all sorts of fun playing with these input and interaction methods and determining how to use them in your social media program.

The iPhone isn't the first mobile device, however, to use these types of applications. The early Palm devices were the first ones to come out with gestures as a means of user interface shortcuts and data entry.

Fitting Mobile into Your Social Media Practices

As a marketer, your job is to communicate, deliver, and exchange value with your audience, and the practice of doing those things with and through mobile devices is referred to as *mobile marketing.* Mobile marketing isn't mystical; neither does it fall outside the practice of traditional marketing. The definition of *mobile marketing* is straightforward: marketing on or with a mobile device such as a smartphone.

Mobile marketing also includes the following:

>> **Communicating:** Imparting information and news about your offerings and related activities to your audience members: customers, clients, partners, prospects, leads, employees, advisors, investors, the press, and all the other people and organizations that play a role in your business, as well as society at large. Communicating spreads the word about what your organization does and the value it has to offer.

You probably use any number of traditional and new-media channels (TV, radio, print, live events, outdoor media, point-of-sale displays in stores, the Internet, email, telemarketing, social media, and so on) to communicate indirectly or directly with members of your audience. *Direct marketing communication* occurs when you initiate contact directly with individual members of your audience, as in the case of sending emails or initiating phone calls. Direct marketing communication also occurs when a customer visits your broadband or mobile Internet website. *Indirect marketing communication* happens when you advertise or present some other form of promotional message through mass-media channels (such as TV, radio, or print) to expose members of your audience to your communication, but you leave it up to individual audience members to initiate direct contact with you.

>> **Delivering:** Providing your products or services and exceptional customer service to members of your audience.

>> **Exchanging:** Swapping value (which we define later in this list). Often, you exchange your goods and services for money, but you can determine for yourself what to take in exchange.

>> **Offerings:** The products and services produced by your organization.

>> **Value:** A sense of worth. People value something when they perceive that the item's worth exceeds what it costs them to obtain, consume, or use.

>> **Mobile-enhanced traditional and new-media channels:** Marketers rely heavily on traditional marketing channels (including television) and new media channels (including websites) to build awareness among members of their audience and promote their offerings. Adding *mobile-enhanced* to the mix simply means that you're marketing to people who are accessing the media in those channels from smartphones and other wireless devices.

In addition, a *mobile marketing call to action* is a set of instructions promoted in the media that shows someone how to use his phone or mobile terminal to participate in a mobile marketing program. For example, one mobile call to action might be "Text SONC to 20222 to donate $5 to support Special Olympics Northern California Athletes. Your donation will be billed to your mobile phone bill, and 100 percent of the proceeds is received by the charity."

Defining mobile marketing and its place within the social media context

As we mention in the previous section, there are two forms of mobile marketing: direct and indirect.

>> **Direct mobile marketing:** Refers to the practice of reaching out and engaging individual members of your audience via their mobile phones. It also includes individuals reaching out and engaging with you in your marketing campaigns.

WARNING

You can proactively engage consumers — that is, text-message and/or call them — if they've given you explicit permission to do so. If you don't have permission, you can't directly reach out to consumers.

>> **Indirect mobile marketing:** Because mobile marketing requires that individual customers give you permission to interact with them on their mobile phones, you can use indirect mobile marketing to expose people

to your offerings and invite them to give you permission to contact them directly. Therefore, indirect mobile marketing is the practice of enhancing your traditional and new-media programs (TV, radio, print, outdoor media, Internet, email, voice, and so on) by inviting individual members of your audience to pull out a phone or mobile device and respond to your mobile call to action. On television, for example, your call to action may ask viewers to text a keyword to a short code to cast a vote. (Think about the TV show *The Voice,* in which the audience votes on Twitter or Facebook.) Or you may ask participants to fill out a form on the web or on the mobile Internet, giving their mobile phone number to participate in the program.

Uniting mobile marketing with social media

The mobile aspects of social media marketing occur within both direct and indirect mobile marketing contexts. As a marketer, you can directly engage your audience either by having its members reach out to you, or vice versa.

Within the indirect context, you can interlace mobile marketing within your traditional and new media channels — including your website, magazine ads, and so on — by adding mobile calls to action. For example, you may

>> **Offer a text alert service.**

You can send participants updates on your programs in text messages. Create a form on your website in which you ask participants to enter their mobile phone numbers and opt in to receiving text messages from you. Or you may invite them to join by asking them to text a specific code to a phone number that you've set up to receive these messages.

TIP

If you would like to collect more data on your customers than their mobile phone numbers (their preferences, for example), use the web form for opt-in, including fields for the additional data you need, and add the customers to your database. However, be aware that asking for such information may limit participation in the program because people may not want to fill out the form or provide much personal information.

>> **Ask for feedback or content.**

Have participants take pictures of themselves using the product with their mobile phones and send them to the community. Or you can ask them to contribute their ideas about the name for your next product, or give a shout-out to a friend.

>> **Remind participants to share.**

Encourage users to share rewards from a program, such as a coupon offer, with their friends.

GROUP DECISION MAKING

Group decision making in mobile marketing is just what it sounds like: using the aspects of mobile to stimulate interactions with groups. Mobile allows people to participate in group settings wherever they are, which makes the membership of the group even larger and more diverse than ever before.

Think about something as simple as planning a party. Using a mobile phone, you can invite all your friends in your address book by sending a text message. Then you can ask your friends what food they would like to bring to the party and keep a running tally of guests who plan to attend. Additional messages can go to those who haven't replied, and soon you have a full menu ready to go. Next you can ask everyone to bring music. And a few button presses later, the evening shapes up nicely.

Community engagement is all about stimulating interaction between you and members of your audience, as well as among community members. You want them talking to each other. Mobile devices are perfect for this aspect of the social community; you can take advantage of this connectivity and the ability to share experiences whenever and wherever community members want to.

Supporting a cause

Cause marketing is the cooperative use of marketing strategy by a for-profit business and a nonprofit organization for mutual benefit. The business gets to align itself with the value of the nonprofit organization, and the nonprofit organization gets the opportunity to draw attention to its activities and possibly recruit new volunteers and donors.

The mobile channel is ideal for capturing charitable donations. You can mobile-enhance any social media marketing program and put a call to action in this marketing to elicit a response from your audience. In the case of mobile charitable donation programs, the response you're looking for is a financial contribution. For example, the American Cancer Society (ACS) raises money by encouraging sponsors to donate via text message. See Figure 23-3 for the call to action featured on the ACS website (`https://www.cancer.org/involved/donate/donate-by-mail-or-phone.html`). This is an effective channel for charitable donations because mobile subscribers can participate without registering for a service or using a credit card; the donation can go straight to a subscriber's mobile phone bill, with 100 percent of the donation being passed to the participating charity. The full amount can be donated to the charity because the person who donates pays the phone transaction fee, and the ads are usually donated by the ad server company.

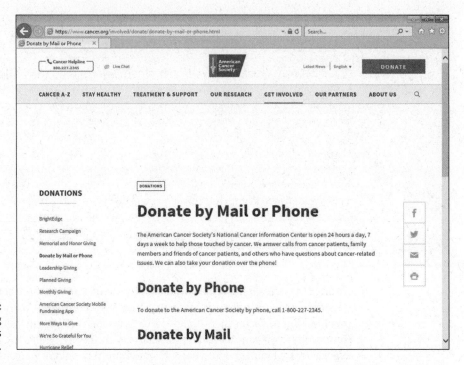

FIGURE 23-3:
ACS accepting donations using SMS.

CHANGING THE WORLD WITH YOUR FINGERTIPS

Jim Manis, one of the mobile industry's most influential players, founded the Mobile Giving Foundation (MGF) after the sale of his company m-Qube to VeriSign in 2007. Manis and the team at MGF set up a program in which MGF-certified charities, partners, and participating carriers can organize charitable-donation programs using premium short-messaging services (PSMS) as the means of capturing mobile subscribers' donations. As in any PSMS program, you promote the call to action; people respond to it and donate, and nearly 100 percent of the donation makes its way to the MGF-certified charity.

A 501(c)(3) or related charity can contact the MGF to go through the certification process and use the mobile channel to raise money. A company that wants to make a difference and be socially responsible can use the mobile channel to promote an MGF-certified program. For more information, visit www.mobilegiving.org.

Building Your Own Mobile-Enabled Communities

Building a mobile-enabled social community isn't as hard as you may think. You can leverage existing social media platforms or build the mobile capability right into your existing interactive marketing channels, such as your website and mobile Internet site.

Leveraging existing online communities

Because people use Facebook and other social networking sites on their phones, they find it easy to accomplish certain tasks, such as uploading photos or posting updates. Some people even prefer to use their mobile phone; it may be much easier to get them to send a picture from their phone than to go home, find the picture on their computer, and upload it to the community. In fact, according to the Global Web Index (`http://globalwebindex.com`), in 2019, people are now spending more time on their mobile than on bigger screen devices (such as laptops and desktop computers).

As a marketer, you can leverage and use existing social community sites and invite your community to keep in touch with you and follow you. Each community site has varying levels of sophistication and capability for mobile accessibility. Two of the most popular are Facebook and Twitter.

Facebook

Facebook (`www.facebook.com`) is the world's leading social networking community. Marketers create Facebook pages for their companies and marketing campaigns so that their community can follow them and keep up to date. Facebook has these existing mobile capabilities that you can leverage:

>> **Keep your Facebook community updated from your phone.**

You first have to register your phone with your Facebook page. (Go to your Facebook page's mobile settings by selecting Edit Page.) You can then configure your page so that you can update it by sending text messages.

>> **Keep your community in sync with you via mobile.**

Ask users in all your marketing media to register on your group or fan page to receive text alerts of your status updates, downloading the Facebook application onto their phones, and following you.

Twitter

Twitter (www.twitter.com), a popular social networking platform, is the journaling of your activities or thoughts in 280-character-or-fewer messages. Twitter has more than 321 million users as of 2019.

As you know, Twitter isn't just for consumers. Companies use it to share their community information. You can create a Twitter account for free and start *tweeting* (the term used for posting to the service). You can then invite people to follow you so that they can receive updates via email, on the web, on the mobile web, and via SMS.

Other social media communities

Countless other social media communities are out there — some general, some targeted niche segments (LinkedIn/Slideshare), and the numerous social media utilities (YouTube, Instagram, Scribd, and others). These all have mobile capabilities, and you can extend others to support your mobile programs. You'll need to do some research to find out who is supporting what and determine how you can best leverage mobile-based marketing in relation to what your competitors are doing (or not doing). You can put your own spin on what they are doing or you can experiment with different tactics. For example, if they send an email on Tuesday each week, you can make sure to send something on Mondays and Wednesdays to get audience attention. If they send an email, you can try a newsletter with discounts.

REMEMBER

If you decide to build your own social media program through the mobile web, use your competitive research to ensure that you're creating something unique and then make sure that the concept is true to your brand.

Creating your own social offerings: applications and widgets galore

You may also want to offer value to members of your audience by creating your own social media offerings or something altogether unique. Even now, you still have plenty of opportunities to create something that hasn't been done before.

You can deploy these services over and through any of the mobile paths, such as SMS, mobile Internet, and downloadable applications. For example, with SMS, you can recruit opinions and comments, blogs, and more. The key is to consider the content format and the most appropriate path for delivering the content to mobile subscribers. One such service is apps.

They make the mobile experience come alive. Think about what makes sense for your customers and how you will make sure it is marketed successfully, and then put your imagination to work!

Applications

One visit to any of the many sites that review applications for various phones shows you how many applications already exist. Thousands contain social media elements. Chat was one of the first to appear, along with mobile versions of most social network sites (Facebook, LinkedIn, and so on).

Adding Social Media Elements to Mobile

You should consider two additional elements while embarking on a mobile social media campaign: social graphs and search. These are important for any social media marketing program, but they're especially important in mobile ones.

Portable social graphs

*Social graph*s are the relationships that people have with each other, within a social network, an application, a site, or across the social web. Think of a social graph as a visualization of relationships — how people connect to each other and what interests they share. But then think about the technical application of this concept. What if you knew who your customer's friends are and then provided user experiences that take advantage of that knowledge?

Facebook Connect allows Facebook data to be integrated into other websites and applications. With Facebook Connect, your customer could use a shopping application for the iPhone or Android and then share mobile offers with their Facebook network. This would be a powerful way to recommend a product.

REMEMBER

Research shows that users are more likely to purchase products or services based on recommendations; friends and family are the most effective referrers.

Searching with mobile

Mobile search is just what the name implies. It's how you find things while on a mobile device, such as websites, people, and restaurants. It sounds as though this type of search should be simple; after all, don't all websites "show up" on your phone when you go to them? But what if you don't know the name of the site, or you're trying to find something and the mobile site address isn't what you thought it was?

Here are a few types of mobile searches:

- » **Search engines:** Just as the web does, search engines and portal sites, such as Google and Yahoo!, have mobile versions. One big difference between the Internet-based and mobile versions is in how results are displayed. For example, when you search for restaurants in a particular city, the listings show the address and phone number (allowing you to easily click the phone number and call the restaurant).

- » **Directories:** Local search and mobile directories are often available through the phone carrier. Some directory services use GPS *(global positioning system)* technology to help determine where you are and provide the right information. Directories assist users in finding sites and are just like the yellow pages of the mobile web.

- » **Recommendation services:** Similarly to technology on the Internet, mobile recommendation engines help users by providing similar or related content as their next step.

For the consumer, mobile search helps unlock the mystery of using the mobile device phone so that people can get the most out of it. As a marketer, you need to make sure that consumers can find the sites and campaigns that you work hard on. In order to be "found" by a mobile search engine, you have to take into account a couple of things:

TIP

- » **Make sure that your mobile site has "good code."**

  Search engines don't like messy sites that contain code errors.

  Have your mobile site tested, and make sure that it gets a passing grade by the code police. Two mobile site testers are http://ready.mobi and https://search.google.com/test/mobile-friendly.

- » **Follow search engine optimization (SEO) best practices.**

  SEO describes how to get websites to appear in search results for specific keywords. Use your most important keywords — the words that your customers use when searching for you — in your pages and your titles. Make sure that the site is accessible by using text links throughout the site. And then submit your mobile site to the mobile search engine, which involves a simple process of going to the mobile search engine submission page and filling out the form.

We'll say it again: You must make sure that your social mobile site is search friendly so that people can find you by phone. People may hear about an application or a fun mobile site from their friends and have to rely on a search service to find it. And your site must be searchable so that people can find each other and the elements of the application. Good user experience goes hand-in-hand with search friendliness.

Harnessing Mobile to Support Social Media

When considering mobile as part of a social influence marketing campaign, plan it like any marketing campaign, with a few added considerations.

>> **Consider how you will support mobile campaigns and calls to action in other channels.**

The mobile campaign won't be successful in a vacuum — you need to market it everywhere.

>> **Take a look at your customer list, and see whether you can determine how your customers use mobile.**

Do they have iPhones, iPads, or other smartphones?

>> **Consider using a tool that can take advantage of the social graph, such as Facebook Connect or other existing social networks.**

>> **Plan mobile applications or widgets, but consider more than the iPhone.**

How can you support Samsung, Nokia, and other smartphones with your widget or application?

>> **Plan for user experience.**

Employ usability testing to ensure that everything you develop is built with the user in mind.

>> **Do your research first.**

Take a look at mobile usage within supporting applications (Facebook Mobile, Twitter, YouTube Mobile, and Instagram) and integrate where it makes sense.

>> **Make sure that you have a good-looking mobile website.**

It allows users to engage with the brand and with each other.

>> **Plan for success.**

Ensure that you know your objectives — what do you want to get out of the relationship with people? — and ensure that you continually measure and report on your interactions.

>> **Be relevant with your communications and with members of the community.**

Deciding When to Build a Mobile App

It's reported that in 2019, iPhone users download an average of 60–90 apps onto their device. Deciding whether your app could be among them is a tricky question. To make it easy, make sure that most or all of the following are true:

>> **You can reach your target market.**

One important question to ask yourself is whether your target market is using mobile and is on the platform(s) you are targeting. This is critical to your success. You need to be sure that your audience is present to consider your app. In other words, fish where the fish are. Does your audience use an iPhone or Android? Do they spend much time on mobile devices? Answer these questions to your satisfaction before you go any further.

>> **You have established goals.**

As with any good plan, you start with your goals. Understand what you want to accomplish by creating this app. Make sure that you're not creating it just because your competitors have one. If it doesn't meet your company's needs, it's a waste of time and money.

>> **You can demonstrate monetization potential or other value.**

Your app should solve a customer problem and provide real value. Apps aren't the novelty that they once were. Your audience won't use an app just because it's available. Also determine whether the app has value to advertisers. If it's appropriate to advertisers, you may be able to entice some of them to be on your mobile app. According to the *Wall Street Journal*, in 2013, apps had already captured $25 billion in sales, and lots of advertisers continue to jump in.

>> **You have the resources and the budget to make it happen.**

This one should be obvious, but often gets obscured in the excitement to build an app. If you don't have internal staff to create it, you'll need to outsource it. That requires a budget. Also, make sure that your IT group has evaluated the linkage required between your app and your e-commerce solution on the web. If you are selling a product that the customer needs to link to, you don't want to create a mess because the app and your site don't work together.

>> **Your content reserves are available and new content is being created.**

No one wants a static mobile brochure. If you don't have good content and the promise of more on a regular basis, don't think it will magically create itself.

>> **You have considered a mobile website.**

Is your website set up for mobile? This may be all you need. Consider the question carefully. It fully depends on what actions you want your customers to take and what platform fits them best.

>> **You have a plan to get in front of your customer with your app.**

According to Tim Cook, Apple's CEO, the Apple App Store has more than one million apps — that's your competition. You have to capture the attention of people who are dazzled every day by new, exciting apps. If you don't have a plan to help your customers discover yours, don't assume that anyone will ever find it. You'll need to do more than just announce it.

Chapter **24**

Encouraging Employees to Advocate for Your Brand on Social Media

When your employees share company messages, they get attention. Social Media Explorer reports that you get a 561 percent increase in reach of brand messages when they are shared by employees rather than an anonymous message from "the brand." When employees advocate for your brand, it:

» Drives brand awareness

» Expands your company's reach

» Attracts valuable talent

» Increases website traffic

» Increases more qualified leads

» Encourages more social engagement

TIP

EveryoneSocial.com says that an employee advocacy program costs one tenth of social advertising and is perceived to be more trustworthy. Make sure that you let your staff know that their participation on social media channels is valuable.

In this chapter, you look at how brand advocacy has changed and why you want to encourage your employees to become part of your social media marketing efforts. In Chapter 26 see more on social media governance.

Embracing the Idea of Employee Collaboration

Companies want their employees to collaborate, communicate, share, and organize into communities of interest the way they do in their personal lives. There's no reason why your employees shouldn't use intranet software built on these consumer-oriented design philosophies, with the collaboration layer built into the core.

The following sections include some recommendations for how you can get your employees to collaborate and socially influence each other in positive ways. These practices are a direct mirror of how you can engage with social influencers, too.

ENERGIZING EMPLOYEES: IT'S NOTHING NEW

This isn't the first time that energizing employees for social influence and knowledge sharing has been discussed. Debates in the knowledge management community on how best to get employees to collaborate date back to the early 1990s. For a long time, companies saw the Holy Grail of knowledge management as the ability to capture everything that was in an employee's head in a database so that if the employee were to leave the company, the company wouldn't suffer.

This thinking evolved to the realization that no firm can truly capture the experiences and knowledge in an employee's brain, and by the time it did so (if that were even possible!), the information or knowledge would be stale. Since then, the focus has shifted to energizing employees to collaborate, exchange information, and motivate one another to increase innovation and employee productivity.

Employees always compete with each other for promotions, bonuses, and better career opportunities. That will never change, and it will always affect their willingness to collaborate and work with each other. As you encourage employees to socially influence each other, be aware of any insecurities they have.

Rewarding teams

Most companies are organized to reward individual performance and promote the rising stars more quickly than other employees. If you want to foster a collaborative environment in which employees learn from each other, share their knowledge generously, and participate in social platforms geared toward harnessing the collective intelligence, think carefully about how you reward performance. You might be well-served by putting more emphasis on team versus individual performance. Bear in mind, though, that you can't just focus on team performance, because in any team dynamic, a few employees do the most while others do less. Those who are performing the best still need to be rewarded uniquely for their efforts.

Treating everyone equally

Employees usually thrive on competition. That's a good thing. But employees who feel left out of the loop or feel that they aren't seen as critical to the organization are less likely to give their time and brain power to the community. Be sure that you treat every employee equally if you truly want to foster collaboration and the free exchange of information among your employees. Employees speak only if you give them ample opportunities and encouragement to do so. You need to let them speak on their own terms, too, whether through the technologies that they prefer, the locations of their choice (team meetings, suggestion boxes, or one-on-one meetings), or with the mentors whom they seek out.

Trusting your employees

Just as it's imperative for you to trust consumers and let them share ownership of your brand, so, too, must you trust your employees to converse, communicate, and collaborate with each other respectfully and productively. If you don't trust your employees, they won't trust you, and they definitely won't want to give their time to furthering the objectives of the organization. This issue of trust matters most when you're trying to energize employees for social influence: It requires a commitment and not just a job description to accomplish.

Creating the right culture

The right office culture is imperative if you want your employees to engage with one another in conversations, be transparent about what they don't know, and be willing to listen and learn from their peers, including the younger or more junior ones. Your culture needs to be one of humility and openness, and one that allows initiative without punishing people too harshly for mistakes. The way you need to behave in the social web to engage with your customers in a meaningful way applies to the way you must engage with your employees, too. And it all starts with culture.

Placing a premium on groups with a purpose

A key ingredient to energizing employees for social influence is to put the right mix of employees in a room (real or virtual) together to brainstorm, innovate, or accomplish a specific task. Bring an eclectic mix of employees together and ask them to collaborate on a specific task at hand. Their diverse skills and personalities result in unique results and can lay the foundation for a more collaborative work environment.

REMEMBER

Collaborating in a work environment is very different from collaborating in one's personal life. You need clearly defined objectives for people to rally around; otherwise, valuable company time may be wasted.

Avoiding excessive snooping

We're always amazed to learn about companies that peek into their employees' email accounts and watch what websites they visit. If you want to create a culture of social interaction in which people in different offices or even countries come together and share their insights and learn from one another online, you need to make them feel that they're not being watched, tracked, or evaluated every step of the way. Treat them with the respect that you give your bosses, and they'll deliver amazing work. Whatever you do, don't snoop around. You'll lose their trust, respect, and commitment.

Picking Social Software for Social Influence

Finding the right solution for your company as you create an environment that energizes employees to use social media can be confusing. Here are several applications you may want to consider when choosing software that encourages your staff to participate in brand advocacy in an approved way.

EveryoneSocial (https://everyonesocial.com/) is a complete platform designed to help employees push brand approved content to your social media channels. It works on all devices and provides analytics that help you determine what content resonates with your audience. See Figure 24-1.

FIGURE 24-1:
EveryoneSocial
home page.

Oktopost (https://www.oktopost.com/) is designed for the enterprise and has several solutions for social media management. Their social media advocacy platform helps staff spread the brand message and distribute it across your channels. See Figure 24-2.

Agorapulse (https://www.agorapulse.com/) is a social media management tool that provides a one-stop dashboard that displays all your messages, your calendar, and your results. See Figure 24-3.

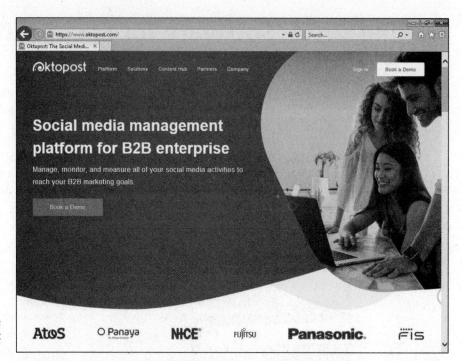

FIGURE 24-2:
Oktopost
home page.

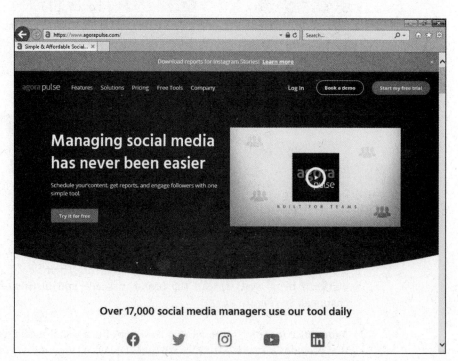

FIGURE 24-3:
Agorapulse
home page.

Rethinking the Intranet

Historically, an *intranet* was defined as an employee-only web-based network for communication, collaboration, self-service, knowledge management, and business decision making. Most intranets were never designed to allow or encourage social influence, even though they're the ideal platforms for furthering collaboration and knowledge sharing within your company.

Many of the intranets were originally *top-down* (management-controlled), rigid, inflexible, and uninviting experiences that served the needs of the Corporate Communications and Human Resources departments but not anyone else. They were used to communicate messages from CEOs and senior management, distribute company announcements, and provide human resources and finance self-service forms to employees.

Intranets slowly evolved to include basic collaboration features and the ability to create and manage department-level pages; they also grew to include key performance indicator dashboards for senior executives. Yet for the most part, these intranets were static, top-down, rigid tools that by their very nature discouraged collaboration and social influencing.

For your intranet to go social and truly encourage collaboration and social influence to take place, you must adapt it to enable clear communication, collaboration, navigation, search, accessibility, and more. We give you some tips on optimizing your intranet in the sections that follow.

Getting rid of the buzzwords

When you design your intranet, move away from the business and technical jargon that you may have used to describe the intranet or label features on it. Don't use words like *portals, knowledge management, digital dashboards, taxonomies, enterprise collaboration,* and *codification.* Use more inspiring language, words that employees can relate to, in all your communications. In other words, humanize the intranet through language but also through its design.

For example, the original intranet at one of Shiv's previous companies, Razorfish, was called "Mom 3000," largely because, like a mother, it had all the answers to questions that employees had. Because it was so advanced, the "3000" was added to it. Needless to say, the employees all loved the intranet and grew attached to it, not just because of all its features but because of its personality.

Don't try to control too much

Most intranet managers now realize that collaboration functionality is essential for the success of any intranet. But many still launch those collaboration tools with overly restrictive controls limiting the amount of collaboration that can take place. Whether it's wiki functionality or group and department pages, make the default setting on all pieces of functionality open to everyone.

By default, let everyone view and edit every page on the intranet unless something has specifically been designated as confidential. And while you're at it, don't dictate how and with what tools your employees should collaborate; let them make those decisions.

Surfacing the connections

Instead of focusing only on publishing information and providing business applications to the employees, look for ways to connect people to one another. Let the intranet reveal strong and weak ties between people and create communities based on the information and collaboration needs of employees.

Make it as easy as possible for the employees by building functionality into the intranet so that people who have shared interests and objectives are linked to each other automatically. This doesn't mean publishing organizational charts but rather quite the opposite — having the *intranet* tell people who else within the organization has similar interests or objectives and encouraging them. The Google employee intranet, Moma, approached this by having each employee's goals and objectives visible on the intranet right next to contact information. That way, an employee would know whether their proposed conversation or project recommendation would be of high or low interest to the other employee even before contacting her.

Taking search social

Intranet managers generally believe — and rightly so — that search is the killer application (in a good way) of their intranet. They also recognize that search is extremely difficult to get right, primarily because employees expect the search to work as well as Google or Bing, even though the intranet search budget is miniscule compared to how much those companies invest in search.

One way to mitigate this is by incorporating social features into the search experience and by combining it with the telephone directory. When you prioritize search results based on what other users find to be useful and link the results with the specific users who find the results valuable, the perception of search increases dramatically because people in an organization are typically interested in the same content that others find useful. And very often, they have deeper questions beyond the content — and are always seeking people who can answer those questions. All the major enterprise search vendors, such as Endeca (www.endeca.com), which is now owned by Oracle, and Apache Lucene (lucene.apache.org) offer some form of social search.

Allowing alternative access

Critical to the success of any intranet today — and even more so if it's one that needs to spur collaboration — is the ability to provide multiple ramps into the intranet. You must build functionality so that employees can install a desktop widget that serves as a mini-window that's easily accessible to the intranet, updating them on who has posted what and making it extremely easy to upload content and share it themselves.

Similarly, building a mobile version of your intranet is important so that employees can get updates on their smartphones and iPads about new information published and collaboration spaces that they are participating in. Notifications are extremely important tools that further collaboration and social influence. Each time someone submits something to a collaboration space, the other members should be notified (if they so choose).

Promoting the value of historical record

Wikipedia (shown in Figure 24-4) has done an immense amount to teach the value of a historical record. Whether your intranet has wiki functionality (the ability for anyone to format and edit the page), definitely make sure that the pages have *roll-back functionality* (the ability to see previous versions of the page).

REMEMBER

With roll-back functionality (or *version control,* as some people call it), employees can always look at previous versions of pages. Or in the case of discussion areas, employees can view earlier collaboration, which often provides great insight as time passes. But more than that, the transparency that comes with having roll-back functionality builds trust and openness in a way that no top-down communication can.

Giving your intranet a pulse

Intranet managers can learn a lot from the social web. Probably the most important lesson is for you to give your intranet a pulse. To fuel those social connections and encourage employees to collaborate with each other on the intranet, you must make sure that the intranet provides the ongoing motivations for people to collaborate.

FIGURE 24-4:
Wikipedia,
the mother
of all wikis.

The most important way to motivate your employees is to showcase the pulse of the intranet. Think of it as a Twitter-like pulse, which shows all the intranet-related activities of a person's social graph in a streaming list. This streaming list encourages the employee to return frequently to the intranet and learn how others are using it. But most important, it encourages the employee to respond to the activities of others on the intranet. The streaming pulse should include documents uploaded, comments made, searches conducted, groups joined, discussions initiated, and the like. It should also include the ability for users to publish status updates and comment on the updates of others. Practically all the intranet software vendors offer this functionality out of the box.

Aiming to destructure

What is often a company's greatest strength is also its greatest weakness, and that is its organizational structure. A company's structure enables resources of all kinds to work harmoniously to enable the company to achieve its objectives. However, it also means that employees have to be fragmented and divided into teams and departments that in time have difficulty working and communicating with each other.

The social intranet helps to break down those organizational barriers. It also encourages people to make decisions and collaborate free of positional bias. To encourage collaboration and the natural social influence that usually takes place, encourage destructuring, which means limiting how your corporate structure affects the intranet user experience, and build online communities of employees where people are encouraged to be honest, transparent, and willing to declare what influences their points of view. With that in place, you'll be well on the path to having an intranet that truly energizes employees and allows for the social influence to take place most naturally.

Giving employees other choices

Irrespective of how well you design your intranet, there will always be employees who will want to use some external products or websites for their collaboration needs. Some may even want to stick to sharing documents over email and using a file server.

That's fine. Don't force people to migrate to your intranet. Ideally, people should gravitate toward it if it is indeed the best solution. If not, let people use what they want. Collaborating and influencing one another is far more important than having them use the intranet. Let them make that choice.

Chapter **25**

Changing Tactics and Metrics

Your customer's buying behavior has changed. They evaluate your products on the channels they prefer and control when and how they buy. So, when behavior changes, the tactics and metrics to measure them must change. It's time to rethink your marketing campaigns and begin to capture more of the data that matters. The good news is that technology advances have made it possible to track and measure this new behavior. The bad news is that you can't coast along, continuing to capture the same analytics you did before and be successful.

There was a common myth several years ago that social media marketing wasn't even measurable. Many a strategist said that you couldn't measure the value of a conversation. These strategists believed that measuring a social phenomenon was difficult. The truth is that these days, social media marketing is as measurable as any other form of marketing.

Today, tools, techniques, and methods are available to measure social media marketing in all its media configurations (chatbots, video, and so on). There are specific campaign- and program-oriented metrics that you can capture, analyze, and map to other performance indicators. These may be in the category of a YouTube video, a Facebook Messenger campaign, or a live streaming broadcast.

In this chapter, we look at tactics that marketers have used to achieve successful marketing outcomes and how they can impact the kind of data you should collect.

Correlating Data with Business Objectives

Capturing metrics about your social media marketing efforts is always crucial, whether they're broader social media metrics or specific ones around a particular platform. However, marrying these metrics with other marketing measures to see how they correlate to business objectives is the key to business growth.

REMEMBER

The most crucial challenge in social media marketing is not measuring individual platforms but rather correlating that data to meet key performance indicators (KPIs).

Here are a few general KPIs to consider. Obviously, you need to pick the ones that match your goals.

>> Rate of customer conversion

>> Performance of marketing campaigns

>> Customer turnover rate

>> Marketing return on investment (ROI)

>> Number of customers acquired in the current year over the previous year

>> Customer churn

>> Customer lifetime value

When you put your social media marketing metrics in place, think about how you can use them to determine whether you have met your marketing objectives. Also, look at how you want to interpret them in relation to the rest of your marketing and business objectives. Otherwise, you'll just be capturing meaningless data.

TIP

Revenue growth, sales effectiveness, brand awareness, and leads are still the metrics that matter most to management, so don't lose sight of them.

CUSTOMER LIFETIME VALUE

One measure that you should consider calculating is customer lifetime value (CLV). This is not a new measure, but as data collection becomes more sophisticated than before, marketers now can capture and gain insights from data along the entire customer journey. CLV is a prediction about the value a customer will have to your business based on their whole relationship with you. This measure helps you determine which customers are the most important to pursue. It includes measures such as average order value and frequency of orders.

Focusing on the Tactics That Count

The focus on social media metrics has shifted from simple measures such as the number of followers and likes to real-time engagement measures with such things as messenger apps and personalized customer experience campaigns. Salesforce (http://salesforce.com) conducted a research study called "Trends and Tactics Driving Marketing ROI." The study looked at which strategies and channels marketers are currently using, the current metrics that marketers use to track these strategies and channels, and the impact of artificial intelligence (AI) on their marketing data. They found that the most successful marketers are doing three essential things:

>> **Leading new personalized customer experience (CX) initiatives and carefully tracking the entire customer journey:** Marketing departments are taking the lead in creating and measuring enhanced customer experiences to create more personalized products and services. To do this, they're more deeply evaluating each customer touchpoint (each place the customer interacts with your brand) to satisfy buyer's needs every step of the way.

Action item: As marketers, you should not be reluctant to take the lead in looking at both personalizing your CX and analyzing your customer journey. Consider using personalized engine software. (See the next section for more details.)

>> **Integrating their marketing technology with corporate analytics systems:** Both business to business (B2B) and business to consumer (B2C) companies are finding that incorporating analytics with such tactics as email, social advertising, and website customer communities are providing them with actionable insights.

Action item: Work across your company to pull in all systems and data analytics together to get a clearer view of the customer as a whole. Cooperating with sales and other departments that are typically interested in controlling their data has made a significant difference when seeking to understand customer data.

>> **Using AI tools to drive their marketing efforts through the customer lifecycle:** Consumers have gotten used to the idea that AI will be used by marketers to dig for insights about them. According to the study, 62 percent of customers are open to the use of AI if it improves their online experiences.

Action item: If you haven't already taken steps to bring AI tools into your company, consider doing so now. The study reports that of the 29 percent of the marketers who use AI, 50 percent say they've seen significant ROI.

In the next sections, we look further into how you may apply these tactics to your organization.

Rethinking the Customer Experience

Are you considering whether to more fully personalize your customer experience? If so, you will probably be rewarded for your effort. In today's marketplace, an enticing customer experience is a distinct competitive advantage. According to research done in 2018 by Epsilon (https://us.epsilon.com/), called "The power of me: The impact of personalization on marketing performance," 80 percent of customers are more likely to do business with a brand when it offers a personalized experience. That's a very high percentage. Customer expectations continue to rise, and you need to be competitive by offering a satisfying and unique customer experience.

TIP

According to Epsilon, your data plays a vital role in executing a personalized experience. To compete, you need to think about tying online and offline data together so you can deliver real-time messaging and facilitate how your campaigns are improving the bottom line.

Personalizing the CX

The stakes are getting higher for companies that are lagging in providing meaningful, personalized experiences to their customers. There is no longer a debate about whether customers care about a personalized experience.

>> 86 percent of customers say that their decision to shop is influenced by personalization (https://www.marketingcharts.com/industries/retail-and-e-commerce-39301).

>> 43 percent of customers expect to receive personalized communications (Broadridge Financial Solutions survey, 2019).

>> 25 percent will no longer do business with a company who delivered a mediocre personalized experience (Broadridge Financial Solutions survey, 2019).

What are some things you can do to create a personalized experience? One possibility is to use personalized engine software (or recommendation engine software). This software can collect individual customer profiles that track and analyze behavior patterns and choices. They do this by collecting, storing, analyzing, and filtering data. So, what are some of the things that personalized engine software allows you to do? You can:

>> **Make custom content recommendations:** By creating a customer profile, the engine can see what content your customer has already read and select other items that will move them towards a possible purchase.

>> **Develop tailored offers:** The engine can determine which offers have already been selected (or heavily reviewed) and make new recommendations based on them.

>> **Provide discounts:** Discounts are always popular with customers. When the engine can provide them for the products they use the most, they will use them and deepen their satisfaction with your company.

>> **Customize ads:** Ads that reflect the customer's preferences are not usually considered annoying, but there needs to be a balance. The engine can determine which ads to display.

If you'd like to look at some personalized recommendation engines, you may want to start with a few that the 2019 Gartner report, "Magic Quadrant for Personalized Engines," chose as the top three leaders providing standalone personalization engines. They are:

>> **Evergage** (https://www.evergage.com/), shown in Figure 25-1, uses machine learning to create customer profiles to predict outcomes. It works well for teams and those in retail, technology, and finance.

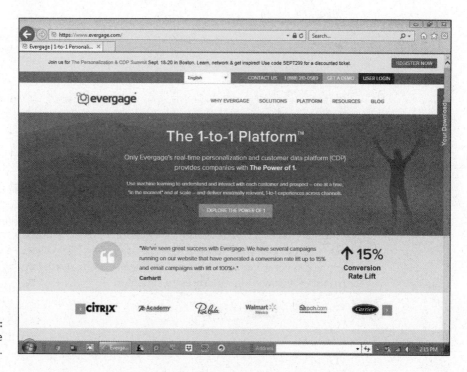

FIGURE 25-1:
Evergage
home page.

>> **Dynamic Yield** (https://www.dynamicyield.com), shown in Figure 25-2, is owned by McDonald's Corporation and is particularly suited for the fast-food/quick-serve industry.

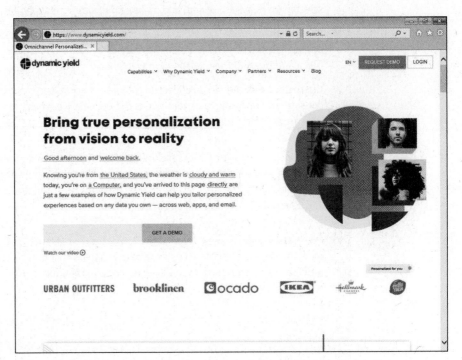

FIGURE 25-2:
Dynamic Yield
home page.

>> **Monetate** (https://monetate.com/), shown in Figure 25-3, works well for those companies that want to create customized experiences. It's recommended for enterprises and mid-market companies.

Measuring your customer experience

As you make changes to the customer experience, it's essential for you to continually measure your customer's satisfaction. According to the User Testing Blog (https://www.usertesting.com/blog/customer-experience-metrics/), there are several metrics that you can use to evaluate the effectiveness of your customer journey. Here are three to consider:

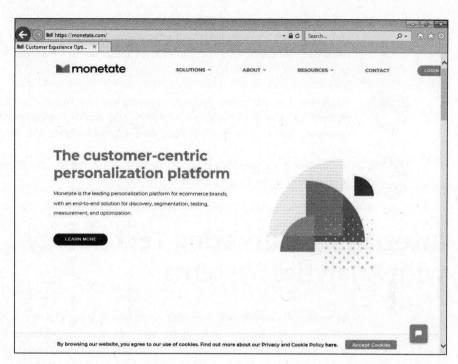

FIGURE 25-3:
Monetate
home page.

- ➤➤ **Net promoter score (NPS):** This score reflects the number of customers who would recommend your service to their friends or business associates. The survey question is typically phrased as, "On a scale of 0-10, how likely are you to recommend our product or service to your friends or colleagues?"

- ➤➤ **Customer satisfaction (CSAT):** This measure is the average of the score that customers give to a specific experience they've had with your company. The survey question is typically phrased as, "How would you rate your experience with x?" Obviously, the higher the score, the better you're doing.

- ➤➤ **Customer effort score (CES):** This measures the amount of effort it takes to accomplish a particular task. The survey item is typically phrased as, "The company made it easy for me to handle my issue."

Analyzing the customer journey

As you know, in decades past, marketers had full control of the customer journey — it was linear. They controlled the message, pricing options, and purchase channels. Of course, those days are a distant memory. Today's customer journey is at best unpredictable and can be hard to track. Customers find information on their own and might buy a product without ever speaking to a salesperson. For that reason, collecting data and analyzing customer behavior in every part of the funnel is critical.

REMEMBER

Analyzing the customer journey requires you to make sure that you provide content on every conceivable channel and social media platform that your customer may find to evaluate your product and interact with your brand.

TIP

In Chapter 3 we provide an in-depth look at navigating the complete marketing funnel from awareness to loyalty.

Integrating Marketing Technology with Analytics Systems

As previously mentioned, the most successful marketers are uniting their marketing technology with their analytics systems. The reason for this is simple. Most marketers are drowning in social media data. What they don't have are customer insights. To gain these insights, you need to combine data from disparate platforms such as your website, mobile apps, email, automation, advertising platforms, call center logs, and your e-commerce sites.

Facing data problems

The key to analyzing data in all the ways that are available to you is to have data that is prepared for analysis. (See the next section.) Unfortunately, this isn't easy for most organizations that are overwhelmed with the volume of data they generate. Here are some of the issues marketers face when trying to bring all their data together. Do some of these problems sound familiar to you?

>> **Data trapped in department silos:** Departments are protective of their data and don't want to release it to others for fear it will be misused or degraded in some way. This prevents the organization from benefitting from a more comprehensive look at the customer.

>> **A lack of automation systems in place:** Your organization is doing a lot of work with spreadsheets rather than using automated processes. This wastes a lot of time and prevents you from analyzing the data at the level you need it to extract insights.

>> **A lack of accurate data:** When was the last time your data was cleaned? Has it been checked for duplicates, wrong addresses, and out-of-date purchase

information? If not, your data is useless, and customers see that you don't really have a handle on their relationship with your brand. They assume they don't matter to you. They also don't have a single source of truth, which is crucial for the organization.

>> **Combined data that is not optimized:** When you combine disparate data, are you making sure to optimize it? Just throwing different data sets into a database makes it unworkable. You could be taking valuable data and destroying its value.

>> **A way to identify customers across channels while maintaining their privacy:** You need to be able to identify your customers by their various names across channels. This is key to having a 360-degree view of the customer. However, you also want to make sure that their data is protected and secure. If customers think you don't respect their data, they will cease doing business with you.

>> **The right staff to do the job:** If you're pulling in unqualified staff from other departments to manage and analyze your data, you're damaging what should be a valuable corporate asset. Hire qualified people who can get the most from your data.

>> **Budgetary constraints:** Bringing together data from across the organization and preparing them to be used in all the systems and analytics tools can be an unanticipated expense. Make sure that you can enumerate the benefits of doing this for the entire organization.

Preparing your data

Clean data free of such things as errors and duplicates ensures that your analytics is useful to you. To help companies understand the process for preparing their data for AI tools, Rob Thomas, General Manager IBM Data and Watson AI, created the "AI Ladder." This details the steps to take using a ladder metaphor. The ladder has four rungs as you progress to the top. They are:

>> **Collect:** Data should be made accessible. Make sure you collect all the data hidden away in silos. Then you want to modernize it (prepare it to handle all data types) so that it is in a form that can be analyzed with current tools and systems.

>> **Organize:** After the data is collected, you should organize it and have governance rules (rules for who and how it can be used) in place.

>> **Analyze:** Scale it to be used wherever needed. Determine the AI tools you will use to analyze it.

>> **Infuse AI:** Operationalize it with transparency to be used across the organization.

REMEMBER

AI data can automate decisions, processes, and customer experiences, but if your data is in bad shape, the new tools and systems you put in place won't be able to provide you with the customer insights you need to grow your business.

Deploying AI Tools

As you can see, AI is currently being used in many business and consumer applications. This also includes machine learning (ML) for such things as getting Netflix recommendations or asking Siri what the weather is. (See Chapter 19 for more about personal digital assistants.)

TIP

Machine learning refers to a subcategory of AI whereby algorithms are created that predict behavior without specifically being programmed to do so. It uses patterns and inferences from previously collected data to learn what the right answers should be.

Your job as a marketer is to use AI tools to learn as much about your customers as you can, and figure out how to help them get the information they need across the customer lifecycle.

TIP

Gartner recommends that when using AI tools to measure customer experience, you should aim for "early quick wins," that you can easily track to determine whether they're a success or failure. A quick success helps propel your initiative forward.

THE 'DOCTOR' WILL SEE YOU NOW

AI is bringing significant savings to the health field with less investment. According to a 2018 white paper by Accenture called "Artificial Intelligence: Healthcare's New Nervous System," the health care economy will see an annual savings of $150 billion by 2026. The top five applications that they predict will provide the most value are robot-assisted surgery, virtual nursing assistants, administrative workflow assistance, fraud detection, and dosage error reduction.

Chapter 26

Understanding Social Media Governance

S ocial media has had a pervasive influence on marketing. In large organizations, it fosters new types of collaboration, processes, policies, and governance structures.

What's more, SMM influences corporations in substantive ways beyond the realm of marketing and into public relations, sales, customer service (or consumer relations), and the legal department. Having strong social media governance and tools is now more important than ever.

Recognizing How SMM Impacts Other Company Functions

Early in the book, we discuss SMM as it relates to brand marketing and direct response. We also frame social media marketing in the context of customer service and real-time marketing. In this chapter, we look at how social media marketing touches some of these other corporate functions and then we review good governance practices. After that, we discuss the different governance models.

Public relations

Marketing and public relations have a symbiotic relationship, and in some organizations, public relations rolls up into the marketing organization. Both groups have important roles to play in the world of social media, but they come at it from different places.

Fundamentally, the marketing function owns the relationship with the consumers and is the steward of the brands. With the relationships often being formed and nurtured in social media, it becomes critical for the marketing function to lead all social media marketing efforts. This means that the following activities are typically led by the marketing team:

>> Defining the brand's social voice

>> Managing the social media platform pages

>> Owning and driving social calendar activities

>> Running social media campaigns across social media

>> Planning and buying all social media advertising

>> Coordinating all community management efforts

However, in larger organizations public relations has a critical role to play, too. They manage relationships with the media and other key influencers, who in turn heavily influence consumer perception. Often, the mainstream media treats social media as the place to distribute its stories. Furthermore, the most successful and largest social influencers online often behave like media companies as well. As a result, the place at which marketing and public relations intersect in social media marketing is also where influencer management takes place. When it comes to social media influencer management, both the marketers and the PR professionals have valuable and important roles to play. It is in this area that tight collaboration is required.

The following activities are typically led by the PR team:

>> Leading all mainstream media relationships

>> Driving core communication plans with outbound PR efforts

>> Running all communication crisis management efforts

>> Jointly managing social influencer relationships

Customer support

Marketing and customer support activities often happen within minutes of each other on the social media brand pages (regardless of whether the brands want this to be the case). A good example is that in any given moment on a brand page in Facebook, one consumer may be expressing her love for the brand and talking about fun brand-related activities while another may be complaining about a defective product. In such a scenario, who manages what? There are no set rules, and they vary by industry. Typically, the first line of response to a consumer is the social media marketing team because that team serves as the voice of the brand on the platform. If the situation demands a serious response very quickly or is an issue that escalates suddenly, it's handed off to customer support.

Although these divisions of labor are easy to write in a process document, the truth is that when it comes to customer queries, the social media marketers and the customer support professionals need to collaborate and partner very closely. Each group brings different skills and experiences to the table, and who is posting what largely doesn't matter — the most important aspect is the collaboration between the two groups. The same need for collaboration applies to marketing and public relations, but a stronger governance model comes into play. The volume of messages in the consumer relations realm, versus more general marketing conversations, drives how tight that collaboration needs to be.

Sales

If SMM were quite literally and narrowly about marketing, it wouldn't be half as interesting to companies as it is today. What makes it special is that within the domain of SMM, you have facets of customer support, public relations, and sales, too. As discussed earlier in the book, offering sales and discounts for customers serves as a very strong incentive to Like a brand on Facebook or follow it on Twitter.

Promoting the deals via the Facebook and Twitter pages of the brand usually makes sense. In that case, the publishing should be managed by the same social media coordinators in the marketing organization who are responsible for the page.

Another, more complex scenario is when the brand has e-commerce enabled on its Facebook or Instagram page. In such a scenario, the page must be managed by the e-commerce team or a digital team that may (or may not) sit in the marketing department. But here, too, the management of the community and the social voice of the brand should be driven through one team and one social media marketer, so tight coordination is required.

Legal

The people who are the most worried about social media are usually the folks on the legal teams. They get concerned about whether something that is published can violate someone else's copyright or make the company liable in some form. The legal teams are definitely justified in their fear, and although there are no potentially overlapping responsibilities between the legal team and the social media marketers, it's important to set clear rules covering what can and can't be published on the social media platforms. In scenarios that don't conform to those parameters, the social media marketers should meet with the legal teams to discuss the exceptions. The more the legal teams understand what the marketers are trying to accomplish via social media strategically, and the more the marketers understand the rules and regulations — both internal ones and those established by government agencies — the stronger the partnership between the two teams will be. Legal involvement becomes critical when reviewing licensing rights to images and video, especially as those rights pertain to celebrities, athletes, and competitor logos.

TIP

Having the legal teams review every single response and every single comment published may not be realistic. But as long as the proper rules, escalation strategies, and processes are in place, the legal teams should be comfortable with social media marketers publishing content on a regular basis without direct approvals. The rules, however, probably need to vary dramatically from industry to industry. In some more regulated industries, approvals of every piece of content might be a necessary evil.

Introducing Social Media Governance Models

Every organization requires social media governance. Whether large or small, if you're a company using social media, you require governance models in place. The hypercollaboration required to succeed (as witnessed by the topics discussed previously) necessitates strong governance models between both marketing and other functions and within marketing, too.

Coordinating this collaboration gets increasingly complex when you have global and local marketing teams and also marketing teams broken up by product lines.

Following are the key governance models to consider:

>> **Centralized governance:** In a centralized social media governance model, one team is responsible for SMM and drives the daily management of the

brand outposts on the various social platforms. This group also drives influencer management in partnership with the PR teams. They loop in legal, consumer relations, sales, and other department representatives as needed. This model is effective in smaller organizations or companies that aren't geographically distributed or do not have a significant number of product lines.

» **Hub-and-spoke governance:** In the hub-and-spoke model, you have both global and local social media marketing teams. Each team is responsible for a core set of activities. Accounts that are more global in nature are managed by the global team, whereas those that are local are managed locally. As more brands move to social media management platforms such as Salesforce Marketing Cloud, Sprinklr, khoros, and Oracle's Vitrue, the need to have both global and local teams (with different permission policies, roles, and responsibilities) gets increasingly important. Clear differentiation in roles and responsibilities with specific process documents and tone and voice guidelines are necessary to make this model a success. For example, a given Facebook page may have global content on it (managed by the global team) and local content that the local teams publish to regularly.

» **Distributed governance:** A distributed governance structure has a very small, centralized SMM team (or it's nonexistent). Each product line or geographic territory has its own social media teams and its own corresponding social media profiles. Coordination happens more informally between the different markets by sharing social media calendars, redistributing content, and sharing tone and voice guidelines, but little else is shared. Each geographical region or each product line chooses how best to approach SMM and does it in its own fashion, with its own philosophies, tools, and processes.

» **Extreme distributed governance:** This model has practically no coordination between different marketing teams responsible for social media across different geographies and product lines. This approach is not recommended, because it can result in the same brand being represented in different ways in different countries or even simply on multiple brand pages. This lack of cohesion quickly results in confusion for the customers. Without even minimal coordination, influencer management becomes challenging because the same influencer may be hearing different messages about the same brands from two different people in one organization.

Some organizations also put committees or councils in place to encourage

- Greater cross-functional collaboration

- The establishment of social media policies and guidelines

- The facilitation of group decision-making

- Conflict resolution

- Crisis management

> Depending on the size of your organization, how your company is structured, and whether organic, spontaneous collaboration takes place, extreme distributed governance may be an evil necessity to put in place for the short term.

Social media policies and guidelines

Every organization needs strong social media policies and guidelines. The policies are best defined as articulating what employees can and cannot do. They are often used to drive what can be published and by whom on a social media platform (when representing the brand) and what procedure you should go through to get to that publishing.

Guidelines, in contrast to policies, are typically defined as best practices covering how to participate in social media as a brand or as an employee representing the company. In the guidelines, you typically see recommendations, examples, rules, and best practices. Organizations large or small need to practice social media marketing effectively.

The major components of a social media policy typically include the following:

>> Guidelines for identifying oneself as an employee of the company

>> Confidentiality clauses — what you are free to publish and what you shouldn't

>> Respect and privacy rights components pertaining to others whom you may talk about

>> Legal components and liabilities; often, just expressing that the opinions are your own can help limit brand reputation risk

>> Rules for participation on social media platforms during work hours and beyond

>> Best practice examples of how to engage — especially on company social media pages

You can write a social media policy document in many different ways. Every organization is different, and you need to have something that's suitable to your organization's needs, philosophies, value system, and culture. However, looking at other social media policies can help. See Chapter 5 for links to examples of social media guidelines.

TIP

Social media policies need to be living documents. As the Internet evolves and social media platforms change, you need to update your company's social media policies to keep pace with that change. Therefore, be sure to revisit your social media policies on a regular basis to determine that they are up-to-date and reflect the current needs of your company.

Tips and tricks for social media governance

Moving to effective social media governance is a journey that requires continuous iteration, planning, re-planning, and structural tweaking. Following are some tips and tricks that can help you institute stronger social media governance in your organization quickly:

>> **Define its purpose.**

Social media governance is one of those initiatives that can quickly become a lot bigger or broader than it's supposed to be. When it gets larger, it often gets unwieldy. As a result, when you're starting to establish social media governance, begin by defining its purpose, scope, and connection points to other governance structures in your organization. List the specific channels, employee groups, and scenarios that will be covered under the governance model.

>> **Develop strong processes and practices.**

No governance model or policies and guidelines will be effective without robust processes and practices put in place early on. As soon as you define the purpose, start thinking about the right processes and practices for your organization. The right ones are probably different for every organization. The best way to choose the right ones are to see what types of processes have been successful for other initiatives in the organization.

>> **Keep policies and guidelines concise.**

As discussed earlier in the chapter, policies and guidelines are extremely important. However, you can easily get carried away and make them long and cumbersome. In their first iterations, try to keep your policies and guidelines as concise and simple as possible. If your employees don't understand the simple versions, they will be more intimidated by something complex and long.

>> **Establish ongoing training and education.**

Establishing governance models, processes, policies, and guidelines are all important. But they're only as good as their rate of adoption. That's why putting training and education processes in place is extremely important. Sometimes the training may need to be just a series of webinars or online classes. In other instances, periodic electronic communication or in-person "lunch and learns" can be more helpful. Use whatever approach has worked for other similar initiatives in your organization.

>> **Do continuity planning.**

In lots of large organizations, a person is never in one job for a very long time. You may be charged with developing and implementing a governance model today, but you may be in another job a year from now. Therefore, a key task is to identify people in the governance structure who know enough about the model and practices to be able to take over from you if your role changes.

>> **Keep legal departments involved.**

Some participants in the social media governance model may feel that the legal department needs to be only peripherally involved. With the FTC (Federal Trade Commission) and other governmental organizations playing a stronger and stronger role in defining social media policies for companies, legal departments need to be actively involved. Stakeholders with vested interests should also be included. Don't leave them out.

Dealing with a Social Media Crisis

As a brand, you may do something that angers your community and you may be hit by a social media crisis. Something may happen to one of your products or services that results in a sudden, sharp backlash from people across the social media ecosystem. If and when this happens, knowing how to respond in the first 24 hours and the first week is absolutely critical. Companies have saved or lost many millions of dollars simply by how they responded to a crisis. Don't make the mistakes that others have.

If you're hit by a social media crisis, the following are key steps to take immediately:

1. **Bring together an emergency response team.**

This team is usually a combination of marketers, consumer relations professionals, PR teams, product managers, and consultants. The core emergency response team should be identified, established, and empowered to make all decisions regarding the crisis.

2. **Listen to the community.**

Using the social media tools discussed in the earlier chapters, try to understand the extent of the backlash and whether it is increasing or decreasing over time. Also, pay particular attention to the complaints and whether there's uniformity in the type of complaints from different people. Also try to understand whether the crisis has geographic boundaries or is limited to a certain set of people who share demographic traits. Try to unearth whether they are new customers, existing customers, or neither.

3. Identify and solve the problem.

You have no better way to deal with a social media crisis than by addressing the problem that is at the heart of the crisis. Devote extra energy and resources to understanding what the problem is, why people are complaining, and what the potential remedies may be. This may seem obvious, but many a company in the midst of a crisis has focused a little too much on protecting its reputation and not enough on truly understanding and solving the root source of the crisis.

4. Create lists of key influencers and research their positions.

If appropriate, you will probably want to contain a social media crisis with the participation of key influencers. Create lists of these influencers — some of whom may be aligned with your brand and your position in the crisis, and some against them. Regardless of their opinions, you need to know who is most influential on the subject. Determine who may be able to tip the scales and help with your message.

5. Respond frequently and with transparency.

Even if you do not have a response to the crisis and are still trying to understand what is going on, respond to the community. It is critical to show that you're hearing their complaints and to explain that you're seeking solutions. A social media crisis demands hypertransparency. If you do not operate with that frame of mind, you're certain to turn off even more people than you may have with the core issue.

6. Be open to having the community influence and define the outcomes.

In a social media crisis, many people respond by being even more guarded, closed, and corporate in their approach to all communications. Although a crisis may indeed be a tricky time, it doesn't mean that you should create additional distance between you and your customers. Instead, depending on the nature of the crisis, ask the community for ideas on how best to shape the outcomes. Sometimes, community members may be the ones who will be best able to provide answers.

Chapter **27**

Using Real-Time Marketing

R eal-time marketing is all about going from strategy and consumer insights to messaging and advertising in a matter of seconds or minutes instead of a matter of months or even years. Until the advent of "always on" social media and real-time buying, it seemed a pipe dream. But with the increased digitization of the entire media ecosystem we now get real-time consumer insights as they are formed by consumers. We can design creative experiences responding to those insights and even run them in digital media locations — all in a matter of minutes.

Introducing Real-Time Marketing

In the 5th edition of "State of Marketing," Salesforce found that although real-time engagement is a marketers highest priority, it's also their biggest challenge. To make real-time marketing practical for your business, you need to understand its core components. These components are real-time

» Insights

» Response

- » On the fly
- » Co-creation
- » Distribution
- » Engagement

Each of these components is discussed in the following sections. They all are built on the foundational principles of SMM, except that now, with real-time marketing, the principles and practices of social media marketing are brought into real time and amplified to achieve an even broader and more dynamic scale than before. In this chapter, we discuss each of these core concepts to illustrate how.

Real-time insights

As of June 2019, more than 500 million tweets are sent by consumers around the world on a daily basis. Add to that the billions of comments on Facebook, conversations on public discussion boards, and blog posts written every day, and suddenly marketers have a rich trove of data to analyze. They use this data to infer consumer interests, tastes, and preferences. Some of this data may be more accessible than others. What's certain is that there's so much new data, often with both time and location stamps (meaning that you know the time and place where the message was posted), that it simply cannot be ignored.

This data is used to draw deep longitudinal insights about consumers, but it can also be used to infer immediate, actionable, short-term insights and consumer preferences. For example, do you know what the most popular show on television is this week? You can tell not just by the number of people who watched the show but also by the number of people who talk about it favorably. Of course, the fact that a show fits into a specific social media demographic also plays a part. Similarly, do you know which artist's music is being talked about the most online in this very moment, or whether one pop culture event is more significant than another?

You can capture real-time insights about your consumers in three ways. The first is more prescriptive in nature, whereas the second is more observational. The third is completely technologically driven. They are as follows:

- » **Prescriptive real-time insights:** If you know three or four different events taking place on a given day but cannot guess which will be the most important to your consumers, you can use social media to determine which is the most important. You can analyze the volume and type of conversation around each on that day.

>> **Descriptive real-time insights:** Several different tools and social media platforms in the marketplace can tell you which conversational topics are trending as the most important. Following these on a regular basis can help you determine what your consumers are thinking about and what's considered topical, of deep interest, or simply hot for them in that given time. Knowing this information can help you alter your advertising messaging and how you engage with those consumers on social media platforms, as well as potentially influence which products you choose to push.

One of the easiest ways to gather these real-time insights is by looking at the Trends for You topics list on Twitter. This list tells you what topics are being talked about the most in any given moment by Twitter users. You can then further narrow down the list to determine the most popular conversation topics for a particular city or country. Other services built on top of Twitter help you easily sort through the most popular music, movies, sports events, and other pop culture activities. Another example is Buzzsumo's Trending Now tool (`https://app.buzzsumo.com/research/trending`).

In a similar fashion, Google Trends helps you draw real-time insights with similar geographic filters by analyzing the comparative popularity of different search terms. These tools help you understand what consumers are thinking and engaging with at any given moment.

>> **Technologically driven real-time insights:** The third way to get to real-time insights is by using technological tools that analyze conversations on a mass scale as well as review the popularity of keyword search terms in Google and Facebook advertising. Based on the cost of those keyword terms, these tools can tell you what topics matter most to consumers and which are most likely to elicit a response from them.

Real-time response

The next concept in real-time marketing is real-time response. This is the type of response that's typically covered in any social media marketing effort. It's the response that you do through the social media channels in as timely and culturally relevant a fashion as you can. It's an organic response, through the voice of the brand, and it's targeted as much as possible to consumers who care. One point to note is that although the response is organic, you may want to "boost" the response with paid media to make sure it gets the attention it deserves. We talk more about this later in the chapter.

But there is one fundamental difference between real-time response and the more traditional SMM initiatives that you may undertake. Real-time responses are organic responses through the lens of real-time marketing insights. So, for example, if you sold soccer shoes, and you knew that a particular soccer game was the most-talked-about thing on that day, you'd use that cultural event to start conversations across Twitter, Facebook, Instagram, and other social channels with your key consumers. Because you can target different consumers by location on Facebook, you would probably target specific conversation types for the fans of each team.

This is a real-time response. You're joining popular online conversations that matter to specific customers of yours in specific locations in an extremely timely, culturally relevant fashion. They're all built off real-time insights in ways that add value to the conversation. The critical difference between real-time response and traditional SMM is that instead of depending on a predefined calendar for your communications, you're responding to real-time insights and happenings in the real world.

Real-time "on the fly"

With easy-to-use platform tools such as InstaStories and Snapchat, you can create real-time content on the fly that disappears after 24 hours. This type of content can capture the excitement of events and product announcements with the click of the record button. You can create behind-the-scenes moments and capture people's responses as they happen.

TIP

See more about using Instagram and Snapchat in Chapters 12 and 13, respectively.

Real-time co-creation

The next concept in the real-time marketing framework is real-time co-creation. There's no use doing real-time insights or real-time response, or even creating compelling content, if it doesn't have a real-time co-creation dimension to it. Real-time co-creation is all about bringing consumer feedback into the marketing process. Co-creation is an iterative process that improves content by exposing it to feedback and revision by both customers and the company.

This is extremely important with real-time marketing. You're doing so much so quickly that you can easily miss the right vibe and cause your brand irreparable harm in your rush to get something out. The only way to mitigate that possible harm is with real-time co-creation efforts. Real-time co-creation efforts can be done in a variety of different ways. The following are some options:

>> **Digital ad creative testing:** If you're running paid digital advertising on Google or a platform like Facebook or Twitter, you can optimize the creative very quickly based on how well it performs. Often, in fact, the ad serving system automatically optimizes the creative for you.

For example, suppose that you're running advertising and want to test three different versions of ad copy. You can run all three, and depending on how each performs (the number of clicks each version gets), the ad serving solution shows the one that's doing the best. You can use this format to test ad creative that is run in other locations, too.

>> **Seeding with a private community:** Many brands launch and run private online communities in which they ask consumers for feedback on production innovations, marketing efforts, and future business plans. If you're creating a piece of content (whether for SMM or elsewhere), you can first run it in your private community and solicit feedback before using it on a much larger public scale.

>> **Tapping into individual third-party content creators:** Another alternative is to tap into content creators directly to help create your marketing communications. Companies such as Tongal (www.tongal.com) and CrowdContent (www.crowdcontent.com) source content creators from their huge community of writers. It happens very quickly, with the greatest benefit being that you're using their communities to help find the right content creator instead of vetting someone on your own. Other companies that can help in this space are FullScreen (www.fullscreen.com), and Soul Pancake (www.soulpancake.com), which does something similar for video content on YouTube.

Real-time distribution

The vision of real-time marketing can only truly come to life if you have a real-time distribution system in place. There's no use gathering powerful insights, creating powerful content, and testing it with consumers if you can't then distribute it on a mass scale. As we say in the "Real-time response" section, earlier in this chapter, the first step is in launching and running the responses through the organic social media channels.

However, you have other ways to distribute the content, experiences, and various forms of communication. Following are some of the key forms of distribution to consider for your real-time marketing content:

>> **Social media platforms:** This is probably the easiest way to distribute your real-time content, but you should start with your own social media channels. Why? Because it's critical to first meet the needs and provide early access to advocates of your brand. They're typically the ones who follow you on Twitter or have Liked you on Facebook. Distributing real-time content on your own channels first takes the shape of organic engagement on the social media platforms, but beyond that engagement, it occurs through paid social media engagement. However, note that because of Facebook's changes in its

newsfeed publishing algorithm, reaching your fans without spending money to boost your social media posts has gotten increasingly *harder*. Some paid investments are required.

>> **Websites:** It's sometimes easy to forget, but your own website is an important content distribution channel. Contrary to all the public hype, people do still visit company websites. If you have it structured in a meaningful way, the website can serve as a great place to engage your consumers in real time. Take a look at the Pepsi website (www.pepsi.com) or the GE web presence (www.ge.com) for examples of websites that look and feel more like media companies in how they publish content.

>> **Digital advertising:** Arguably, the quickest way to get mass reach for your real-time marketing efforts is by leveraging the scale of digital advertising. Increasingly, you can buy digital advertising on a real-time basis and swap creative in and out in the moment. You can even put social media content (a Twitter feed, for example) into the display advertising. Digital advertising is an important arrow in the quiver of your real-time marketing efforts because it often gives you significant scale very quickly.

>> **Email programs:** Your email programs can serve as an important real-time marketing distribution engine for your real-time marketing efforts. Don't shy away from using these programs effectively. In fact, even with the rise of social media, email continues to be a complementary means of communication. The challenge is in making it work effectively without overburdening your consumers.

REMEMBER

All the previously listed options can be activated in a matter of minutes. In fact, we are already seeing that with real-time video ad targeting. What's more, for the first time ever, the real-time marketing efforts can be done on a mass scale — a scale that historically was limited to traditional marketing efforts only.

Real-time engagement

After you've tapped into your consumer's real-time insights, co-created real-time experiences, and triggered the engagement with them, the last key piece is real-time engagement. This is arguably the hardest to do in a scalable way. Expect to have fewer consumers engage meaningfully with you when you move beyond pushing content or experiences to them and ask them to participate on an ongoing basis.

Real-time engagement can take many different shapes. For example, it can focus on building and nurturing daily engagement with your consumers through Facebook, Twitter, Instagram, Tumblr, or Pinterest. After you've triggered consumer engagement driven by real-time insights, you can then use that engagement as an opportunity to engage with consumers on a more regular basis. What follows are some tips and tricks to consider for real-time engagement:

>> **Make paid, owned, and social media work together.**

The best forms of real-time engagement are the ones that use the reach of paid media, harmoniously coupled with the deep engagement of social and owned media.

>> **Make sure to think about mobile.**

With the majority of Facebook, Instagram, and Twitter usage happening on mobile platforms, planning engagement on these platforms is very important. Engage your audience with real-world scavenger hunts, tips at special locations, and physical-world reward systems. See Chapter 23 for more about mobile campaigns.

>> **Partner with media companies that practice real-time marketing.**

Some media talk to consumers every single day through television and the Internet. You can partner with them to find ways to engage with consumers on a daily basis.

>> **Harness Twitter Trends for You to engage in real time.**

Nothing is stopping you from participating in conversations that are trending on Twitter. Determine meaningful ways to join and contribute to those conversations, and use promoted tweets to strategically amplify your own engagement efforts.

Organizing for Real-Time Marketing

Practicing real-time marketing successfully requires an interdisciplinary team coming together and partnering extremely closely. Just because you need to move really quickly doesn't mean that you shouldn't do so in a very collaborative, inclusive fashion.

In large companies, real-time marketing teams typically include representatives from brand strategy, social media marketing, legal, media, public relations, and consumer relations functions. In small companies, the SMM team typically carries the responsibilities for real-time marketing and operates with predefined guidelines and processes.

REMEMBER

The most challenging piece of real-time marketing is knowing which consumer trends to market against and which ones to avoid. Some trends will no doubt be much more relevant to your brand and your specific consumers than others. However, discovering which those are comes only in time, by testing and viewing the responses.

To help jump-start your real-time marketing efforts, take the following actions:

>> **Create a list of key topics.**

You cannot participate in every consumer trend or pop culture moment. But by creating a list of priority topics that are of interest to your consumers and matter to your brand, you'll know which trends to prioritize over others when things start popping. For example, if you're a shoe company, tapping into a real-time trend around running will be far more important than one about reality TV shows.

>> **Create a global calendar of major pop culture events in the year.**

Having a calendar of events will help you determine which major pop culture events are worth activating against. However, not every pop culture event in the year has meaning for your brand. (For example, does Mother's Day have particular resonance for your brand? If you're Hallmark, the answer is obviously yes). Choose the days on which you want to activate with real-time marketing carefully, because you're probably like most marketers and have limited resources.

>> **Put aside some media dollars for paid advertising.**

Create a small bucket of advertising dollars to support your real-time marketing efforts around those specific topics or days in the year. Use these dollars to amplify any real-time marketing activity against the trends and topics that matter most to your consumers. This is important because without the paid investments, you probably won't reach enough consumers who matter to your brand.

>> **Pay attention to trends as they're popping.**

Trends are most valuable if you can ride their growth and exposure to more and more people. Keep an eye on trends that are just starting to pop; they may be more valuable and cheaper to market against than a trend that has already hit the mainstream.

>> **Listen to key influencers in your space.**

Sometimes the best way to discover a trend that matters to your customers and your business is by watching what key influencers in your space are talking about. Often, they're the ones who talk about trends first and take them mainstream.

>> **Start small; test and learn.**

Real-time marketing is tricky, and getting it right in ways that match the scale and budget of your brand can be difficult. The only way to practice real-time marketing successfully is to test different tactics, observe how they perform, and then build to bigger and bigger programs from there.

Taking TV into Real-Time Marketing

Approximately 60 percent of people watching television have a laptop, a mobile phone, or a tablet computer open in front of them. In fact, iPads are used the most when people are watching television. Here are some tips for taking TV into real-time marketing if your brand runs TV advertising:

>> **Use traditional buttons.**

The ends of television ads that include calls to action for the brand are called *buttons.* Be sure to include your Facebook URL or your Twitter handle in them at the end.

>> **Make sure to track conversations.**

If you are advertising on television, typically for the show you are advertising against, there are lots of online conversations going on. Think about buying Twitter search terms against those conversations so that your message is amplified. You can then craft your Twitter communications to be contextually relevant to the show and anything else happening in the media ecosystem in that moment.

>> **Make dynamic calls to action.**

Depending on what you're advertising, you can benefit from more dynamic buttons in your TV advertising. For example, if you know that the advertisement is going to run during the Grammy awards, your call to action at the end of the ad can be about going online and seeing which artist is the most talked about. This approach puts your call to action in real time and makes it relevant and contextual.

>> **Treat the TV ad as a piece of a broader narrative.**

It is easy to forget, but television advertising can be an important part of a broader narrative of a brand that's centered in real-time digital engagement. As you plan your TV advertising, think about what else may be happening in the world on the day it runs and what types of conversations consumers will have online in that moment. Factor those aspects into your planning.

Chapter **28**

Data and Privacy

With data breaches and questionable digital marketing practices becoming more common, data and privacy couldn't be a more important and sensitive topic for marketers today. From data breaches at Yahoo, Facebook, Marriott, Equifax, and others you can't presume data is ever as safe as you think it is. Practically every week, there is a data breach somewhere in the world where people's data gets compromised.

We want to believe that those data and privacy horror stories are at the more extreme end of the spectrum and far away from the marketing that we all do. However, that isn't the case. Marketing in the digital world can be a slippery slope towards breaking laws and betraying the trust of consumers. It's important to know what best practices to consider when you're marketing using data. The laws in parts of the United States and across the European Union have changed as well. Knowing what you are allowed and not allowed to do is critical to understand. And more so, it's important to learn what this means for marketing in the future.

Knowing What Data You Have to Play With

Social media has become such an intrinsic part of people's lives that they don't pay attention to how and where data is gathered about them. They realize so many benefits with using social media from being able to connect with friends, gather news, participate in groups, find products, and further professional relationships that they forget to think about the value exchange at play.

Social media platforms are able to offer their services for free because they gather data on consumers that is then used by businesses to market on their platforms.

The same applies to company websites and advertising efforts — data is gathered by businesses (not just the social media platforms) that is then used to market more effectively. It's just the nature of how marketing works. To better understand what data you have available to you to play with as a marketer, it's necessary to learn about first-, second- and third-party data.

>> **First-party data:** This is the data you have directly collected from consumers who have bought your product and services. It can also be data that you have collected from consumers who have visited your website, used your service, or simply engaged with you in some fashion. First-party data is typically of high data quality and can be used in precise ways for marketing, such as for retargeting advertisements in Facebook (running ads on Facebook to people who have already visited your website). This data requires you to explicitly ask your consumers for permission before collecting or using.

>> **Second-party data:** This is data other businesses may have collected about consumers whom you may want to market to. The data quality is typically not as strong as first-party data and has narrower targeting reach but can be used to run effective marketing campaigns. You typically have to buy these data sets or form partnerships with those businesses to use their data. It's key that the businesses that provide you with this data not only have permission from the consumers to collect and use the data but also to allow third parties like you to use it.

>> **Third-party data:** This is the data collected by third parties from multiple sources and combined into larger data sets and then segmented based on specific characteristics. Not surprisingly, the quality of these data sets can be of varying quality and the ability to market effectively with them can be limited. Even though the data sets can be very large, it's often outdated. Here too, the rules of making sure that consumers have granted permission to the business to collect, use, and sell the data to other businesses are critical to follow.

Typically, any marketer is probably dealing with a combination of first-, second- and third-party data in their marketing efforts. For example, you may collect email addresses on your website (first-party data), combine it with purchasing data from a retailer that is selling your product (second-party data), and eventually match all that information in Facebook to create custom audiences (third-party data) that you can then advertise against. That's how advertising works and is par for the course for most advertisers.

However, between these different types of data collection and usage methods, a lot can go wrong. And that's why understanding data best practices and knowing the most important data and privacy laws of today are critical.

Harnessing Data & Privacy Best Practices

One of the greatest strengths of social media marketing is that you have access to much more personalized data about your potential customers. This allows you to identify them with laser-focused precision, target them when they're most likely to respond to your marketing messages, and also adjust the communication so that it resonates based on how they are behaving in that moment of time. Without a doubt, for many this is the holy grail of marketing — reaching customers at the right time, in the right place, and in the right format based on how exactly they're behaving and knowing what they'll most likely respond to.

WARNING

But at the same time, this is a double-edged sword. Without realizing it, you may find yourself learning so much about your customers that you're not just convincing them to make a purchasing decision but instead are unintentionally manipulating how they think.

To really understand what data you can play with and how exactly you should use it, here are some key best practices to follow:

>> **Write easily understandable terms of service and privacy policies.** Most privacy policies are designed for and by lawyers. While that worked for a long time, it isn't the right thing to do. You run the risk of upsetting your users by not properly informing them how you will use their data if it is in language they cannot understand. A good litmus test to use is to ask yourself whether a layman can understand your terms of service.

>> **Educate customers on how you will use their information.** It's one thing to be collecting the data, but another is in how you use it. Explain to your customers how you're going to use the data and how you're also going to protect their privacy at the same time. Your customers need to understand how you use their data not only on your website but across your entire business.

>> **Establish a global data policy first.** If you run a business across countries, create a stringent global data policy. Then augment those rules based on local laws that may result in specific country nuances that would typically be tied to where and how the data is stored. It's one way to guarantee you will be more careful with your customer data.

- >> **Be extra careful if you sell to minors.** The rules for what you can or cannot do when selling to minors are even more stringent. If you're in a business that may market or sell to minors (or have minors unintentionally buy the product), conduct an inventory of your data practices immediately. You have to be very clear on what you are allowed to collect and use. Keep in mind very often parental consent will be required.

- >> **Protect the data as if your life depends on it.** Your customers are trusting you when they share their data with you. Protect it as if your life depends on it. If you get hacked or worse — sell their data to a third party without explicit permission — you'll lose the customer trust indefinitely. Also know, that your customers will also hold you responsible if the third party gets hacked and their private data is exposed.

- >> **Don't creep out your customers.** Everyone's gotten into the habit of accepting privacy policies on the Internet without reading the fine print, and not realizing what they're agreeing to most of the time. When you're marketing to customers, don't creep them out with marketing messages that demonstrate you know a lot more information about them than they may have realized.

- >> **Use good judgment when developing data practices.** The most important rule when it comes to using a customer's data or to advertising on a social media platform is to ask yourself whether it's the right thing to do. Ask yourself whether you'd be comfortable with someone else using your own personal data in the same way that you're planning to. Sometimes that serves as the best check of all.

Understanding New Data and Privacy Laws

Data and privacy laws are quickly changing in the European Union and the United States. We highlight these two in the following sections.The net effect: Your ability to target potential customers via social media platforms may be less potent in the future.

General Data Protection Regulation

In Europe, the GDPR (General Data Protection Regulation) governs all data for individual citizens in the European Union, including the transfer of personal data outside of the EU. To summarize, GDPR requires marketers to secure explicit permission from their customers for data driven activities in the European Union.

What this means in a practical sense is that if you're wishing to use behavioral data from your prospective customer to re-market to them in the future, you need to request explicit permission to do so. You can't start using behavioral data on your website to engage with them elsewhere without them actively allowing you to do so. To gain access to the data, the consent needs to be active (instead of passive) representing a conscious choice to give you the data. This is why many websites now explicitly require you to click a button to allow the use of cookies on their sites.

Included in GDPR is also a requirement around data portability. What this means is that a customer has the right to access, modify, erase, or move the data that you have on them. This rule, while specific to the European Union, has significant ramifications for how much businesses value the collection and usage of data. Whereas data used to be uniquely valuable to a company, now that it can be moved by the individual to a new service, its longer-term value is less.

For more information on the GDPR, see `https://gdpr-info.eu`.

California Consumer Privacy Act

In a similar fashion to GDPR, the state of California passed new data privacy laws that took effect in January 2020. This law stipulates that consumers have the right to be informed about what kinds of personal data companies have collected and why it was collected. The law also stipulates that consumers have the right to request the deletion of personal information, opt out of the sale of personal information, and access the personal information in a "readily useable format" that allows them to move the data elsewhere. In many ways as you can see, the law is similar to GDPR and it's probably only a matter of time before other states or the U.S. government enacts a similar law.

With the California Consumer Privacy Act (CCPA), personal information may include geolocation, biometric data, Internet browsing history, psychometric data, and the like. This is all data that companies use to market to consumers in a more targeted fashion today. So what does this mean for you in a practical sense?

The most direct impact of CCPA is on the social media platforms that need to be more stringent in how they collect, use, and allow third parties (which includes advertisers like you) to leverage all the data. For example, if customers start to lose interest in a platform like Twitter or Facebook, they can ask those platforms to delete all their user data. This will hinder your ability to market on those platforms whether it's to those customers itself or to other customers who are just like them. Another influence of these changing laws are the limits placed by the social media platforms. This will affect how much their algorithms can combine data from millions of users to present content and advertising to end users.

For more information on the CCPA, see `https://www.caprivacy.org`.

So What Does This All Mean for Your Marketing Effort?

Understanding data and privacy in the context of marketing can feel daunting. After all, it can involve so many different parts of your company or your team. Not to mention lawyers who may make you very nervous.

REMEMBER

As you think about data and privacy in the context of your business and social media marketing, keep the following tips in mind:

» **Data fuels marketing in positive ways.** While it's very important to comply with all state, federal, and international laws around data management, data is what allows you to reach customers who would be most interested in your products and services. Data-driven marketing, especially on social media platforms, simply works both for the brand and for the customers.

» **Social media platforms have new responsibilities.** Without a doubt, the social media platforms have been lax when it comes to protecting customer data. They're determined to change and with every passing day are getting better at data management. That's a good thing. It also means that you shouldn't hesitate to interrogate them on their data practices to make sure nothing gets missed.

» **Technology makes a big difference.** Often data leakages happen on your own website. Cybersecurity threats can quickly spiral into major customer data breaches that can affect how you're able to market within social media as well. Be sure to stay close to your technology team so that you're aware of what protections they're putting in place.

» **Personally identifiable information (PII) is sensitive.** If you're a business that deals in personally identifiable information, start by protecting that first. Any information that identifies a person, needs to be handled with extra care. You may be used to having conversations with customers in social media but you have to watch for when they share personal information. As soon as that happens, you need to take the conversation out of any public channel.

6

The Part of Tens

Learn about the ten must-read blogs that will keep you updated with the world of SMM and digital marketing more broadly.

Discover the top ten online SMM tools to try.

Find out how to avoid fakeness in the social media world.

Chapter **29**

Ten SMM-Related Must-Read Blogs

Achapter with just ten must-read social media marketing blogs can't do justice to the wealth of information online that covers social influence marketing. Still, you have to start somewhere, and here are ten of our favorite blogs that help us further our own thinking in SMM. You'll notice that these blogs are listed in alphabetical order. They're all so good that we didn't want to rank them.

Brian Solis

https://briansolis.com

Brian Solis is a principal analyst at Altimeter, the digital analyst group at Prophet and a global thought leader. He is also a best-selling author of such books as *Lifescale: How to Live a More Creative, Productive, and Happy Life*. He's always on the cutting edge of business and technology, and his blog is an important read.

Content Marketing Institute

https://contentmarketinginstitute.com

The Content Marketing Institute (CMI) was founded by Joe Pulizzi in 2007, and is one of the foundational companies created to foster education about content marketing. It also runs the very popular annual Content Marketing World Conference. Their blog is a one-stop resource for all things content marketing and their newsletter boasts over two hundred thousand subscribers.

Convince and Convert

https://www.convinceandconvert.com/blog/

Jay Baer's blog Convince and Convert has been rated the Number 1 Content Marketing Blog in the World, by Content Marketing Institute. His books include *Talk Triggers: The Complete Guide to Creating Customers with Word of Mouth*. He covers all social media topics in a clear and helpful way and is always on the cutting edge.

Copyblogger

http://copyblogger.com

Brian Clark started this blog in 2006 with emphasis on teaching. His philosophy is that by educating your clients, you can help them understand why they should buy from you. This blog is always on top-ten lists and worth your time.

Marketing Profs

http://www.marketingprofs.com/marketing/library/articles/

This blog has a university-level set of articles, podcasts, guides, videos, and webinars. It offers both a free level and a membership level. If you make an effort to peruse the content, you will find information on almost any marketing topic. Ann Handley is at the helm as Chief Content Officer, and she does a wonderful job of keeping everything on the cutting edge. In addition, her book *Content Rules,* with C.C. Chapman, is a must read.

Neil Patel's Blog

https://neilpatel.com/blog

Neil Patel is a well-regarded blogger and entrepreneur. He has started several very successful companies and offers an audio podcast called "Marketing School." His blog has many long-form articles on social media topics that will help you grow your business. His blog is a must-read.

Razor Social

https://razorsocial.com/blog

This blog, written by the talented Ian Cleary, is subtitled, *"Marketing Technology Blog for B2B Marketers."* He really delivers on this promise. He is constantly able to find new tools and remind you about the use of old favorites that you've forgotten about. What makes this blog so useful is that he chooses timely topics for social media marketers in search of new ideas.

Seth Godin

https://seths.blog

This blog is a must-read for all marketers. Seth is ahead of almost everyone in his thinking about both the digital future and how to make the most of marketing right now. He has been writing his blog since 2002, and it's as fresh and powerful now as it was at the beginning. Also, don't forget to check out his list of extensive marketing books.

Shiv Singh

www.goingsocialnow.com

Going Social Now is coauthor Shiv's blog, covering all things social media marketing.

Social Media Examiner

https://www.socialmediaexaminer.com

This blog is written by talented author Michael Stelzner and lots of great guests. It's billed as "your guide to the social media jungle."

The Examiner tackles the thorny issues surrounding social media and relentlessly offers solutions. The blog is written in an easy style that is sure to help you learn while you have fun.

Chapter **30**

Ten Top SMM Tools

When you're launching a social media marketing campaign, a good first step is to measure the size of the social activity on the web. When you see the numbers of possible customers (who fit your demographics, psychographics, and technographics) you can reach using social tools, it's usually a no-brainer that a social media campaign is a good thing. Fortunately, several reliable online tools show how to measure social activity on the web.

Many of these tools are free and serve as a good starting point for your listening and research efforts. But remember, no single tool is perfect for capturing web usage. Therefore, it's always useful to use multiple sites together to get the best data. Also, looking at the relative changes in the statistics over a period of time (versus the raw numbers, which may not always be totally accurate) may be a safe approach to take. Keep this list of tools handy when you're doing your research.

Buffer

```
https://bufferapp.com
```

This app enjoys great popularity because of its ability to automate social media delivery. After linking your accounts, you can choose when to deliver your posts (individually for each account). You can also choose items to post directly from your browser (Chrome, Safari, or Firefox) or your mobile device. Another plus is that you can get data about the response to each of your posts to determine how on target they were.

BuzzSumo

`https://buzzsumo.com`

BuzzSumo is a top-rated tool that has a variety of uses. It has a content analyzer and lets you see how a particular post did on such platforms as Facebook, Twitter, Pinterest, and Reddit and what its total engagement score is. You can also see who shared the content. It will show you the questions being asked about the topic on platforms like Quora, Amazon, and Reddit. There is a specific Facebook analyzer tool.

Facebook Insights

`www.facebook.com/insights`

Insights is a valuable Facebook tool to help make the data from Facebook trackable. Until this tool's introduction, determining exactly what was happening in your "corner" of Facebook was difficult. With this suite of analytics tools, you can find data about such things as demographics and readership. Facebook developers can dive even deeper. There are two main sections — Users and Interactions — so that you can determine what actually works with your particular readers.

Followerwonk

`https://followerwonk.com`

Followerwonk helps you identify the right Twitter users for your community. Then it analyzes those users and helps you compare and contrast your users with that of your competitors. It also enables you to optimize your follower list for reach.

Hootsuite

`https://www.hootsuite.com`

One of the chief complaints that most business people have about social media is that it takes a lot of time — time that they don't have. Hootsuite is popular because it acts as a dashboard for all your social media activities. You can link up your accounts (Hootsuite has links to more than 20+ platforms) to get data, listen to your followers, and plan marketing activities from one location.

Later

https://later.com/

If you want to focus on Instagram and Pinterest you may want to try Later. It lets you visually plan and schedule posts. In addition, it will analyze your Instagram hashtags so you can see which ones are the best performers. It will also provide Pinterest analytics so you can determine how well your profile is doing. You can also use it for Facebook and Twitter.

Mention

https://mention.com

Do you want to make sure you know what's being said about your company and its products? One way is to use Mention.com. It allows you to set up alerts and monitor them in real-time. It's very easy to use and has a central dashboard. You can also use it to monitor competitors and the industry at large. It helps you become aware of potential problems before they become big ones.

SproutSocial

https://sproutsocial.com

SproutSocial is a tool that wants to help you understand your followers. You can publish to several social media platforms, including Facebook, LinkedIn, Twitter, and Instagram, from one central location. In addition, you can monitor your brand in real time.

Tailwind

https://www.tailwindapp.com

Tailwind is used by those who want to up their game on Instagram and Pinterest. You can use a single dashboard to schedule posts and track analytics on multiple accounts. You're able to monitor what's being said about your brand on Pinterest and Instagram and optimize your content.

Tweepi

https://tweepi.com

Tweepi is a great tool for managing your Twitter account. Twitter promotes responsible rules in the effort to prevent spammers, and the Tweepi tool works within those rules to help you analyze your engagement with your followers. You can look at each Twitter user at the individual level so that you can judge whether Twitter is still a good fit for your business audience.

Chapter **31**

Ten Tips to Navigate Fakeness

akeness is nothing new by any means. Misinformation, false information, and propaganda have been around from the beginning of time. We have entered a new post-trust era though, where navigating the fakeness has gotten extremely difficult thanks to all the technology changes we have been witnessing. On November 16, 2016, *Oxford English Dictionary* named "post-truth" its international word of the year, reflecting what it referred to as a "highly charged" political twelve months. In choosing the word, the editors defined post-truth as a state in which "objective facts are less influential in shaping public opinion than appeals to emotion and personal belief."

Without a doubt, the post-truth and resultant post-trust era that we're experiencing is something unique to our time. It describes a new condition we are living in — one with deeply troubling ramifications for all of us as citizens and many of us as social media marketers. With increasing automation, empowered by artificial intelligence and social media infiltrating every part of our lives, our vulnerability to fakeness has only increased. Dealing with fakeness online and in social media in particular has become a fact of life. As a result, here are ten important tips for navigating that fakeness. We hope they help as you embark on your journey as a social media marketer.

Create Shared, Mutual Goals

By its very definition, social media marketing means interacting and working with many different people both within your company and outside it. In fact, the more you engage with people via social media, the more susceptible you are to being conned or harmed by fakeness. Establish objectives for yourself in social media that are aligned with those of the people you're trying to engage with. Have conversations to better understand what your customers are trying to accomplish. This may seem obvious but when you have clear goals and you understand the goals of your customers, it's hard for a third party to mislead you in some way.

Use Reflection to Override Bias

One of the reasons why we tend to fall for fakeness online is because bad actors across the Internet know how to take advantage of the inbuilt human biases we may have. While bias may be bad, it's natural for everyone to have some kind of bias or other. Researchers have found that the ability to reflect is what predicts whether a person can distinguish facts from alternative facts. When forming an opinion, consciously choose to delay arriving at your judgment. Let all the available information sink in and deliberately reflect on it. That way it is less likely that you'll fall for any fakeness.

Engage Openly with Dissent

Most of us choose to avoid conflict. We'd rather run away from it than engage with conflict because it's uncomfortable and even dangerous at times. However, when it comes to social media, if you're trying to understand the facts from fiction and to separate the truth from the fakeness, one important way to do this is by actively engaging with all parties involved in a particular disagreement. Try to get as much of a 360-degree view of the issue as you can before you make any judgments. It may even help you understand whether your own opinion is the fake one!

Challenge Opinion and Ask for Facts

This may seem obvious to do especially because this is exactly what we're taught in school. However, in a fast-moving social media world, where having a strong opinion has significant social currency, sometimes facts are forgotten. Sometimes this behavior also influences how social media marketers act online as well.

The solution: Force an evidence-driven approach to decision-making within your company. Ask for evidence when strong opinions are expressed. Vigorously challenge opinions that are not grounded in fact and don't give them equal treatment to those based on hard evidence.

Encourage Those Who Don't Conform

When you're building a team of social media marketers or hiring in your company (big or small), it's easy to get trapped in finding people who look and sound like you. That's not good enough though. Studies have found that non-conforming employees report being more confident and engaged in their work, display greater creativity, and receive higher ratings on performance and innovativeness from their supervisors. Most critically, they help you combat conformity and groupthink where everyone begins to agree with one another a bit too much. With groupthink comes the inability to separate the truth from the fakeness. To avoid that, have peers and teams who don't conform too neatly to your world view.

Ask Yourself "What if the Opposite Was True"

To fight fakeness it's also important to recognize your own limits. In a social media world where opinions are in abundance and evidence often rare, learn how to evaluate information more critically. One way to do that is to ask yourself, "what if the opposite was true?" It's not simply enough to ask people to be fair and impartial. By asking them (and yourself) to think about the opposite condition to their own conclusions forces them to reflect and removes bias.

Engage in Active, Critical Analysis

As a social media marketer, you have a lot of influence. Very often you make daily judgment calls on what to publish, how to respond to a comment, and whether to use a specific photograph when sharing information with thousands and thousands of customers. It's very important that you don't leave the thinking to anyone else. You're ultimately responsible for the decisions that impact the success of your brand on the social media channels. Take guidance from your peers and external consults but always remember you're the one responsible — both to publish smartly and also to avoid falling for fakeness online.

Question Morally Dubious Directives

As human beings, we are wired to want to please others. And if it is someone who pays your salary, then even more so. But when it comes to social media marketing, you may have unique skills or experiences that few others in your company have. As a result, don't be shy about questioning morally dubious directives. Compliance can have a ripple effect. The more you comply with questionable commands, the more you will continue to do so. If you want to be a successful social media marketer, recognize that the fakeness could be internal as well, especially when it takes the form of a morally dubious directive. You have to be able to recognize it early and question the directive.

Seek Out Allies

You're bound to come across a lot of fakeness in your job if you're a social media marketer. The fakeness can take the form of competitors promoting their products with unverified claims, influencers pushing metrics on you that are exaggerated, criticisms from customers that are unfounded, and misinformation about your brand and your products from unidentifiable sources. It comes with the territory when you market your business online. One way to fight the fakeness, is by seeking out allies who will help you question what is fake. Think of these as uber influencers who aren't only valuable to highlight what's great about your products but also come to your defense and help you fight the fakeness when you're attacked in some form or the other.

Focus on Building Trust First

This one might appear counterintuitive but probably the best way to fight fakeness in social media is not to pay too much attention to it. The more you're able to focus on your customers and their needs, passions, and painpoints, the more success that you'll have. You will build an army of loyalists among your customer base who will come to your defense quickly when you're attacked on a specific social media channel. They'll be there for you when you need them the most. These customers will happily step in to help you if you've built trusted, long-lasting relationships with them first. And once you have that, then everything else becomes easy.

Index

Q

qualitative research, 44–45
quality, Medium and, 243
Quantcast, 40, 123–124
quantitative research, 45–46
quartile view, 172
questions, answering on LinkedIn, 186–187
quotes, as Tumblr media, 234

R

radio frequency identification (RFID), 339
rankings, for competitors, 40
Raven, Bertram (psychologist), 14
Razor Social (blog), 405
read ratio (Medium), 245
reader's interests (Medium), 245
reads (Medium), 245
real-time marketing
    about, 385–386
    co-creation, 388–389
    distribution, 389–390
    engagement, 390–391
    insights, 386–387
    "on the fly," 388
    organizing for, 391–392
    response, 387–388
    social media marketing and, 66–68
    taking TV into, 393
recognition-seeking, Millennials as, 259
recommendation services, 348
recommendations, in LinkedIn profile, 179
Reddit.com
    about, 248
    analyzing content, 250–251
    lingo for, 249–250
    marketing on, 248–249
    setting up, 249
    website, 248
referent influencers, 14–15, 267, 272–275
referrers (Medium), 245
reflection, overriding bias with, 412
remarketing, 61

Remember icon, 2
resonance, creating, 170
resources, evaluating, 127–129
respect, as an ethical value, 114
responses
    to criticism, 92–93
    Medium, 246
    real-time, 387–388
    Twitter, 151
responsibility, as an ethical value, 114
results
    measuring on Snapchat, 208–209
    tracking for campaigns, 84–85
    tracking in Pinterest, 224–225
retweets (Twitter), 148–149
reviewing profiles for Medium, 245–246
rewarding teams, 355
Rheingold, Howard (author)
    Smart Mobs: The Next Social Revolution, 24
rich pins, 220–221
Rise filter (Instagram), 196
Rite Tag, 197
roles
    about, 9–10
    influencers, 12–13
    marketer, 10–12
roll-back functionality, 361
RSS feeds, 55
rules, Reddit, 249

S

sales, governance and, 377
Salesforce (website), 367
Salesforce Trailblazer Community, 313
Sandberg, Sheryl (COO), 135
save pin widget (Pinterest), 214
Savvy Auntie, 77
search engine optimization (SEO)
    about, 310
    websites and, 304
    YouTube and, 163

About the Authors

Shiv Singh helps brands transform with the rise of digital and has worked in executive level positions on both the agency side and with Fortune 50 companies. He is currently the SVP of Global Brand and Marketing Transformation at Visa Inc. Shiv has been recognized by *Ad Age* as a Media Maven and has been featured on the publication's cover. More recently, he was recognized by *Adweek* as a Top 50 Marketer (no. 19).

The award-winning and business-results-producing work done by Shiv and his teams while at Visa Inc. and PepsiCo have been recognized by leading industry and consumer publications from *Fortune Magazine* and *Ad Age* to *Forbes* and *The Harvard Business Review*. This includes the definition and launch of the new, multistakeholder Visa brand platform and communications model, reimagining card innovation for major Visa clients, evolving the Pepsi brand for the digital era by making it a media brand through the creation of a global media network called Pepsi Pulse, and forming the largest multidimensional partnership with Twitter in its history.

Shiv has also written for the *Harvard Business Review* online, *Ad Age*, *Adweek*, and other publications. Shiv sits on the DMG World Media Board of Governors and has advised startups including Buddy Media, Crowdtwist, Beckon, and Social Chorus. He holds a BS in Information Systems from Babson College, and an MSc (Research) from the London School of Economics & Political Science, where he focused on social network theory. You can find him on Twitter: @shivsingh.

Stephanie Diamond is a thought leader and management marketing professional with years of experience building profits in more than 75 different industries. She has worked with solopreneurs, small business owners, and multibillion-dollar corporations.

She worked for eight years as a Marketing Director at AOL. When she joined, there were fewer than 1 million subscribers. When she left in 2002, there were 36 million. She had a front-row seat to learn how and why people buy online. While at AOL, she developed, from scratch, a highly successful line of multimedia products that brought in an annual $40 million dollars in incremental revenue.

In 2002, she founded Digital Media Works, Inc. (contentmarketingtoolbox.com), an online marketing company that helps business owners discover the hidden profits in their business. She is passionate about guiding online companies to successfully generate more revenue and use social media to its full advantage.

As a strategic thinker, Stephanie uses all the current visual thinking techniques and brain research to help companies to get to the essence of their brand. She continues this work today with her proprietary system to help online business owners discover how social media can generate profits. You can read her blog at www.MarketingMessageBlog.com.

Stephanie's other books include *Prezi For Dummies* and *Dragon Naturally Speaking For Dummies*.

Stephanie received a BA in Psychology from Hofstra University and an MSW and MPH from the University of Hawaii. She lives in New York with her husband and her Maltese, Colby.

Dedications

To Barry, who makes all things possible. To my family, for their love and support.

— Stephanie Diamond

To Rohini, Arjan, and Shyam, who mean the world to me. And to my parents and my brother, who've always been there for me from the very beginning.

— Shiv Singh

Authors' Acknowledgments

It has been my distinct privilege to write this book. I want to offer great thanks to my wonderful coauthor Shiv Singh for his brilliance and John Wiley & Sons, Inc. for letting me write this book for their audience of smart readers.

I also want to thank Matt Wagner, my agent at Fresh Books, for his continued hard work and support on my behalf.

Finally, thanks to you for choosing this book to learn about social media marketing. I wish you enormous joy on your exciting journey into social media.

— Stephanie Diamond

I've always wanted to write, a desire that was constantly fueled by my parents, who encouraged me to write first by keeping a diary and then by exploring poetry and fiction, and finally, by nonfiction as I grew older. And the same goes for my brother, who fueled the interest by patiently reading drafts of whatever I've written and providing valuable feedback. Many teachers in school pushed me along in a similar fashion. Without all the continuous encouragement from my childhood days to put pen to paper, no book would have ever been written.

This specific book would have never been completed had it not been for my wife, who sacrificed what should have been many a family weekend to let me sit at my desk and churn out chapter after chapter.

A book like this also could not have been written without the constant inspiration, collaboration, and debate that happens among employees in dynamic organizations like Visa, PepsiCo, and Razorfish. I feel lucky to have been able to work among such talented people whose thinking has undoubtedly shaped me and my views on social media marketing. Every day, I go into work humbled as I learn something new from these star employees.

Finally, but not least, my co-writer Stephanie Diamond, who's been a patient, committed, and thoughtful force, deserves lots of acknowledgement.

— Shiv Singh

Publisher's Acknowledgments

Executive Editor: Ashley Barth
Development Editor: Rebecca Senninger
Technical Editor: Michelle Krasniak

Production Editor: Mohammed Zafar Ali
Cover Image: © SPF/Shutterstock